Nakón-wįco'i'e né ųspénįc'iciyac

· · · · · · · ·  · · · · · · · ·

Practising Nakoda

Nakón-wįco'įe né ųspénįc'iciyac : Practising Nakoda

A THEMATIC DICTIONARY

Vincent Collette, Tom Shawl,
and Wilma Kennedy

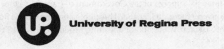

University of Regina Press

Printed and bound in Canada. The text of this book is printed on 100% post-consumer recycled paper with earth-friendly vegetable-based inks.

Cover art: "Untitled Drawing," 2012, By Darryl Growing Thunder, from the collection of the National Museum of the American Indian.
Cover design: Duncan Noel Campbell, University of Regina Press
Interior layout design: John van der Woude, JVDW Designs
Copyeditor: Kelly Laycock
Proofreader: Rachel Taylor, Banoong Editing

Library and Archives Canada Cataloguing in Publication

Title: Nakón-wįco'i'e né ųspénįc'iciyac = Practising Nakoda : a thematic dictionary / Vincent Collette, Tom Shawl, and Wilma Kennedy.
Other titles: Practising Nakoda
Names: Collette, Vincent, 1976- author. | Shawl, Tom, author. | Kennedy, Wilma, author.
Description: Includes bibliographical references.
Identifiers: Canadiana (print) 20240383567 | Canadiana (ebook) 20240383591 | ISBN 9781779400185 (softcover) | ISBN 9781779400192 (hardcover) | ISBN 9781779400208 (PDF) | ISBN 9781779400215 (EPUB)
Subjects: CSH: Nakoda language—Dictionaries. | LCGFT: Subject dictionaries. | LCGFT: Multilingual dictionaries.
Classification: LCC PM1024.Z9 N35 2024 | DDC 497/.524—dc23

10 9 8 7 6 5 4 3 2 1

University of Regina Press, University of Regina
Regina, Saskatchewan, Canada, S4S 0A2
TEL: (306) 585-4758 FAX: (306) 585-4699
WEB: www.uofrpress.ca

U OF R PRESS

We acknowledge the support of the Canada Council for the Arts for our publishing program. We acknowledge the financial support of the Government of Canada. / Nous reconnaissons l'appui financier du gouvernement du Canada. This publication was made possible with support from Creative Saskatchewan's Book Publishing Production Grant Program.

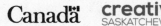

Contents

Foreword

The Nakoda language is a gift of the Creator and is at the very core of Nakoda cultural identity. Nakoda is, through prayers and songs, the means by which important cultural values and spiritual knowledge are transmitted from generations to generations. Even though it was spoken for millennia, Nakoda is now seriously endangered due to the trauma of residential schools, which halted its transmission in the 1950s and '60s. The terrible consequence of this is that now only a handful of elderly speakers know the language in Saskatchewan and Montana, and most have but a few people to speak with since the remaining few speakers are relatively isolated from one another. Nevertheless, many middle-aged Nakoda people—some of whom are semi-fluent speakers or rememberers—strongly feel the need to learn and pass down the Nakoda language to their children and grandchildren, but lack concrete teaching tools to do so. One can always rely on published dictionaries, apps, or verb books, but these materials, however precise and complete they may be, do not teach how to make sentences in order to communicate in a meaningful way with other Nakoda speakers. Since full immersion with native speakers is not possible at the moment, what is crucially needed is a user-friendly book that teaches both the core vocabulary and how to use it in sentences. This is the goal of *Practising Nakoda: A Thematic Dictionary*.

First, the present book contains basic Nakoda vocabulary that is organized into thirty main chapters based on specific themes (e.g., human body, communication, flora and fauna, space and time, etc.). This will give the student the basic words for every theme and a general view of word formation patterns. Second, some sections are meant to enhance daily and ceremonial communication (e.g., dances and songs, ceremonies, ceremonial clothing). Third and most important, the words are not organized alphabetically but are grouped according to the root element or to their meaning. For instance, words having the root -*škada*- 'play' are grouped together even though some of them start with the sounds *a*, *o*, or *w*:

škádA *vi1, vt2*	*s/he plays; s/he plays a musical instrument*
Tągán škáda wo!	*Play outside!*
Mitákona gicí waškáda.	*I play with my friend.*
škatkíyA *vt1-caus*	*s/he lets sb play*
Mihų́ tągán škatmą́kiya.	*Mom lets me play outside.*
aškádA *vt1*	*s/he plays on smth*
oškádA *vi1, n*	*s/he plays inside of smth; playground*
oškáde *n*	*picnic; festival; arena*
oškáde tíbi *cp*	*gymnasium*
wayá'įškadA *vi2-abs*	*s/he teases, plays jokes on people*

On one hand, this way of grouping words makes it harder to look for a word, but on the other hand, it enhances greatly the learner's "morphological awareness." Nakoda is a polysynthetic language, meaning that words are often built up with many elements that attach to the root. Thus, being able to identify the root -*škada*- and those other elements, called "morphemes" (like *o*- 'in, inside', -*kiya* 'cause to do', -*ya*- 'with the mouth, by speech'), is a crucial asset in the student's learning success. The more aware the student is about the makeup of complex words, the more skilled s/he will become at guessing the meaning of more complex words s/he has never heard before. The student is also strongly encouraged to consult *A Concise Dictionary of Nakoda (Assiniboine)* by Collette & Kennedy (2023) or the online dictionary of Assiniboine hosted on the American Indian Studies Research Institute's (AISRI) website at *zia.aisri.indiana.edu* (under Assiniboine) for more details.

This book is based on the fieldwork of Dr. Vincent Collette with the late Wilma Kennedy from Carry The Kettle (Saskatchewan), and with Tom Shawl from Fort Belknap (Montana). Other people who have contributed to this book are Kenneth Helgeson (Lodgepole, MT), Mike Turcotte (Wolfpoint, MT), the late Armand McArthur (Pheasant Rump, SK), Peter Bigstone (Oceanman, SK), and Geraldine Rutherford (Fort Belknap, MT). Even though it is modest in size and evidently incomplete, *Practising Nakoda* is nevertheless another tool for the documentation, revitalization, and strengthening of Nakoda language and culture.

Elements of Nakoda Grammar

Pronunciation

In this book the Fort Belknap spelling is used. In the following tables we have included the pronunciation of the Nakoda sounds as used in Linda Cumberland's forthcoming book, *Grammar of Assiniboine (Nakoda)* (2024).

Vowels

Nakoda alphabet	English equivalent	Nakoda example	Cumberland's *Grammar*
A a	at, hat	*aké* 'again'	a
Ą ą	man (nearest equivalent)	*cą́* 'wood'	ą
E e	bet	*nén* 'here'	e
I i	beat	*nína* 'very'	i
Į į	mean (nearest equivalent)	*įȟá* 'he laughs'	į

O o	open	*ómna* 'he smells it'	o
U u	two	*sudá* 'it is hard'	u
Ų ų	*not found in English	*húgu* 'his/her mother'	ų

Nakoda has eight vowels: five orals, and three nasals. When producing oral vowels *a, e, i, o,* and *u,* the airstream coming from the lungs goes directly through the mouth, as in AAAAAH. However, nasal vowels *ą, į,* and *ų* are produced by letting air escape by the nose and mouth at the same time. The closest English equivalent of nasal vowels occurs in the words *mean* and *bingo*. In the word *mean* the oral vowel *i* is flanked with two nasal consonants *m* and *n,* and so it is slightly nasalized, while in *bingo* the vowel is fully nasalized. Nasal vowels are indicated by a small hook underneath, as in *ą, į,* and *ų*. The vowels *e* and *o* are never nasalized in Nakoda.

Consonants

Nakoda alphabet	English equivalent	Nakoda example	Cumberland's *Grammar*
B b	bat, tab	*basnóhą* 'to push'	p
C c	chill	*cába* 'beaver'	c^h
C' c'	*not found in English	*cic'ú* 'I give it to you'	c'
D d	damp	*dágu* 'what, thing'	t
G g	gum	*gúwa* 'Come!'	k
Ǧ ǧ	*not found in English	*ǧí* 'it is yellow'	ǧ
H h	happy	*hiyá* 'no'	h

Ȟ ȟ	*not found in English	*ȟóda* 'it is grey'	ȟ
Ȟ' ȟ'	*not found in English	*ȟą́* 's/he behaves'	ȟ'
J j	jam	*júsina* 'it is small'	c
K k	keep	*kuwá* 'he chases him'	kʰ
K' k'	*not found in English	*k'ú* 'he gives it to him'	k'
M m	mine	*mína* 'knife'	m
N n	night	*nųwą́* 'to swim'	n
P p	Peter	*pahá* 'hair'	pʰ
P' p'	*not found in English	*cup'ó* 'it is foggy'	p'
S s	sit	*sihá* 'foot'	s
S' s'	*not found in English	*-s'a* (habitual enclitic)	s'
Š š	shadow	*šų́ga* 'dog'	š
Š' š'	*not found in English	*š'á* 'it is a roaring sound'	š'
T t	team	*tanó* 'meat'	tʰ
T' t'	*not found in English	*t'á* 'to die'	t'
W w	water	*wá* 'snow'	w
Y y	yes	*yatką́* 'he drinks'	y
Z z	zipper	*zizíbena* 'thin cloth'	z
Ž ž	measure	*ožúna* 'it is full'	ž
'	button [bɐʔn̩]	*wa'ówabi* 'paper'	ʔ

Syllables

Words in English and Nakoda can be divided into syllables. Every syllable consists of one vowel (obligatory) and one or more preceding or following consonant(s), which are optional. Syllables are separated by a hyphen in the following English examples:

no	as-pen	ca-li-ber	se-pa-ra-tion
1	1 2	1 2 3	1 2 3 4

When a word has more than one syllable, one of them is produced with more force or amplitude, as in AS-pen. We call this syllable the "stressed" syllable. It is the one that carries the accent. In Nakoda spelling, the stress (or accent) is indicated by a diacritic sign on top, such as *é* in *duwé* 'who,' which is pronounced doo-wɛ́. For English speakers learning Nakoda, it is difficult to guess which vowel will be stressed. The rule of thumb is that the vowel of the second syllable will carry the stress, but there are counter-examples where the first syllable is stressed.

Second syllable accent

tokána	*grey fox*	škoškóbena	*banana*
mató	*bear*	duwé	*who*
hągé	*half*	škobá	*it is hollowed out*

First syllable accent

néža	*s/he urinates*	**há**ba	*moccasin*
škóbena	*it is slightly crooked*	**má**ni	*s/he walks*
máza	*iron*	**šká**da	*s/he plays*

With words that consist of only one syllable, the vowel will automatically carry the stress. For the sake of consistency, we have decided to keep the accent everywhere, even on monosyllabic words.

tó	*it is blue, green*	**tá**	*moose*
šką́	*s/he/it moves, tries, feels*	**ú**	*s/he/it comes here*

In English the position of the stress in a word can make a difference in meaning between two words, as in the case of *permít* 'to give permission' (verb) vs. *pérmit* 'official document granting someone with an authorization to do something' (noun). These two words have different stress patterns and mean different things. Nakoda too has meaningful stress, and this is why it is always indicated in the spelling. Here are two examples:

ga**na**	*those yonder*	o**há̧**	*s/he cooks smth by boiling*
gána	*s/he is old*	**ó**ha̧	*among, in the middle, in it*

Finally, the sound cluster *tk* can switch to *kt* in some Nakoda communities, like in Carry The Kettle. For some entries both forms are provided starting with the switched form *kt* following by the unswitched form *tk*, as in **wįktókto, ~ wįtkótko** *vs-redup* 's/he is bad, crazy; misbehaves'.

Word Classes

Nakoda has seven types of words: nouns, verbs, adverbs, demonstratives, pronouns, postpositions, and interjections. It also has a fairly large series of enclitics, which are not words but elements that "lean" on the verb.

Nouns describe a person, place, thing, or idea (e.g., *dog, love, faith*).

búza	*cat*
cąpásusuna	*pepper*

Verbs express an action, a state of being, a condition, an event, or a natural phenomenon.

kuwá	*s/he chases, goes after sb, smth*
cíga	*s/he wants smth*
osní	*it is cold weather*

NB: Technically Nakoda does not have a separate class of adjectives like English does (e.g., *nice, big, small*). To express the colour or the size of something, a stative verb is used.

síja	*s/he/it is bad*
wasnókya	*s/he is wise*
sába	*s/he/it is black*

Adverbs modify the action of the verb (e.g., as in arriving *late* or *early*) or indicate a location in time or space (e.g., *there, now*), or manner (e.g., *silently*).

wanágaš	*long ago*
gakí	*over there, yonder*
éstena	*early*

Demonstratives indicate the location and the distance of an entity in relation to the speaker's point of view (e.g., *this* man, *that* house *over there*).

né	*this*
žé	*that*
gá	*that yonder*

Pronouns replace a noun (e.g., *Paul* is sick > *He* is sick; *The plant* is sick > *It* is sick). Some pronouns are used to form interrogative sentences.

íš	*s/he/it/they too; also*
duwé	*who*

Postpositions specify a relationship between two words in a sentence (e.g., <u>Paul</u> is *in* the <u>house</u>; <u>Paul</u> is *at* the <u>theatre</u>). In English, prepositions like *from, to, over*, etc., can fill in the empty space in the sentence *The bird flew* _____ *the house*. Nakoda equivalents to

English prepositions come after the head word, and this is why they are called "postpositions" (*post-* 'after').

ektá	*at*
tín	*in*
gicí	*with another person*

Interjections are used to call out to people, to warn, or in brief to keep open the channel of communication. They are never inflected for person.

Ahé	expression of humility used at the beginning of prayers or songs
Hą́ jé!	*yes, ok, mmh!* (literally, *yes + always*)
Hį́į́!	*Oh my!* (expression of surprise) (female speaker)
Hinága!	*Wait!*
Waná!	*Are you ready!*
Hokwá waná he?	*What's happening now?* (male speaker)
Wągá!	*as if!* (as if it was true, slander, irreality marker)
nų́ške…	*euh…* (when a speaker is thinking about what to say)

Enclitics are forms that attach at the end of a verb. They indicate mood/tense, negation, plural, number, etc.

-kta	potential/future
-bi	animate plural
-šį	negation

Grammatical particles are independent words that follow the verb. They indicate commands and interrogation, but also mood (degree of certainty), and evidentiality (source of knowledge). Some of them are used only by men, others only by women, or both.

no	declaration (male speaker)
he	interrogation (male/female speaker)
wo	order (singular addressee) (male speaker)
ųkáš	*I wish, if only*
hųštá	*it is said*

Word Order

Nakoda word order differs greatly from that of English since Nakoda demonstratives, postpositions, and adverbs are placed after the noun and not before as in English. The verb is almost always at the end of the sentence, and this is why it is often said that Nakoda is a Subject-Object-Verb (sov) language. The following schema will help visualize the Nakoda word order. Note that the brackets, in positions 1 and 2, indicate that the element in question is optional in a sentence. The verb is the only element that is not optional in a fully formed sentence.

1st word	2nd word	3rd word
(noun)	(demonstrative) (postposition) (adverb)	verb

For example, an English sentence like *That dog is running* would be expressed as *Dog that runs* in Nakoda. Here are a few examples reflecting Nakoda word order:

Máni.				*He is walking.*
he.walks				

Wįcá	že	máni.		*That man is walking.*
man	that	he.walks		

Wįcá	háska	že	máni.	*That tall man is walking.*
man	tall	that	he.walks	

Šúga	gá	aktága.		*That dog over there is running.*
dog	that	he.runs		

Wíyą	né	nážį.		*This woman is standing.*
woman	this	she.stands		

Verb Conjugation

Nakoda verbs are the most complicated words to build, and students will have to pay attention to the different types of verbs in order to successfully communicate with other speakers. If you look at the following table you will see that there are four distinct ways to say *I* and *you* depending on the verb class in Nakoda: Class 1 (regular stem class); Class 2 (Y-stem class); Class 3 (nasal conjugation class); Class 4 (nasal+vowel conjugation class). The first three classes of verbs express actions (active verbs), and the last class of verbs expresses states (stative verbs). Note that the third person singular verb (underlined in the table) receives no marker; the bare form of the verb is the citation form.

CLASS 1 (regular stem class) *infixed*	CLASS 2 (Y-stem class) *infixed*
wacíga 'I want it'	mná 'I want it'
yacíga 'you want it'	ná 'you want it'
cíga 's/he wants it'	yá 's/he wants it'
ųcígabi 'we want it'	ųyábi 'we want it'
cígabi 'they want it'	yábi 'they want it'

CLASS 3 (nasal conjugation class) *infixed*	CLASS 4 (N+V conjugation class) *infixed*
mų́ 'I wear it'	mayázą 'I am sick'
nų́ 'you wear it'	niyázą 'you are sick'
ų́ 's/he wears it'	yazą́ 's/he is sick'
ų'ų́bi 'we wear it'	ųyáząbi 'we are sick'
ų́bi 'they wear it'	yazą́bi 'they are sick'

To know if a Nakoda verb is active or stative, examine the translation of the verb in English: if it is a verb that requires the auxiliary *am* or *are* in front (as in *I am sick* or *you are silly*), then the Nakoda verb is a stative verb. This trick works most of the time (but see *wayúpi* below).

The person markers for *I, you, s/he*, etc., can be either **pre**fixed (placed *before* the stem) or **in**fixed (placed *inside* the stem) for each of the verb classes. Here are examples with a verb from each class.

CLASS 1	CLASS 2
(regular stem class) *prefixed*	(Y-stem class) *prefixed*
ma**wá**ni 'I walk'	wa**mn**úpi 'I am skilled'
ma**yá**ni 'you walk'	wa**n**úpi 'you are skilled'
máni 's/he walks'	wa**y**úpi 's/he is skilled'
má'**ų**ni**bi** 'we walk'	wa'**ų**yupi**bi** 'we are skilled'
máni**bi** 'they walk'	wa**y**úpi**bi** 'they are skilled'

CLASS 3	CLASS 4
(nasal conjugation class) *prefixed*	(N+V conjugation class) *prefixed*
ecá**mų** 'I ask it'	**í**ma**pi** 'I am full'
ecá**nų** 'you ask it'	**í**ni**pi** 'you are full'
ec**ú** 's/he asks it'	**í**pi 's/he is full'
ec**ú**g**ú**bi 'we ask it'	ų**gí**pi**bi** 'we are full'
ec**ú**bi 'they ask it'	**í**pi**bi** 'they are full'

Verb Enclitics and Particles

A few important grammatical elements called "enclitics" are attached at the end of a verb. These can indicate meanings like plurality, small size, habitual aspect, etc. Grammatical "particles" are other elements that follow a verb and indicate modality (speaker's attitude toward what is expressed) and evidentiality (source of knowledge), and interrogative, declarative, and imperative sentences. The enclitics follow an order when they occur together. The following table displays the position order for grammatical enclitics (1–8) and particles (9–11).[1]

Ordered positions for grammatical enclitics and particles

		Verb STEM	
Enclitics	1	-*hĄ* (continuative aspect)	
	2	-*ːgA* (durative aspect)	
	3	-*bi* (3PL animate)	
	4	-*na* (diminutive)	
	5	-*s'A* (habitual aspect)	
	6	-*ktA* (potential mood; future)	
	7	-*šį*	-*gen* (negation)
	8	-*ȟ* (intensifier, focus)	-*ȟtiyĄ* (augmentative, emphasizer)
		- *š* (adversative)	-*s* (hortative)
Particles	9	*jé'e* 'always'	
	10	*céyagA* 'should, could'	*otí'igA* 'must'
		hųštá 'it is said'	
	11	*he* (interrogative)	*no* (declarative – male)
		c (declarative – gender neutral)	*'* (declarative – female)
		ce (declarative – female)	*wo* (imperative SG – male)

Here are two sentence examples with verbs that show the order of some enclitics and particles:

Nową́-bi₃-kte₆-ši₇   no₁₁
sing-PL-POT-NEG   DECL.MALE
'They will not sing.' (man/woman speaking)

Waná   ya-kí-n-ųga-bi₃   ceýage₁₀ '₁₁
now   2-arrive.back.there-2-lay-PL   MUST   DECL.FEMALE
'Now, you all must go back to bed.' (women speaking)

Besides the potential/future -ktA and plural -bi, which are very common in speech, the use of some of the other enclitics and particles will seem difficult to master at first, and so students will have to be very attentive to how some of the enclitics and particles are used in storytelling and other verbal performances. See Chapter 30 Structural Words for more details about the use of these elements.

Ablauting Process

Some verbs that end in the sounds a or ą may change to e or į when followed by certain suffixes, enclitics, demonstratives, or particles that trigger the sound change known as "ablaut." This process is indicated by capitalized letters A or Ą in the Nakoda form of a verb in this book.

Two very common ablauting elements include the negative enclitic -ši, which triggers e-ablaut (e.g., wódA > wódeši 's/he does not eat'), and the potential enclitic -*kta*, which triggers *i̧*-ablaut (e.g., *wódA* > *wódi̧kta* 's/he will/can eat').

Abbreviations

adv = adverb

art = article

aux = auxiliary

benef = benefactive verb

coll = collective verb

conj = conjunction

cont = contracted form

cp = *compound*

dem = demonstrative

dit = ditransitive verb

encl = enclitic

imper = impersonal verb

interj = interjection

irr = irregular verb (similar to Class 1)

lit. = literally

n = noun

np = noun phrase

num = number

part = particle

ph = phrase

pl = plural

pos = possessive verb

post = postposition

pro = pronoun

quant = quantifier

recip = reciprocal verb

refl = reflexive verb (verb class 3)

sb = somebody, someone

sg = singular

smth = something

suff = suffix

v = verb

vcont = contracted verb

vi = intransitive verb

vimp = impersonal verb

vs = stative verb (verb class 4)

vt = transitive verb

1 = verb class 1 (regular stems)

2 = verb class 2 (Y-stems)

3 = verb class 3 (N-stems)

~ = indicates local or dialectal variants

1

Greetings and Forms of Address

Greeting, Farewell, and Thanking

háu *interj*
  Háu koná! Dóken ya'ų́?
  Hą́ mišį́! Dágu dókanų?

hello, hi; yes (male speaker)
  Hello friend! How are you?
  Hello my friend! What are you
    doing? (female)

hą́ *interj*
  Hą́, dąyą́ wącímnaga.

hello, hi; yes (female speaker)
  Hello, it's good to see you.

ą́ba wašté *ph*
  Ą́ba wašté yuhá bo!

it's a nice day
  You all have a nice day!

hąyákena wašté *ph*

good morning

ų́ *vi1*
  Dóken ya'ų́? — Dąyą́ wa'ų́.

s/he/it is, lives, exists, stays, feels
  How are you? — I am fine.

pinámayaya *vt1*
  Miyéco žé pinámayaya.

I thank you
  Thank you for inviting me.

wópina k'u *vt1*
  Wópina tága cic'ú no.

s/he gives gratitude
  I give you great thanks.

Departing

iyáya *vi2* s/he sets to go, departs from here

   Imnámnįkte no! *I'll depart, leave!*

   Mitágena dóki inána he? *My older sister, where are you setting to go?*

kná *vt1* s/he goes, returns back to where s/he is from

   Tída yakná he? *Are you going back home?*

wayága *vt2* s/he sees sb, smth

   Aké wacímnagįkte no. *I'll see you again.*

   Éstena wacímnagabįkta. *I'll see you all soon.*

dókaš, dókš *adv* later; in a while

   Dókš wacímnagįkta. *I'll see you later.*

ú *vi1* s/he comes, arrives here from there

   Aké ú. *Come again.*

   Tín ú. *Come in.*

aké *adv* again

   Aké ú! *Come again!*

   Aké wacímnagįkte no! *I'll see you again!*

Establishing Relationships with Others

cažé *n* name

   Dágu cažé nitáwa? *What is your name?*

acáštų *vt1* s/he names sb after another person

   Mikúši acášmatųbi. *They named me after my grandmother.*

   Nikúši nitúgaši acášnitų. *Your grandmother named you after your grandfather.*

egíya, ejíya *vt1* — s/he tells sb smth; s/he/it is called (by a name)

Dóken eníjiyabi he? — How are you called?
—Mary emágiyabi. — —I am called Mary.
Dóken egíyabi he? — How do they call him?

hí *vi1* — s/he arrives here from there

Dóhąc'ehą yahí? — When did you arrive here?
Duwé gicí yahí? — Who did you come with?

dókiyadahą *adv* — from which direction, where from

Dókiyadahą yahí? — Where do you come from?
Huhúžubina žéciyadahą wahí no. — I come from around Regina.

dágu *pro, quant, vs* — thing, something; what; any, none; it is something

Dágu dókanų? —Dágunišį! — What are you doing? —Nothing at all!

Dágu yacíga he? — What do you want?

daguýA *vt1* — s/he has sb as a relative; s/he is related to sb

Wįcá žé dagúwaya. — I am related to this man.
Koná! Dagúciye no. — Friend! I am related to you.
Mitúgaši né mitáwa. — This is my grandfather.

duwé *pro, n, quant, vs* — who; person; nobody; s/he is sb

Niyáde, nihų įš duwé he? — Who are your mother and father?

né *dem* — this

Né nikúši he? — Is this your grandmother?
Né mitúgaši. — This is my grandfather.

3

2
Human Body

Head Parts

tawácį *n, vs*	mind; his/her mind, mindset, goal; s/he thinks thus
Tawácį ús iyéskabi.	They converse using their mind.
Dóken nitáwacį?	How do you think?
pá *n*	head; nose (only in some constructions)
Pá ksúya.	He injured his head.
Pá knuk'ék'eğešį!	Don't scratch your head repeatedly!
pahá *n*	hair
Pahá cįcá.	He's got curly hair.
Pahá kpakcá!	Comb your hair!
pahá gisų́ *vt1-pos, n*	s/he braids his/her own hair; braid
ugísų *n*	braid
šų́bi *n*	braid
hį́ *n*	hair, fur, pelt
pesnéde, ~ pesnéda, ~ peyéde *n*	crown of the head
Pesnéde én wacíhe įkóyaga.	She has a plume on top of her head.

nasú *n*	*brain*
nažúde *n*	*nape of the neck, occiput (back of the skull)*
nawáde *n*	*temples*
núǧe, núǧe *n*	*ear*
Micų́kši núǧe įkpáȟnoga.	*My daughter pierced her ears.*
nųȟcóga	*interior of the outer ear*
nųȟ'óȟnogana	*earhole*
núǧeǧiǧija, núǧecą́šįšįna *n*	*earwax*
tahú *n*	*neck*
Tahú yubémni.	*He twisted its neck.*
tahúką *n*	*tendons at the base of the neck*
pahú *n*	*skull bone*
įté *n*	*forehead*
Įté mabíža.	*My forehead is wrinkled.*
įdé *n*	*face*
Įdé kpakída.	*Wipe your face.*
įdéhįšmą	*facial hair*
įštá *n*	*eye*
Įštá sąní wąyága.	*He sees with one eye.*
įštáha	*eyelid*
įštáhį	*eyelashes*
įštáȟe	*eyebrow ridge*
įštáȟehį	*eyebrow, hair of the eyebrow*
įštásu	*eyeball; pupil*
paȟnáda *n*	*bridge of the nose*
póǧe *n*	*nose*
Póǧe nitágac.	*You have a big nose.*
poȟ'į́kpa	*tip of the nose*
póǧe oȟnóga, poȟ'óȟnoga	*nostrils*

6

pasú *n*   *beak; tip of the nose*

tapų́ *n*   *cheek*

    Tapų́ šagíya.   *He painted his cheeks in red.*

    Tapų́ gaskába.   *He slapped his face.*

    Įštá maȟníȟni.   *I have gummy eyes.*

pudé´ *n*   *upper lip*

    Pudé knašná!   *Shave!*

    putį́ȟį   *whiskers, beard*

    pudéȟįšmą   *mustache*

įští *n*   *lower lip*

    Įští maȟpúȟpu.   *I have chapped lips*

ihá´ *n*   *lips, both lips*

    Tadé né ų́s ihá maȟpúȟpu.   *My lips are chapped because of the wind.*

í *n*   *mouth*

    I'ábi hą́da í wanį́jabi.   *When they* (aliens) *speak they have no mouth.*

    Í nagítaga.   *Close your mouth.*

cagá *n*   *palate, roof of mouth*

noȟé *n*   *gills; jowls*

hiyábate *n*   *gums*

hí *n*   *tooth*

    Hí mayúšnoga.   *He pulled my tooth out.*

    hímaza   *gold tooth*

hiské *n*   *tusk, fang, eyetooth, canine tooth*

ceží *n*   *tongue; gun trigger*

    Ceží waknáȟtaga.   *I bit my tongue.*

    cežížina   *tonsils*

cehúba *n*
    Miní žé cehúba žén ehą́'i.
    Cehúba mayázą.
įkú *n*
    Įkú togíya.
nodé *n*
    Nodé badį́da.
    nodé pšųpšų́

chin and jaw area; jawbone
The water reached his chin.
My jaw hurts.
chin
She tattooed her chin.
throat, neck
Her neck is stiff.
Adam's apple

Trunk Parts

tacą́ *n*
    Tacą́ šayá áya.
    wįcátacą
ogáza, huhá *n*
coníca *n*

ha´ *n*
    Tągán ų́bi né'ųs, há zí.

    ha'ágam
    há okmábi
jísą *n*
hiye'de *n*
amnó *n*
acóga, acógena *n*
    Acóga hįšmą́.
ahcó *n*

body
His body is turning red.
human body
limbs of the body (arms, legs)
flesh; meat and the meat of fruits
   and vegetables
skin; pouch, box, container of any sort
He is continuously outside, and
   because of this his skin is tanned.
on the skin
birthmark, tattoo
birthmark
top of the shoulder
shoulder blade
armpit
He has hairy armpits.
shoulder (below the shoulder joint on
   the outer side of the arm)

taȟpá *n*	*back*
Taȟpá mayáząą.	*I have a back ache.*
taȟpáhu	*backbone*
cemnóhu *n*	*clavicle, collarbone*
ceška *n*	*upper chest*
azé *n*	*breast*
azépįkpa	*nipple, teat* (human and animals)
makú *n*	*chest*
makú įyúskice, makúskice	*brassiere*
makúhuhu	*sternum*
cuwí *n*	*waist, chest; body* (human and animals)
cuwí ókšą	*around the waist*
cuwíc'iba	*travois*
cuwícogąą	*in the middle of the chest, breast*
cuwíknąga	*coat; shirt*
niǧúde *n*	*flank, part below the ribs*
nįdé *n*	*lower part of the back, above the rump; hip*
Nįdé mayáząą.	*My rump hurts.*
cucúšte *n*	*ribs*
cekpá *n*	*navel; umbilical cord*
cekpá yámni	*triplets*
cekpábina	*twins*
įkpí *n*	*front of torso and lap; abdomen*
mįcá *n*	*loin*
nįȟcé *n*	*area between navel and groin*
ųzé *n*	*buttocks*
Ųzé ȟniȟní.	*He has rashes on his buttocks.*
ųzóȟnoga	*anus*
sįdéhuhu, sįdédena *n*	*coccyx*

Arm and Leg Parts

įstó *n*	*arm*
Įstó mabádį míjibawįda.	*My arm is stiff; rub it for me.*
Įstó kpáweǧa.	*He fractured his arm.*
įspá *n*	*lower part of the elbow*
įspáse *n*	*point of the elbow*
Įspáse ksúwagiya.	*I injured my elbow.*
nąpcó *n*	*outer area of the upper arm; tenderloin*
nąbé *n*	*hand*
Nąbé táwa žé pąžéna.	*Her hands are soft.*
Nąbé miní omážuna.	*My hand is full of water blisters.*
Nąbé mayúza.	*Hold my hand. / Shake my hand.*
nąbé pšųkáya	*fist*
nąbé okíhąge	*finger joints*
nąkpą́ *n*	*wrist*
nąkpą́huhu	*wrist bone*
nąmką́ *n*	*veins of the wrist*
nąpcóga *n*	*palm of the hand*
Nąpcóga en oknága.	*He put it in his palm.*
nąpsíhu, nąpsú, nąbáwąge *n*	*finger*
nąbáwąge jjínųba	*middle finger*
nąbáwąge jjíwažį, wa'ébazo	*first finger, index finger*
nąbáwąge jjíyamni	*ring finger*
nąbáwąhųge tága	*thumb*
šašté *n*	*little finger*
nąpáhu, nąpáwąge *n*	*thumb*
šagé *n*	*nail, hoof, claw*
sipášage, sišáge, sihášage	*toenail*
nąpsíhušage	*fingernail*

hąwístesteye n	cuticles, little moons on fingernails
hú n	stem, stalk, leg
Hú sąní nážį.	He stood on one leg.
cejá n	thigh; leg of smth (chair, table)
cejáką	muscle on outside of thigh
cejúde	thigh
niséhu n	thigh
onúde n	thigh; hip joint
taȟáge n	knee
taȟáge huhú, taȟágena	kneecap
cąkpé n	shin; knee
cąkpéhu, humnó	shin bone
sicą́ n	shin
siką́ n	ankle, calf
hucóǧą, husní n	calf
sicógądu, sicóga, sicą́de n	arch of the foot
sihú n	bone of the lower leg; sole of the foot
sihútką	muscle or tendon of the ankle
sicúha n	foot sole
Sicúha mašóga.	My foot soles are calloused.
sihá n	foot
Sihá sʼámna.	He has stinky feet.
Sihá nibó.	You have swollen feet.
sihášage	toenail
siyéda n	heel
siyédaką	Achilles tendon
sipá n	toe
Sipá waknášuža.	I stubbed my toe.
sipášage	toenail
sišášte n	little toe

Internal and Reproductive Organs, Body Fluids

wé *n, vs*	blood; *s/he/it bleeds*
Nína wé.	*It bleeds a lot.*
páwe	*s/he has a nosebleed*
wé'opta *n*	*vein, artery*
ką́ *n*	*muscle, gristle, tendon; vein, artery*
Ką́ mayútiba	*I have a muscle cramp.*
kątą́ga	*heart artery; large blood vessel*
huhú *n*	bone, bones
Hoǧá žé huhú ožúna.	*That fish is bony.*
Šúga žé huhú yamnúǧa.	*That dog is crushing a bone.*
wįcáhuhu	*skeleton*
cubá, ~ cubé *n*	*marrow*
tacúba	*animal marrow*
niǧé *n*	*stomach, abdomen, tripe* (edible lining of an animal stomach)
Niǧé yazą́.	*He has a stomach ache.*
niǧé húde, niǧé įhókun *cp*	*lower part of the stomach below the navel*
šubé *n*	*guts, intestines*
šibúde *n*	*groin* (area below the navel)
cądé *n*	*heart; seat of emotions, feelings, sentiment*
Cądé įmánažį žehą́.	*I had a heart attack then.*
caǧú *n*	*lung*
Wįcá íyąges'a žé, caǧú wašté yuhá.	*That man is a runner, he has good lungs.*[2]

---

2   Fourstar 1978, 10.

pí *n*	*liver*
tapí *n*	*ruminant liver*
pizí *n*	*gall bladder*
pišnéja, tapíšnude *n*	*spleen*
nɛ́žeha *n*	*bladder*
šubégažada įcáğa *n*	*appendicitis*
ažų́kta, ~ ažų́tka *n*	*kidney*
Ažų́kta mayázą.	*My kidneys hurt.*
caná, caną́ *n*	*area inside the thigh from hip to the knee; crotch, genital area*
canópa *n*	*crotch*
Canópa naȟtága.	*He kicked him in the crotch.*
cé *n*	*penis*
cehį́	*man's pubic hair*
cetápą *n*	*male genitalia (penis and testicles)*
snúga *n*	*foreskin; idiot, a person who is pretending not to know anything*
susú, susúna *n*	*testicles*
šą́ *n*	*vagina*
šąhį́	*woman's pubic hair*
įštámniğe *n*	*tear (as in crying)*
asą́bi *n*	*milk*
Asą́bi žé sewí.	*That milk is sour.*
įjášpe *n*	*phlegm*
ȟ'ą́ *n*	*scab*
tažó *n*	*saliva, spit*
ímneze *n*	*drool, saliva*
tų́ *n*	*pus*
paȟní *n*	*snot, mucus*

cešní, ųkcé *n*	*shit, feces*
paȟpúȟpu *n*	*dandruff*
hecéšpu *n*	*wart*

Animal Parts

hiské *n*	*tusk, fang, eyetooth, canine tooth*
šųkhį́ *n*	*wool*
sįdé *n*	*tail*
ȟubáhu *n*	*wing*
ho'ábe *n*	*fish fins*
sįsį́ *n*	*fish scales; slime*
šų́, wíyaga šų́ *n, cp*	*longest feathers on the wing*
wíyaga *n*	*feather*
wó'įšte, ~ wóhįste *n*	*eagle feather, plume, down feathers*
wacį́he *n*	*feather, plume tied up in the hair*
hé *n*	*horn*
tanó *n*	*meat, flesh*
įkní *n*	*grease obtained from marrow, or from thin and soft layers of fat inside the stomach*
tabó *n*	*ruminant duodenum (part of the small intestine)*
azé *n*	*breast*
azépįkpa	*nipple, teat* (human and animals)
dáza *n*	*inner, fleshy part of a cow's udder*

14

Bodily Functions and Actions

knébA *vi1*
Mayázą hį́kna waknébe no.

s/he vomits
 I am sick and vomiting.

knemkíyA *vt1-caus*
Tanó žé knemmą́kiya.

s/he/it makes sb vomit
 This meat made me vomit.

abámnu *vi1*
Ecágen awábamnu.

s/he/it belches, burps
 I often belch.

wį́dukA *vs*

s/he relieves him/herself (urinate,
 defecate); *uses the bathroom*

Wį́duke í.

 He went to the bathroom.

cesní *vs, n*

s/he/it defecates, takes a shit;
 feces, dung, shit

Nén nicésnįkta he?
Cesnį́kta.
Cesní oyátaga.

 Are you taking a shit here?
 She is going to the bathroom.
 She is constipated.

néžA *vi1, n*
Yanéžįkta he?
Hokšína né nežémna.

s/he/it urinates; urine
 Are you going to urinate?
 The boy smells of urine.

onéžA *vt1*

s/he urinates on/in smth; s/he pees
 in bed

Owága onéžįktešį ų́spéwakiya.

 I taught him not to urinate in bed.

anéžA *vt1*
Cą́ awáneža.

s/he urinates on smth
 I urinated on the tree.

tažóšA *vi1*

s/he spits, expectorates

atažóšA *vt1, n*

s/he spits on smth; spittoon

céyA *vi1*
Dágucen yacéya?
Mitáwjju! Céyešį wo!

s/he cries
 Why are you crying?
 My wife! Do not cry!

gíjiceyA *vt1-benef*	*s/he cries for sb*
įštámnįğe *n*	*tear* (as in crying)
wé *n, vs*	*blood; s/he/it bleeds*
wé hiyáyA	*s/he/it is bleeding*
weȟáȟa	*s/he has a hemorrhage,*
	bleeds constantly
weyÁ	*s/he causes sb to bleed*
páwe	*s/he has a nosebleed*
o'óye *n*	*scar*

Cosmetics and Grooming

įbákca *n*	*comb*
Įbákca žé mitáwa.	*That's my comb.*
pahá įbákca *cp*	*hair brush, comb*
kpakcá *vt1-pos*	*s/he combs his/her own*
Pahá kpakcá.	*Comb your hair.*
cicá *vs*	*s/he/it is curly* (hair)
Pahá cicá.	*He has curly hair.*
gisų́ *vt1-pos*	*s/he braids his/her own hair*
Mikúši dąyą́ gisų́s'a.	*My grandmother always braided*
	her hair nicely.
págisų *vt1-pos*	*s/he braids his/her hair*
pahá gisų́	*s/he braids his/her own hair; braid*
pahá gíjisų	*s/he braids his/her hair for him/her*
knukcá *vt1-pos*	*s/he undoes his/her own braids*
tapų́šage *n*	*rouge for the cheeks*
íšagiya, įštíšage *n*	*lipstick*

yužáža *vt2*

Dáguškina yužáža.

Žená yužážabišį.

knužáža *vt1-pos*

Tacą́ waknúžaža.

Cuwíknąga knužáža wo!

gíjiyužaža *vt1-benef*

Hayábi wįcágijiyužaža.

s/he washes sb, smth by rubbing

Bathe the baby.

Those are not washed.

s/he washes his/her own thing

I washed my body.

Wash your shirt!

s/he washes sb, smth for him/her

She washed their clothes for them.

3

Food and Drinks

Eating and Drinking

wódA *vi1*

Mį́š wówadįktehtįyą.

Waná wo'ų́das.

Né wowádįkte né'įš
pinámayaye no.

yúdA *vt2*

Dóhą yúda?

Wóyude mitáwa žé iyúha yúdabi.

Škoškóbena wąží núda he?

oyún wašté *vs*

Dágu co'ų́ba né oyún wašté.

wók'u *vt1*

Gugúša žé wók'u.

Šúga wówįcak'ubįšį.

nodį́n t'A *vs*

Nodį́n t'a ayéšį.

Nína nodį́n mat'a áya.

s/he/it eats

I want to eat too.

Let us eat now.

For what I am about to eat,
I thank you.

s/he/it eats smth

When did she eat it?

They ate all of my food.

Are you eating a banana?

it is good to eat; it tastes good

What she cooks tastes good.

s/he feeds sb, an animal

Feed that pig.

The dogs were not fed.

s/he/it is hungry, starving

He is not that hungry.

I am getting really hungry.

19

temyÁ *vt1*
Owá temwáya.

ípi *vs*
ínipi he? — Nína įmápi,
pinámayaye no.

įyútA, ~ iyútA *vt2*

Taspą ohnáte co'úbabi né įyúta.

waštémna *vs, n*
Ağúyabi né waštémna.

hųwí *vs*
Tanó žé'įš hųwí.

yaktÁ, ~ yatkÁ *vt2*
Dágu natká?
Dágu yatkábi yacígabi he?
Búza skána gá asábi yatká.

yağóba *vt2*
Miníwaką yağóba.

mni'ít'a áyA *vs*
Šúgataga žé mni'ít'a áya.
Nína mni'ímat'a áya.

s/he/it eats it all, devours smth
I devour them all.

s/he/it is full, sated
Are you full? — I am very full,
thank you.

s/he tests, tries, measures smth
(food, drink, clothes, task)
Try this apple pie.

s/he/it smells good; horsemint
This bread smells good.

it has a rotten smell
That meat too has a rotten smell.

s/he drinks smth
What are you drinking?
What do you all want to drink?
That white cat over there is
drinking milk.

s/he sips a beverage
He is sipping a whisky.

s/he/it is thirsty
The horse is thirsty.
I'm really thirsty.

Food

wóyude, ~ wóyuda *n*
Wóyude óda ųyúhabi.
Wóyude awágu.

food, groceries
We have a lot of food.
I brought food.

tanó *n* meat

  Cąknágiyą žén tanó oktégiya.   *She dried her meat there on the drying rack.*

  Tanó edáhą manų́.   *He stole some pieces of meat.*

  Táȟcamnoga tanó žé wąkánašį.   *That stag meat is not tender.*

  tanó maksáksabi, tanóyukpąbi *n*   *ground beef, hamburger*

  tanó obáząbi   *sausage*

wacónica *n*   *dried meat*

wašáša *n*   *berry, berries* (generic)

taspą́ *n*   *hawthorn fruit; apple; fruit* (in compounds)

  Asą́bi yatką́ wo, hį́kna taspą́ ǧí yúda!   *Drink your milk, and then eat your orange!*

  taspą́ ǧí, taspą́ǧiǧi   *orange*

  taspą́ pestóstona   *pear*

  taspą́hįtųtų, taspą́ ǧí hįšmą́, taspą́ hįšmą́   *peach*

  taspą́ ǧí tága   *grapefruit*

  taspą́ ǧí tutá   *lemon*

wį́bazoką *n*   *Saskatoon berries*

  Wį́bazoką ųgónes.   *Let us go search for Saskatoon berries.*

wįyą́teja *n*   *cranberry*

wažúšteja *n*   *strawberry*

taką́heja *n*   *raspberry*

škoškóbena *n*   *banana*

  Škoškóbena wąží núda he?   *Are you eating a banana?*

cąpá *n*   *chokecherry, pin cherry*

  Cąpá gakpá.   *Pound the chokecherries.*

  Mikúši cąpá yušpí yá.   *My mother is going to pick chokecherries.*

cį́kta, ~ cį́tka *n*	raisin
ȟ'eyáyana *n*	grapes
waȟpé įjáhibi *cp*	salad
waȟpé tága *cp*	cabbage; lettuce (lit., great leaf)
Waȟpé tága įcáȟwayįkte.	I'll grow lettuce.
į́kšukšuna, ~ ų́kšukšuna *n*	bean
ų́'į *n*	hazelnut
yaȟúgabi *n*	peanut, any kind of nut
Yaȟúgabi žé duȟáȟa.	The peanuts are dimpled.
yaȟúgabi tága *cp*	coconut
tį́psina *n*	turnip
Pąǧí, tį́psina, wakmúhaza	She cooked potatoes, turnips,
įš špąyą́.	and corn too.
pąǧí *n*	potato
Waná pąǧí maȟ'ú.	Now she is peeling potatoes.
pį́ȟpįǧana, tį́psinaǧi *n*	carrot
tį́pšina skúye, tį́pšinašaša *cp, n*	beet (lit., sweet turnip)
wakmúhaza, ~ wakmúhąza *n*	corn
wakmúhazaskuya	sweetcorn
wakmúhazakneǧe	Indian corn
wóžabi *n*	Saskatoon soup, berry soup; gravy, stew
Mikúši wóžabi gáǧįkta.	My grandmother will make gravy.
wahą́bi *n*	soup, broth
Wahą́bi edáhą gáǧa.	Make some soup.
wayáȟoda *n*	oats
Adé wayáȟoda óda įcáȟya.	Dad grows a lot of oats.
gugúša yúde *cp*	barley
aǧúyabi *n*	flour; bread, bannock
aǧúyabi baská	dough
aǧúyabi mįmą́	round bannock

aǧúyabi mnúna	*flour*
aǧúyabi océti ągán	*bannock baked on a stove*
aǧúyabi skuskúyena	*cookie*
aǧúyabi šnoyábi	*fried bannock*
aǧúyabi zipzíbena	*pancakes*
aǧúyabisaga *n*	*toast, cracker*
Hąyákena štén aǧúyabisaga nagų́ asą́bi wacíga.	*In the morning I want toast and milk.*
aǧúyabiskuya *n*	*cake, cookie*
Aǧuyábiskuya edáhą yúda.	*He is eating some cake.*
oȟnáte co'ų́babi *cp*	*pie*
taspą́ oȟnáte co'ų́babi	*apple pie*
tanó oȟnáte co'ų́babi	*meat pie*
cį́kta oȟnáte co'ų́babi	*raisin pie*
cąšmúyabi *n*	*maple syrup; sugar, refined sugar*
cąšmúyabi pšųkáka *cp*	*candies*
Cąšmúyabi pšųkáka tutá.	*These candies are sour.*
Cąšmúyabi pšųkáka jónana mak'ú.	*Give me a few candies.*
cąšį́ *n*	*chewing gum*
Cąšį́ žé awódabi mahén ayáskam.	*The chewing gum is stuck under the table.*
štušténa *n, vs*	*salt; it is salty*
Eháš štušténa óda ecų́.	*She used too much salt.*
Štušténa agána.	*He pours salt on it.*
Nína štušténa.	*It is very salty.*
cąpásusuna, štušténa sába *n, cp*	*pepper*
Cąpásusuna yuką́ he?	*Is there pepper?*
Cąpásusuna agána.	*He spreads pepper on it.*
tuȟmą́ǧa cesní *cp*	*honey*
asą́bi sudá *cp*	*cheese*

asą́bi wį́kni *cp*	*butter*
wį́kni *n*	*fat, grease*
wį́kniskana	*lard*
wį́tka, wį́kta *n*	*egg*
Ábahotuna wį́tka óda tų́.	*The chicken laid many eggs.*
Eyáš wį́kta óda yúhabi.	*They have enough eggs.*
šų́ga káda *cp*	*hot dog*
gugúša šį́ *cp*	*bacon*
caȟyúkpąbi *n*	*ice cream*

Drinks

yatką́bi, ~ yaktą́bi *n*	*beverage, drink*
miní *n*	*water*
Miní įbíǧa.	*The water is boiling.*
Miní mnéza.	*It is pure water.*
Miní edáhą wacíga.	*I want some water.*
minískuya *n*	*pop*
Minískuya wąží mak'ú wo.	*Give me a pop.*
miní sudá *cp*	*alcohol*
minį́biǧa *n*	*beer*
Minį́biǧa núba opéwatųkta.	*I'll buy two beers.*
hąbí *n*	*juice*
taspą́ hąbí	*apple juice*
taspą́ ǧí hąbí	*orange juice*
waȟpé *n*	*tea, leaf*
Waȟpé nągú asą́bi mnuhá.	*I have tea and milk.*
Waȟpé edáhą mak'ú!	*Give me some tea!*
Waȟpé nówa škąšká.	*All the leaves are shaking.*

waȟpé acáǧa *cp*
 Duwé waȟpé acáǧa gáǧa?
asą́bi *n*
 Asą́bi žé sewí.
huȟnáȟyabi *n*
 Huȟnáȟyabi wįcáwejaǧįkta.
 Huȟnáȟyabi yacíga? — Há,
  edáhą wacíga.

iced tea
 Who made iced tea?
milk
 That milk is sour.
coffee
 I will make coffee for them.
 Do you want coffee? — Yes,
  I want some.

Cooking and Cooking Implements

špąyÁ *vt1*
 Pąǧí, típsina, wakmúhaza
  į́š špąyá.
wašpáyÁ *vi1-abs*
 Mikúši nína wašpáyąbi wayúpi.

 Mihų́ nakų́ mitų́wi į́š wašpáyąbi
  ógiyabi.
co'ų́bA *vt1*
 Mihų́ tanó co'ų́ba hį́kna wožábi
  gáǧa.
 Miyé cowá'ųba.
wacó'ųbe *n*
wacó'ųbA *vi1-abs*
 Wacó'ųbabi ogíhiši.̨
wį́kni owáco'ųba, įwáco'ųba,
 ~ įwáco'ųbe *cp, n*

s/he cooks, bakes smth
 She cooked potatoes, turnips,
  and corn too.
s/he cooks things
 My grandmother is very skilled
  at cooking.
 My mother and my aunt also
  helped her cook.
s/he roasts smth; s/he fries smth
 My mother roasted meat and made
  gravy.
 I cook my own dish.
baker
s/he roasts, fries, cooks things
 She cannot cook.
frying pan

ohĄ *vtı*
s/he cooks smth by boiling

O'ápe šákpe ohą.
Boil it for six hours.

Iná pasú agástaga ohą žé nína
The turkey my mother boiled

tągáȟtiyą.
is very big.

wóhĄ *viı-abs*
s/he cooks things by boiling

Wóyahą he?
Are you cooking?

įwóhe *n*
cooking pot

štúnyA *vtı-caus*
s/he thaws, defrosts smth

Tanó štúnya!
Thaw the meat!

agánA *vtı*
s/he pours liquid on sb, smth;

s/he spreads, sprinkles smth on it

Cąpásusuna agána.
He spreads pepper on it.

bapsų́ *vtı*
s/he pours, spills a liquid out;

s/he empties a container

Wį́kni bapsų́.
He spilled oil.

įjáhiyA *vtı*
s/he blends, mixes smth together, with it

Asą́bi wį́kni įjáhiwayįkta.
I will mix it with butter.

įjášoša *vtı*
s/he mixes smth into it to thicken it

mína *n*
knife

Dukté'ega kóšta mína wacíga.
I want any knife.

įcápena *n*
fork

Įcápena mak'ú.
Give me a fork.

kiškána *n*
spoon

Kiškána niyúha wabáwiyakpa.
I polished all the spoons.

kiškána tága *cp*
ladle

į'íjuna, íjuna *n*
cup, glass

Į'íjuna wąží yaknúha he?
Does she have a cup with her?

Íjuna óda.
There are a lot of cups.

wahíyoknąga *n*
bottle, glass, jar; cooking pot

Wahíyoknąga žé žąžą́.
That jar is transparent.

iyógapte, ogápte *n*
  Iyógapte ecúmakiya.
  Iyógapte oȟní žená baȟpú.
iyógapte sába *cp*
iwóbaska *n*
océti *n*
  Océti gakná nawážį.
  Océti natága!
océti waką́ *cp*

plate, dish; shell; dipper
  She makes me do the dishes.
  Scrape those dirty plates.[3]
frying pan
bread pan
fireplace, hearth; stove, oven
  I am standing beside the stove.
  Turn the stove off!
microwave oven

---

3   Fourstar 1978, 8.

4

Clothing and Getting Dressed

Articles of Clothing

hayábi *n*
    clothes, costume, suit
  Wówaši hayábi wéc'ų.
    I put on my working clothes.
  Hayábi wįcágijiyužaža.
    She washed their clothes for them.
  hayábi oktéyabi
    clothes hanger
  hayábi opíye
    suitcase
  hayábi owópetų
    clothing store
gağábi *n*
    clothes
  dáguškina gağábi
    children's clothes
hatéja *n*
    new clothes
zizíbena *n*
    cloth, fabric
  Zizíbena izį́mna.
    The cloth has a burnt smell.
  zizíbena cuwíknąga *cp*
    T-shirt (lit., fabric shirt)
  zizíbenaskana
    muslin
wapáha *n*
    cap, hat, bonnet
  Wapáha tó žé waknúha.
    I have my blue hat with me.

cuwíknąga *n* — coat; shirt

    Cuwíknąga knužáža wo! — *Wash your shirt!*

    cuwíknąga háska — *long coat, shirt*

hųská *n* — pants, leggings

    Hųská né duktén opéyatų he? — *Where did you buy these pants?*

    hųskána — *stockings*

    hųskáto — *blue jeans, denims*

    wíc'į hųská — *chaps*

mahén hųská *cp* — long johns, thermal underwear

mahén ų́bi, mahén hayábi *cp* — underwear

oyák'ų *n* — socks, stockings

    Oyák'ų gic'ų́šį. — *He is not wearing his socks.*

hą́ba *n* — moccasins, shoes

    Hą́ba né įyúta. — *Try these moccasins on.*

    Hą́ba né ogáȟnokwagiya. — *I got my shoes wet.*

    hą́ba kšúbi — *decorated moccasins*

    hą́ba oskábi, hąbóska — *quilled moccasins*

    hą́basicų — *moccasin soles*

    cą̨šíhąba — *rubber boots*

    osníhąba — *overshoes*

cą́hąba *n* — shoes

    cą́hąba owópetų tíbi — *shoe store*

    cą́hąba háske — *cowboy boots*

    cą́hąba įsámye — *shoe polish*

psé, wahą́ba *n* — snowshoes

    Psé žé maštį́ja wąží wįcášta wįcák'u. — *A rabbit gave the people a pair of snowshoes.*

    Wahą́ba gic'ų́! — *Put your snowshoes on!*

siyéda wagą́du *cp* — high heels

įpíyaga *n* — belt

įjáše *n* — button, safety pin

o'ópiyeda *n* — pocket

    O'ópiyeda yubáǧe. — He pulls it out of the pocket.

įpíyaga įjášeye *cp* — belt buckle

nąbíkpa *n* — gloves, mittens

    Nąbíkpa yaknúha he? — Do you have your mittens with you?

sąksája *n* — dress

    Waȟcá né sąksája awágaǧeǧekta. — I will sew this flower on the dress.

šiná *n* — blanket, robe, shawl

    Wįkóške né šiná ayázabi ú. — This young woman was wearing a beaded shawl.

nąpsíoȟną'į *cp* — ring

    Nąpsíoȟną'į wiyákpaya yįgá. — The ring is shiny.

nuȟ'ó'į *n* — earrings

    nuȟ'ó'įkiyA — s/he puts earrings on sb's ears

įštáyabi *n* — eyeglasses

    įštáyabi sába — sunglasses

makú įyúskice, makúskice *cp, n* — brassiere

Wearing

įc'ícuwa *vi3-refl* — s/he gets dressed

    Waníyedu osnókyabi háda įc'ícuwabi. — They knew about winter and how to get dressed.

ú *vi3* — s/he wears smth

    Wapáha né núkta he? — Are you going to wear this hat?

    Cuwíknąga ziyéna žé mú. — I am wearing a yellow shirt.

gic'ú *vti1-pos* — s/he wears his/her own (clothes, jewelry)

    Owá gic'ú. — Wear all your clothes.

    Oyák'ų gic'úšį. — He is not wearing his socks.

gitų *vt1-pos* — s/he wears his/her clothes or smth over the upper body part

Įdéha gitų. — *Wear your face mask.*

ųkíyA *vt1-caus* — s/he makes sb wear smth

Cuwíknąga žé ųkíya. — *Make him wear his coat.*

ohĄ́ *vt1* — s/he wears a shoe

į *vt1* — s/he wears smth on the shoulder

Šiná wąží į́. — *She is wearing a blanket over her shoulders.*

nap'į́ *vt1* — s/he wears smth on the neck

Nawáp'įc. — *I wore it specifically on the neck.*

įknúšnogA *vt1-pos* — s/he undresses him/herself, takes off his/her clothes

įknúžužu *vi3-refl* — s/he undresses him/herself

Įknúžužu hį́kna įyúga. — *He undressed and went to bed.*

įknų́zA *vi3-refl* — s/he dresses him/herself in a certain way

Cosyá mįknų́zįkta! — *I will dress warm!*

Wací įknų́za. — *She is dressed in regalia.*

Owá dąyą́ įknų́zabi. — *They are all well-dressed.*

šnišníyena *adv* — naked, with no clothes on

Šnišníyena mįštímįkte no! — *I will sleep naked!*

įyútA, iyútA *vt2* — s/he tests, tries, measures smth (food, drink, clothes, task)

Hą́ba né įmnúta. — *I tried these shoes.*

Ceremonial Clothing

hą́m'ayazabi *n* — beaded moccasins

hą́m'oskabi *n* — quilled moccasins

wąžú *n*	*quiver*
tešnága *n*	*bandana, crown* (any head dress)
wa'ážutųbi *n*	*regalia, decorated outfit*
wókoyage *n*	*clothes, fancy clothes, outfit*
įwáci *n*	*dance outfit*
wací įknúza *n*	*s/he is dressed in regalia*
wíyaga wapáha *cp*	*feather hat; war bonnet*
wíyaga wapáha sįdéyųke *ph*	*war bonnet with trailer*
cągáȟage *n*	*trailer of a war bonnet*
wacíȟe *n*	*plume*
pahį́ pahá *cp*	*porcupine quill hat*
teȟpí *n*	*buckskin*
teȟpí sąksája	*buckskin dress*
teȟpí hųská	*deer hide leggings*
teȟpíȟąba	*hide moccasins*
teȟpípąpą	*soft hide* (like deer hide)
coknága *n*	*breech cloth*
cokną́kkitų	*s/he wears his/her breechcloth*
óska *vt1*	*s/he decorates smth* (outfit, rawhide)
	with porcupine quills
óskabi	*it is quilled*
hą́ba oskábi, hąbóska	*quilled moccasins*
wóska *vi1-abs*	*s/he does quillwork*
Iná wóska:ga.	*Mom was quilling.*
hą́ba kšúbi *cp*	*decorated moccasins*
owį́ža basísA *vi1*	*s/he quilts, does quilt work*
šnašnána *n*	*dancing bell*
šnašná sąksája	*jingle dress*
wanáp'į *n*	*necklace*
huhúwanap'į	*breastplate, necklace*

tatága wapáha *cp*	*buffalo headdress*
įjápsįde *n*	*whip*

Washing and Mending Clothes

šába, šam- *vs*	*it is dirty*
šam'įc'iyA *vi3-refl*	*s/he/it dirties him/her/itself*
Škáda hą́da ní:::nah̃ šam'įc'iya.	*When he played he always got very dirty.*[4]
šnušnúda *vs*	*s/he/it is dirty*
šnušnúnkiya *vt1-pos*	*s/he dirties his/her own*
Hųská šnušnúnkiya.	*He dirtied his pants.*
gah̃náda *vs*	*s/he/it is stained*
gíjah̃nada *vs3-pos*	*s/he has a stain on his/her own* (clothes)
Cuwíknąga mijáh̃nada.	*I got a stain on my coat.*
yužáža *vt2*	*s/he washes sb, smth by rubbing*
Žená yužážabišį.	*Those are not washed.*
wayúžaža *vi1-aux*	*s/he washes things by scrubbing; does laundry*
Ą́ba yužáža hą́dahą wamnúžaža.	*On Saturdays I do laundry.*
knužáža *vt1-pos*	*s/he washes his/her own thing*
Dágu nówa knužáža hį́k gabúskiya.	*She washed all of her things and dried them in the sun.*
gíjiyužaža *vt1-benef*	*s/he washes sb, smth for him/her*
Hayábi gíjiyužaža.	*She washed their clothes for them.*
įbáskij, įwábažáža *n*	*washboard*

---

4   BigEagle 2019, 4.

owáyužažabi *n*	*laundry*
įyúžaža *n*	*soap, laundry soap*
įyúžažamno *n*	*laundry soap* (granular)
gaǧéǧe *vt1-redup*	*s/he sews smth*
Sąksája žé wąží wagáǧeǧe.	*I sew this dress.*
wagáǧeǧe *vi1-abs*	*s/he sews things*
wagáǧeǧe wíyena	*seamstress*
agáǧeǧe *vt1-dit*	*s/he sews, stitches smth onto it (ribbon, patch)*
Waȟcá né sąksája agáǧeǧe.	*Sew this flower on the dress.*
gíjaǧeǧe *vt1-benef*	*s/he sews smth for him/her*
Cuwíknąga né míjaǧeǧe.	*Sew this shirt for me.*
basísA *vt1*	*s/he sews, stitches smth*
Mikúši šiná basísa.	*My grandmother sewed the blanket.*
abásisA *vt1*	*s/he sews smth on it*
Sąksája awábasisa.	*I sew it on the dress.*
wabásisa *vi1-abs*	*s/he sews, mends things*
įbásise, įbásisa *n*	*needle, safety pin*
įwábasisa, ús įbásisa *n*	*sewing machine*
tahį́špa juk'ána *cp*	*sewing needle*
Tahį́špa juk'ána ús wagáǧeǧe.	*I sewed it with a needle.*
owópiyena *n*	*woman's sewing bag*
wabámnaya *n*	*s/he irons clothes*
įwábamnaya *n*	*iron*
ȟaȟúda *n*	*thread, rope*
Ȟaȟúda žé jjáška.	*He tied the rope to it.*
ȟaȟúda įwágaǧeǧe	*sewing thread*
jjášna *n*	*scissors*

yuksá *vt2*

Nųpín yuksá.

abáȟnadA *vt1*

Niyé abáȟnada!

hayábi oktéyabi *cp*

hayábi opíye *cp*

hayábi owópetų *cp*

baȟnógA *vt1*

Wi'óti žé baȟnóga.

kpaȟnéjA *vt1*

Cuwíknąga tága wakpáȟneja.

yuȟnéȟnejA *vt2*

Hųská žé ųmá knušnóga hį́k yuȟnéȟneja.

yuȟcína *vt2*

Šiná žé yuȟcínabi.

---

s/he breaks, cuts, trims smth off with scissors

   Cut it apart.

s/he stitches, pins smth on it; ribbon; silk, silk cloth

   Pin it on yourself!

clothes hanger

suitcase; dresser

clothing store

s/he pierces, makes a hole by pressure

   He pierces a hole in the tent.

s/he tears, punctures his/her own by pushing

   I tore my coat.

s/he tears smth in strips manually

   He took off one of his leggings and tore it up.[5]

s/he/it tears, frays smth (cloth, blanket, coat)

   They tore the blanket in rags.

---

5   Parks & DeMallie 2002, 16.

5

Living Arrangements

Building, Buying, or Renting a House

tíbi *n* — house, dwelling, any type of structure
    Tíbi žé yuhókšubi. — *They destroyed the house.*
    Tíbi né miyé wagáǧa. — *I'm building this house myself.*

wašíju tíbi *cp* — *framed house*

tí *vi1* — *s/he lives somewhere* (house, place, area)
    Duktén yatí? — *Where do you live?*

tijáǧa *vi1* — *s/he builds a house*

ti'ágam *n* — *roof*
    Ti'ágam gaȟmóga. — *The wind blew off the roof.*

ti'ánaȟ'am, ~ tináȟ'am *n* — *wall*

tihókun *n* — *cellar, cold storage room; downstairs*
    Tihókun ékne. — *Put it in the cellar.*
    Micíkši tihókun ú. — *My son is downstairs.*

amúǧiya tí *cp* — *garage*
    Amúǧiya tí žé ékne. — *Put it in the garage.*

ti'óba, tiyóba, tiwóba *n* door
  Ti'óba žé yušpábi? *Is the door opened?*
  Ti'óba natága wo. *Shut the door.*
tiyóba šnašná *cp* doorbell
tiyóba oyúze *cp* doorknob
ti'ų́ma *n* room
  Ti'ų́ma gá žé ékne. *Put that in the room over there.*
  Ti'ų́ma ektá yá. *Go in the other room.*
tibúspA *vii* s/he daubs a house, plasters a hole in a wall
ticé *n* roof, top of tipi; ceiling
ti'óne *vii* s/he looks for a home to buy, room to rent
ti'ónoda *vii* s/he rents a house
ti'ógijinoda *vti-benef* s/he rents a house for sb else
  Micų́kši ti'ówejinoda. *I rent a house for my daughter.*
otí *n, vii* dwelling; s/he lives in a dwelling
  Né tíbi né owáti. *I live in this house.*
įwą́knage *n* mirror; glass, window
  Zitkána įwą́knage apá cén t'á įȟpáya. *A bird hit the window and fell down dead.*
į'áni *n* ladder
  Į'áni žé ų́s iyówahi. *I reach it with a ladder.*
į'ų́tų *vti* s/he paints smth
  Tíbi žé į'ų́watų. *I painted the house.*
cągážibe, cągážiba *n* carpenter
wakéya *vii* s/he puts up a covering, lodge, shelter
cą'ówą *n* floor
  Mína žé cą'ówą én yįgéšį. *The knife is not on the floor.*

cą'ówįža, cą'ówiža n
  Cą'ówįža žedáhą wabáhi.
  Cą'ówįža žé wapíwacįšį.

owókšubi n
  Mikúši owókšubi én ų́.

o'į́štima vi1, n
  Waná cįkší o'į́štima knužáža.

owášpąyąbi, owášpąye n
  Owášpąye én océti mnusníšį
  cén ti'ókada.

én yągábi ph

o'į́knužaža n
  O'į́knužaža én hayábi nitáwa
  éya wo.

**owį́dukabi, owį́duka, owį́duka
tíbi** n, cp
  Owį́dukabi oḣnóga mahén hįḣpáya.
  Micų́kši owį́duka yaknúžaža cá.

į'ókanye n
įjánųzakiya n
ti'óganu n

wooden floor, mat
  I picked it up from the floor.
  The floor is not clean.

garden
  My grandmother is in the garden.

s/he sleeps inside smth; bed, bedroom
  Now, son, clean your bedroom.

kitchen
  *I did not turn off the stove in the
  kitchen so it is hot in the house.*

living room

bathroom; washbasin, sink
  *Take your clothes from the
  bathroom.*

toilet; bathroom, outhouse

  He fell into the toilet hole.
  My son is cleaning his bathroom.

heating, heater
electric fan
house fan

Household Work and Objects

yudáda vt2
tiyúdada vi2
tiyúwąga vi2
  Koškábi nówa tiyúwągabi.

s/he cleans smth (sweep, dust, wipe)
s/he cleans, tidies up a house
s/he takes a lodge down
  *All of the young men took the
  lodge down.*

wapíwacįšį *vi3*
Wįcá žé wapíwacįšį.
Cą́ówįža žé wapíwacįšį.

s/he is dirty, sloppy, unkempt
That man is slovenly.
The floor is not clean.

bakį́dA *vt1*

s/he wipes, brushes sb, smth off;
cleans the surface of smth

Awódabi bakį́dešį.
Awódabi bakį́da ócijiyakta.

He did not wipe off the table.
I will help you clean the table.

basmíyą *vt1*
Awódabi wabásmiyą.
įbásmiyąyą *n*

s/he clears, cleans the surface of smth
I cleared the table.
anything used to clean, polish smth
(polishing cloth, steel wool)

yužáža *vt2*
Dáguškina yužáža.
Iyógapte yužáža wo.

s/he washes sb, smth by rubbing
Bathe the baby.
Wash the dishes.

knužáža *vt1-pos*
Dágu nówa knužáža.
Cuwíknąga knužáža wo!

s/he washes his/her own thing
She washed all of her things.
Wash your shirt!

gíjiyužaža *vt1-benef*
Hayábi wįcágijiyužaža.

s/he washes sb, smth for him/her
She washed their clothes for them.

wayúžaža *vi1-abs*

s/he washes things by scrubbing;
does laundry

Ą́ba yužáža hą́dahą wamnúžaža.

On Saturdays I do laundry.

wóžaža *vi1-abs*
tiyúžaža *vi2*
įwáyužaža *n*
owáyužažabi *n*
įyúžažamnu *n*
owážaža *n*
ogáǧe *vt1*

s/he washes things
s/he cleans a house; washes the floor
washing machine
laundry
laundry soap
washtub
s/he gathers smth in it (as when one
picks up dust after sweeping)

bahí *vt1* — s/he gathers, picks up smth
  Cąsága wabáhi. — I gather some twigs.
  Makóce dahą́ bahí. — He picked it up from the ground.

sakyÁ *vt1-caus* — s/he dries smth that is wet
  Hą́ba mitáwa ogą́hnoga cén sakwáyįkta. — My moccasins got wet so I'll dry them.

busyÁ *vt1* — s/he dries smth
  Coníca busyá jé. — He always dries the meat.
  Hayábi buswáye no. — I dried the clothes.
  Hayábi buswákiya. — I dried my clothes.

gabúsyA *vt1-caus* — s/he dries smth, lets smth dry in the wind, sun
  Oktéya hį́kna gabúsya. — Hang it and let it dry.

gabúskiyA *vt1-pos* — s/he dries, lets his/her own (clothes, blanket) dry in the wind, sun
  Dágu nówa knužáža hį́k gabúskiya. — She washed all of their things and dried them in the sun.

won'ékne *vi1* — s/he sets the table

mína *n* — knife
  Mína yukmą́! — Grind the knife!
  Mína žé nína péna. — The knife is very sharp.

įcápena, įcápe *n* — fork
  Įcápena mak'ú! — Give me a fork!

kiškána *n* — spoon
  Kiškána né gigída. — This spoon is sticky.

iyógapte, ogápte *n* — plate, dish; shell; dipper
  Iyógapte ecúmakiya. — She makes me do the dishes.
  Iyógapte mnužáža. — I wash the dishes.
  iyógapte sába — frying pan
  iyógapte škokpá, ~ iyógapte oškókpa — bowl

iyógapta opíye, iyógaptopi	*cupboard*
iyógapta įyúžažena	*dishwasher*
iyógaptopi, į'íjuna o'égiknąga *n, cp*	*cupboard*
awódabi *n*	*table*
Awódabi žé ktášį.	*That table is not heavy.*
Awódabi agáŋ yúda!	*Eat it at the table!*
natágA *vt1*	*s/he closes, locks, shuts smth; it (wind) closes it, turns it off*
A'óžąžą né natága.	*Shut the lights off.*
Wíyą žé ti'óba natága.	*The woman shut the door.*
yu'įktų, yu'įtkų *vt2*	*s/he/it lights, turns smth on (light, stove, fire)*
Miyé mnu'įktų.	*I turned on the lights myself.*
Péda žé yu'įktų!	*Light the fire!*
cą'ókpa *n*	*sawdust*
mąkámnuna *n*	*dust*
yusmíyaya *vt2*	*s/he polishes smth*
Cą'ówįža mnusmíyayac.	*I polished the floor.*
gadódo *vt1*	*s/he shakes, brushes, sweeps, dusts smth off; s/he/it pecks sb, smth (tree, ground)*
Wá žená ųgádodobi.	*We swept the snow off.*
otígadodo *n*	*broom*
gağé *vt1*	*s/he rakes, gathers, sweeps smth together (leaves, snow)*
Waȟpé žená gağé.	*Rake the leaves.*
Sihá ús gağé.	*He raked it together with his foot.*
owógana *n*	*trash pile*
wašíjaȟpą *n*	*junk, trash*

wóyude, wóyuda *n*	*food, groceries*
Wóyude awágu.	*I brought food.*
wą́éya *n*	*provisions; lunch*

Home Furnishing

o'į́štime, o'į́štimabi *n*	*bed, bedroom*
ticé *n*	*roof, top of tipi; ceiling*
océti	*fireplace, hearth; stove, oven*
Océti gakná nawáži.	*I am standing beside the stove.*
Océti natága!	*Turn the stove off!*
o'ékne *n*	*countertop*
agán wa'éknebi *ph*	*shelf*
o'į́knužaža *n*	*bathroom; washbasin, sink*
onų́we *n*	*bathtub*
įyáweȟtįyą, owókma wąyágabi *n, cp*	*computer*
įwą́knage *n*	*mirror; glass, window*
o'į́štima *vi3*	*s/he sleeps inside smth; bed, bedroom*
o'į́štimabi *n*	*bed, room*
owį́ža *n*	*quilt, bedding sheet, blanket;*
	mattress, bed
Owį́ža mahén yįgá.	*Stay under the blanket.*
Owį́ža žé yumnáya.	*Spread the blanket.*
cą́ówįža agáȟpe *cp*	*carpet*
šiná *n*	*blanket, robe*
Mikúši šiná basísa.	*My grandmother sews the blanket.*
Mary šiná gága žé opéwatų no.	*I bought the blanket Mary made.*
wókoyage owópiyabi *cp*	*wardrobe, dresser; clothes closet*

įktúyąbi, pedį́žaža n	light, lamp
Įktúyąbi žé sní.	The lamp went out.
pedį́žaža n	oil lantern, lamp
Pedį́žaža žé ayúsni!	Dim the lamp!
owádA vs, n	it is lit; lights
Owáda žé yusní.	Turn off the lights.
yu'į́ktų, yu'į́tkų vt1	s/he/it lights, turns smth on
	(light, stove, fire)
Miyé mnu'į́ktų.	I turned on the lights myself.
Péda žé yu'į́ktų!	Light the fire!
a'óžą́žą vimp, n	it is sunny, lightened up; light
A'óžą́žą né natága!	Shut the lights off!
įžą́žą n	light, candle
Įžą́žą žé yusní.	Turn off the light.
awódabi n	table
Awódabi anų́k iyódągabi.	They sat on both sides of the table.
agą́n wókmabi, agą́n wóyabi cp	desk
įbáhį n	pillow
cą'ágą, cą'ágą yįgábi, cą'ágą yągábi n, cp	chair
Cą'ágą yągábi né mak'úbi.	They gave me this chair.
Cą'ágą yįgábi awódabi iyápa éknąga!	Put the chairs along the table!
Įbáhųhųza n	rocking chair
huȟnáȟyabi awódabi cp	coffee table
agą́n yągábi cp	sofa
cowópiya n	box, trunk
hayábi opíye cp	dresser
owánaȟ'ųbi n	radio
įwábazo n	television
wašką́šką škádabi, škąšká'ų cp, n	video game
Škąšká'ų škáda.	He plays video games.

6

Human Characteristics

General Characteristics and Values

wašté *vs*
> it is good, nice (event, temperature, object)

  Nína wašté.
> It's very good.

  Šúga né wašté.
> This dog is nice.

  Waštékta šką́.
> He is trying to be nice.

įwáštena *adv*
> slowly, carefully, softly

  Įwáštena wagú.
> I came back home slowly.

waštéjaga *vs*
> s/he is kind, good, good-natured, pleasant to live with

  Nidáguyabi wįcágiwaštejaga wo!
> Be kind to your relatives!

cądéwašte *vs*
> s/he is kind, good-hearted

  Nína cądéniwašte no!
> You are very kind!

síjA *vs*
> s/he/it is bad, hard, difficult, harmful, unpleasant; s/he/it is ugly

  Dágu síja awácį.
> He is tormented.

sijá akípa	s/he encounters, is afflicted with bad luck; it is bad luck
sijáyA	it is wrong
sijáya	badly, poorly
sijáyekna	s/he feels sad, badly
síjecų	s/he does smth bad
síjehtįyĄ	s/he/it is the worst, wildest, meanest, ugliest
oh'ą́sijA	s/he behaves badly
cądé yasíjA	s/he makes sb feel bad by speech
wósijA *vi1-abs, n*	s/he causes trouble, does bad things; something bad, evil, disastrous
Wįktóktobi cén wósijabi.	They did bad things because they were misbehaving.
Dóken ecágen wósija hų́n.	I wonder why he always causes trouble.
wósija akípa	s/he encounters, is afflicted with bad luck; it is bad luck
wósijeya	acting problematically, troublesome
sin-, ~ **šin-** *vcont*	bad
šin'ákipa	s/he encounters smth bad; s/he is afflicted with bad luck
watéhina *vi1-abs*	s/he is stingy
Wašíju né nína watéhina.	This Whiteman is very stingy.
cóǧA, cógA *vs, n*	s/he is honest; truth, honesty
cóǧeh *adv*	honestly, in an honest manner
Cóǧeh ecámųkta.	I will do it honestly.
cóh *adv-cont*	absolutely, truly, honestly, really
Cóh wįjáyakešį.	You are not absolutely honest.

Cóȟ žeyá? · *Did he really say that?*

Cóȟ cíga. · *He really wanted it.*

cóȟtįyĄ *vs* · *s/he/it is very honest; it is the truth*

Comáȟtįyą wįcášta žemáca. · *I am a very honest man.*

wa'úšina *vi1-abs* · *s/he pities people, is kind to people*

wawá'ųšigina *vi1* · *s/he is kind, good-natured, likes people*

Micúkši wawá'ųšigina. · *My daughter is good-natured.*

ohídigA *vi1* · *s/he is brave, fearless*

Agícida žé nína ohídiga. · *That soldier is very brave.*

ohídiga įc'ína *vi3-refl* · *s/he thinks of her/himself as brave, fearless*

wíyukcąšį *vi2* · *s/he bold, brave*

Wįcá žé nína wíyukcąšį. · *That man is very brave.*

yužágA *vt2* · *s/he mistreats, bullies, picks on sb*

Mayúžągešį wo! · *Do not bully me!*

Ecágen yužága. · *He always picks on her.*

yužą́k *vcont* · *mistreating, bullying, picking on sb*

Yužą́k makúwa. · *She is mistreating me.*

ksábA *vs* · *s/he is wise, intelligent, prudent*

Hųgá žé ní:::na ksabé cá. · *The chief was a reeeally wise man.*[6]

ksamyágen *adv* · *rather wisely, prudently*

Ksamyágen i'á. · *He talks rather wisely.*

waktá *vi1* · *s/he is expectant for sb or smth to happen; s/he/it is alert, careful, aware of smth*

Waktá mągá. · *I am sitting expecting it.*

---

6   BigEagle 2017, 9.

Mitášųga nína waktá.	*My horse is very alert.*
Nína waktášį.	*He is very careless.*
dąyágen *adv*	*carefully, fairly well, properly, with ease*
Wįcá žé dąyágen ókšą éduwą.	*The man looked around carefully.*
Dąyágen ecų́.	*He did it fairly well.*
wókogipe kná *vi1*	*s/he is fearful of, cautious of out of fear, apprehensive of*
Wókogipe wakná.	*I'm fearful of it.*
įštéjA *vs*	*s/he is bashful, shy, easily embarrassed, ashamed*
Wįkóške žé hí hą́da nína įštéja je'e.	*When that girl comes around he's really shy.*
įštéješį *adv*	*shamelessly*
Įštéješį i'á.	*She spoke shamelessly.*
įštén *vcont*	*embarrassing*
įštén įc'íyA *vi3-refl*	*s/he makes a fool of, embarrasses him/herself*
įštényA *vt1-caus*	*s/he embarrasses, shames sb*
Misúgabi įšténwįcawaye no!	*I shamed my younger brothers!*
Koná įšténmayaya.	*Friend, you shamed me.*
wį́šteja *vs*	*s/he is shy, modest, bashful; to be ashamed*
Wamą́tejanac'ehą nína wį́maštejac.	*I was very bashful when I was young.*
scúgą, scú *vs*	*s/he is shy, bashful*
Wįkóške žé mį́kayena hą́dahą mascúgą jé.	*I'm always shy whenever that young woman is near me.*
įtų́pa *vt1*	*s/he avoids sb out of embarrassement; s/he is shy*
Mikų́ įtų́wapa jé'e.	*I always avoided (out of respect) my mother-in-law.*

įcómni *vs* — s/he feels lonely, sad, homesick
 Ecágen įnícomni'! — You are always sad!
 Kiknábi cén įmącomni. — They went back home so I am lonely.
šikná *vi1* — s/he/it is mad, angry
 Waktá šiwákna! — Beware, I am angry!
 Šikná stéya no. — He is angry it seems.
šiknákiyA *vt1-caus* — s/he is mad at sb
šiknáyA *vt1-caus* — s/he makes sb mad
šiknáya *adv* — angrily
 Šiknáya i'ábi. — They talk angrily.
šiknáyagen *adv* — kind of angry
 Šiknáyagen ų́. — She is feeling kind of angry.
asásya *vt1* — s/he is proud of him/her; s/he makes sb proud

 Asásmayaya he? — Are you proud of me?
 Ecágen asásciya. — I am always proud of you.
a'íc'isaza *vi3-refl* — s/he is proud of him/herself
agísaza *vs* — s/he is proud (with negative connotations)

 Nína agísaza otí'įga. — I guess he is very proud.
agísas *vcont* — proudly
 Agísas mawáni. — I walk proudly.
 Agísas nážį. — He stands proudly.
knaškíyą *vi1* — s/he is crazy, out of control, insane
 Knaškíyą ų́šį wo. — Do not be crazy.
 Né knaškíyą. — This one is out of control.
knaškíškįyą *vi1-redup* — s/he is very crazy, out of control
 Žé nína knaškíškįyą — That one is very crazy.
wįktó, ~ wįtkó *vs* — s/he is crazy

wįktókto, ~ **wįtkótko** *vs-redup* s/he is bad, crazy; misbehaves

 Wįktókto cén wagábe. *He misbehaved so I spanked him.*

 Wįktóktobi cén wósijabi. *They ruined it because they were bad.*

wįktógağA, **wįtkótkogağA** *vi1* *s/he makes a fool out of him/herself*

 Owá wįktó'ųgağabi. *We all made a fool of ourselves.*

awįktoktoga, ~ **awįtkotkoga**

 vs-redup *s/he is somehow crazy, retarded*

 Wįcá né awįtkotkoga. *This man is kind of crazy.*

yaktúžA *vt2* *s/he makes sb crazy by talking*

yaktúš *vcont* *talking crazily*

 Yaktúš i'á. *She is talking crazily about him.*

agíktųža *vt1* *s/he goes crazy over sb, smth;*

    s/he forgets smth

 Nécen agíktųžabi cá. *They go crazy over it in this way.*

The Five Senses

naȟ'ų *vt1* *s/he hears, listens to sb, smth; s/he*

    obeys sb

 Nacíȟ'ų no. *I hear you.*

 Dąyą́ nawáȟ'ų. *I hear well.*

 Iná nawáȟ'ų ecámųkta duká! *I should have listened to mom!*

onáȟ'ų *vt1* *s/he hears about smth*

naȟ'úšį *vs* *s/he is deaf*

anáğoptą *vt1* *s/he listens to sb, smth*

 Adé anáwağoptąšį. *I did not listen to dad.*

 I'á štén anáğoptą wo. *When he talks you listen to him.*

 wa'ánagijiğoptą *s/he listens to what sb has to say*

 wa'ánağoptą *s/he listens to things*

-mna *suff*	*s/he/it smells*
ómna	*s/he/it smells, sniffs sb, smth*
ecámna	*it has a smell, odour; it smells*
nežémna	*s/he/it smells of urine*
ošódemna	*s/he/it smells like smoke*
pédamna	*s/he/it smells like fire, smoke*
šųgámna	*s/he/it smells like a dog*
temnímna	*s/he/it smells of sweat*
ųkcémna	*it smells like feces*
waštémna	*s/he/it smells good*
wąyágA *vt2, vi2*	*s/he/it sees sb, smth; s/he/it sees;*
	s/he has sight
Aké wącímnagabįkte no.	*I will see you all again.*
Duktén šúga žé wąnága he?	*Where did you see the dog?*
Wąmnága owágihi.	*I can see.*
wągíknagA *vt1-pos*	*s/he sees his/her own* (relative)
wą'íc'iknagA	*s/he sees him/herself*
yu- *pref*	*manually* (with the hand, fingers), *by*
	pulling; s/he/it causes sb, smth to be
yubémni	*s/he twists smth manually*
yuškóba	*s/he bends smth manually*
bažíbA *vt1*	*s/he pokes, touches sb, smth lightly*
įyútA, ~ **iyútA** *vt2*	*s/he tests, tries, measures smth*
	(food, drink, clothes, task)
Wahpé né įyúta.	*Try this tea.*
įgíjiyutA *vt1-benef*	*s/he tries, measures, tastes sb else's*
Wožábi įmíjiyuta!	*Try my gravy!*
oyún wašté *vs*	*it is good to eat; tastes good*
Dágu co'úba né oyún wašté.	*What she cooks tastes good.*

yunwášteya *adv*   *in a tasteful manner*

   Dágu nówa yunwášteya ecú.   *She makes everything taste good.*

įyágų *vi2*   *s/he gags because of an awful taste in the mouth*

7

Feelings, Instincts, Emotions, and Motives

cądé *n*

Cądé ksuwágiya.
Macądeskuya cądé mayúksa.

cądésuda *vs*

Cądémasuda no.

cądéšinyA *vt1-caus*
Mnasíja cén cądéšinwaya.

cądéwašte *vs*
Nína cądéniwašte no!

cądéwašteya *adv*
Cądéwašteya omáwani no.

cądé úšiga *vs*
Cądé úmašigas'a duká.

cądé yasíjA *vt2*

cądé yuká *vs*
Cądé mayúką cén úšiwana.

heart; seat of feelings, emotions,
sentiment
I hurt my heart (because of her).
My sweetheart broke my heart.
s/he is strong-hearted, unaffected by
the adverse, stubborn
I am brave.
s/he makes sb sad; breaks sb's heart
I spoke ill of her and made her
feel sad.
s/he is kind, good-hearted
You are very kind!
with a good heart
I travel with a good heart.
s/he is timid
I used to be timid.
s/he makes sb feel bad by speech
s/he is considerate
I pity him because I am considerate.

cądé wanį́jA *vs*
   Nína cądé wanínįjac!
teȟína *vt1*

   Temáyaȟina he?
   Hą́ tecíȟina no!
   tegíciȟinabi
įyúškį *vt2*
   Hokší įyúškį.
   igíjiyuškį
wašténa *vt1*
   Šá žé miyé waštéwana.
   Huȟnáȟyabi, asą́bi cóna waštéwana.
waštégina *vt1-dat*
   Nína wacíbi waštéwagina.
waštégicinabi *vi1-recip*
   Wanágaš koǎká waštéʼųgicinabi.
owáštenkina *adv*
owášten-kiyA *vt1*
waȟténašį *vt1*

   Wayáwabi waȟtéwanašį.
   Ecágen ecúbi waȟtéwanašį.
kišné, akíšne *n*
   takíšne
   mitákišne
kišnégiciyabi *vi1-recip*

   Kišnéyeciyabi hųštá.

s/he is inconsiderate
   You are very inconsiderate!
s/he loves, holds on to smth, prizes,
   cherishes sb/smth
   Do you love me?
   Yes, I love you!
   they love one another
s/he admires sb, smth
   He adores the baby.
   s/he admires sb, smth for sb else
s/he likes, loves sb, smth
   I, myself, like the colour red.
   I like coffee without milk.
s/he enjoys, loves, is pleased with smth
   I really like dancing.
they like, love one another
   Long ago a boy and I were in love.
happily
s/he enjoys, is happy about sb, smth
s/he hates, dislikes sb, smth (taste,
   task, person)
   I do not like to study.
   I hate doing it all the time.
lover, boyfriend
   her beau
   my lover
they love one another; they are going
   out together
   You loved each other, it is said.

kišnéyA *vt1*
s/he loves sb romantically, steadily; s/he has a lover; s/he makes love to sb

Duwéȟ kišnéyaya?
Do you love someone?

Wanágaš hádahą kišnéya.
Long ago he loved her steadily.

naȟmá kuwága *vt1*
s/he has a love affair with sb

įhákta *vt1*
s/he is concerned for sb out of love

Kúgišiktu įhákta cén kníšį.
He was concerned for his grandmother so he did not come back home.

piná *vt1*
s/he is thankful for smth

Nína dąyą́ pi'ų́nabic.
We are very thankful for it.

pináyA *vt1-caus*
s/he pleases sb, makes sb be grateful; s/he thanks sb

Micį́kši pinámaya.
My son pleased me.

Né wowádįkte né'įš pinámayaya.
For what I am about to eat, I thank you.

wópina *n*
thanks, gratitude

"Wópina!" epá.
"Thanks!" I said.

wópina k'ú *vt1*
s/he gives gratitude

Wópina tága cic'ú no.
I give great thanks.

Ą́ba wašté né wópina wak'ú no!
For this beautiful day I give thanks!

wópinayA *vt1-caus*
s/he makes sb thankful

owópina *vs*
s/he is thankful, grateful

Nína owópina.
He is very thankful.

awácį *vt3, vs*
s/he feels, thinks about smth, has smth on the mind; it is a purpose

Dágu síja awácį.
He is tormented.

Né dágu awácį?
What is the purpose of this?

tawácį dąyą́šį *vs*
s/he is moody, feels bad

Wíhamne né ų́s tawácį dąyą́šį.
He is moody because of a dream.

síjA *vs*

Yawábi síja.

Dágu síja awácį.

įšíjA *vs*

Dágu įmą́šija.

sijáyekna *vs*

Įšną́na yįgá cén sijáyekna.

Sijáyekna i'éšį.

kna *aux*

Nągáhą né osní ųknábi.

šką́ *vt1*

Waštékta šką́.

Nína šką́.

Wéskuya táwa šką́ he?

Mikúši dóken yašką́ he?

Iyéyįkta wašką́.

ų́ *vi1*

Né téhą niyáhą ya'ų́kta!

Waná nén wa'ų́.

Dóken ya'ų́? — Dą̨yą́ wa'ų́.

Síjah ųk'ų́bi.

wacį́'iyogipi *vs*

Ą̨bédu nén wacį́'iyomagipi.

s/he/it is bad, hard, difficult, harmful, unpleasant

It is hard to read.

He is tormented.

s/he feels bad because of it

There is something wrong with me.

s/he feels sad, badly

She feels sad because she is alone.

Don't talk with bad feelings.

s/he feels, senses

These days we find it cold.

s/he tries to do smth; s/he is busy; s/he moves, behaves; s/he feels thus

He is trying to be good.

She is very busy.

How is her diabetes level?

My grandmother, how are you feeling?

I'm trying to find it.

s/he/it is, lives, exists; s/he stays, lives somewhere; s/he feels, exists, is in a certain way

You will be living for a long time!

Now I live here.

How are you? — I am fine.

We are getting along badly.

s/he feels happy

I feel happy today.

įgážąga *vs*
s/he is anxious, worried, bothered because of the lack of smth (like money)

Iná dáguniȟ įgážągešį.
Mom is not lacking anything.

Mázaska įmágažąga.
I'm hard up for money.

watókąkna *vi1-abs*
s/he feels uneasy around strangers

įcómni *vs*
s/he feels lonely, sad, homesick

Ecágen įnícomni'!
You are always sad!

Kiknábi cén įmącomni.
They went back home so I am lonely.

oȟpáyA *vs*
s/he is sad, lonely

Dóhąniȟ omáȟpayešį.
I am never sad.

įnįhą *vs*
s/he fears, is worried, apprehensive

Įnįhą yįgá.
He sits in fear.

įnįhąyA *vt1-caus*
s/he/it makes sb worry

Dókiya yá hąda įmąnįhąą.
When he goes away it makes me worry.

kogípA *vt1-dat*
s/he fears sb, smth

A'ókpazą hąda tągán yábi kowágipa.
I am afraid to go out in the darkness.

okópA *vi1*
s/he is fearful, uneasy, wary, apprehensive, on one's guard

Wanágaš okópa niyáhą ųbi.
Long ago they were always on alert.

ogícikopabi *vi1-recip*
they fear one another

wóginihąga *vs*
s/he/it is fearsome, dangerous, ferocious

Wakpá žé wóginihąga.
The river is dangerous.

yahókudu *vt2*
s/he denigrates sb

įknáhokudu *vi3-refl*
s/he denigrates him/herself

Dóhąni įknáhokudušį.
Never denigrate yourself.

otéȟigA *vs* — it is difficult, hard, problematic, sad

Dágu nówa otéȟiga ecúkta šką́šį. — He did not try to solve all of the problems.

Né wįcóyazą né otéȟiga. — This pandemic is difficult.

naháŋįštaš *part* — I wonder, I wish

Naháŋįštaš híbi. — I wish they could have come.

as'į́ *vt1* — s/he wishes for sb, smth

Wįcá žé as'į́:ga. — She wishes for that man.

wa'ás'į *vi1-abs* — s/he wishes

iyógipi įc'íyA *vi3-refl* — s/he enjoys him/herself

wó'imaǧaǧa *vs* — s/he/it is amusing, enjoyable

wó'imaǧaǧa'įc'iyA *vi3-refl* — s/he enjoys, amuses him/herself

iyógipi *vs-dat* — s/he is happy about sb, smth

Iyónigipi he? — Are you happy about it?

Niyé iyómagipi no! — I am happy for you!

Ą́ba iyógipi! — Happy birthday!

iyógipišį *vs-dat* — s/he is displeased about sb, smth

iyógipiyA *vt1-caus* — s/he/it makes sb happy, satisfied

Wį́yą žé iyógipiwaya. — I made that woman happy.

Híc'ehą iyógipimaya. — When she came she made me happy.

iyógipi įc'íyA *vi3-refl* — s/he enjoys him/herself

iyógipisijA *vs* — s/he is sick, sad, grieving

iyógipisinyA *vt1-caus* — s/he saddens sb, makes sb feel bad, sorry

iyógipišįyA *vt1-caus* — s/he offends sb

Iyógipišįciya he? — Did I offend you?

iyógipišįyą *adv* — feeling sad, displeased about smth

Iyógipišįyą wa'ų́. — I am feeling depressed.

ų́šina *vt1*
　Ų́šimana wo.
　Cądé mayúką cén ų́šiwana.
įȟé'įc'iyA *vi3-refl*

　Įȟé›įc'iya yįgá.
tayúkašį *vt3*
　Žéci yábi tayúkašį.
　Wíyą žé gicí i'ábįkta tamúkašį.

įštéjA *vs*

įštéješį *adv*
　Įštéješį i'á.
įštén *vcont*
įštényA *vt1-caus*
　Misúgabi įšténwįcawaye no!
įštén įc'íyA *vi3-refl*

wį́štejA *vs-abs*
wo'į́štéjaga *vs*
wó'įštenyagen *adv*
kibážį *vt1*
　Sųgágu kibážį.
įšką́ *vs*

gų́ *vt1*
　Wįkóške wąží wagų́ cén.

s/he pities, has compassion for sb
　Pity me.
　I pity him because I have a heart.
s/he grins, laughs at him/herself
　unpleasantly
　She is sitting grinning at herself.
s/he is reluctant to do smth, dreads smth
　He dreads going there.
　I am reluctant to speak with that
　woman.
s/he is bashful, shy, easily embarrassed,
　ashamed
shamelessly
　She spoke shamelessly.
embarrassing
s/he embarrasses, shames sb
　I shamed my younger brothers!
s/he makes a fool of, embarrasses
　him/herself
s/he is ashamed
s/he/it is shameful
shamefully
s/he is against, jealous of sb
　He is against his younger brother.
s/he/it is horny, feeling lustful, sexually
　aroused
s/he desires sb, wishes for sb
　I desire a young woman.

nawízi *vi1*

Waná aké nawízi cén.

Wį́yą žé šikná cén nawízi.

nawís *vcont*

Nawís wa'ų́.

s/he is jealous

And so now he is jealous again.

The woman was angry because she was jealous.

jealous

I feel jealous.

8

Thinking

nasú *n*

wací *vi3, n, part*

Nową́bi ecų́ wacą́mį.

Tawácį wašté no!

Dágúškina ǫǧúǧįkta wací.

tawácį *n, vs*

Tawácį wašté žé mnihą́.

Dóken nitáwacį?

tawácį dąyą́ *vs*

tawácį dąyą́šį *vs*

Ecų́šį cén tawácį dąyą́šį.

Wį́hamni né ų́s tawácį dąyą́šį.

tawácį ecédušį *vs*

Hokšína žé tawácį ecédušį.

tawácį hą́skA *vs*

brain

s/he feels like doing smth; mind, plan,
goodwill; it is about to happen;
intentive, prospective, or imminent
event

I feel like singing.

She has a good mind!

The baby is about to wake up.

mind; his/her mind, mindset, goal;
s/he thinks thus

A good mind is strong.

How do you think?

s/he is considerate

s/he is moody; s/he feels bad

She did not do it because she felt bad.

He is moody because of a dream.

s/he is stupid

That boy is stupid.

s/he is patient

tawácį núba *vs*	*s/he is undecided*
tawácį otóką *vs*	*s/he is strange*
tawácį síjA *vs, n*	*s/he has a wicked mind; bad habits*
Wagágana žé tawácį síja.	*That old lady has a wicked mind.*
tawácį wašté *vs, n*	*s/he has a good mind; good mind*
awácį *vt3, vs*	*s/he feels, thinks about smth, has smth on the mind; it is a purpose*
Dágu síja awácį.	*He is tormented.*
Dágu awácį ecų́ he?	*What is the purpose of doing that?*
agíwacį *vt1-pos*	*s/he thinks about his/her own*
wacį́tųšį *vi1*	*s/he/it is thoughtless*
Dąyą́ wóknagabi žená wacį́tųšį no.	*Those nice stories are thoughtless.*
wacį́mnezA *vs*	*s/he thinks clearly*
snokyÁ, snohyÁ *vt1, vi1*	*s/he knows sb, smth; s/he understands*
Dóken ecų́bi snokwáyešį.	*I do not know how to do it.*
Snokyáyešį no.	*You do not understand.*
Duwé onówą snokyá?	*Who knows these songs?*
snokyékiyA *vt1-caus*	*s/he lets sb know smth, lets smth be known*
Iná snokyékiyešį!	*Do not let mom know!*
osnókyA, ~ osnóhyA *vt1*	*s/he understands smth, is knowledgeable about smth*
Osnóhya wacíga.	*I want to understand it.*
wasnókyA, wasnóhyA *vi1-abs, n*	*s/he is clever, knowledgeable; wisdom*
Wasnókya he?	*Is she clever?*
Mary nína wasnókya.	*Mary is very clever.*
Wįcáȟtįyą žé wasnókya wįcá žecá.	*That elder was a clever man.*
wasnókyabi *n*	*knowledge*
wasnókkiyA *vt1-caus*	*s/he teaches smth to sb*

wasnókya-įc'ína *vi3-refl*	*s/he thinks him/herself clever, knowledgeable*
wasnókye įc'ína *cp*	*know-it-all*
wasnókye wacį́ *cp*	*nosy person*
wasnókyeja *vi1-abs*	*s/he is intelligent, knowledgeable, knows a lot of things*
Wįcášta nína wasnókyeja.	*This man is very knowledgeable.*
wókcą *vi1*	*s/he thinks, plans on doing smth*
wókcąšį wįcášta *cp*	*thoughtless person*
awókcą *vt1*	*s/he has thoughts about sb, smth*
owókcą *n*	*thought*
Mitówokcą wašté no.	*My thoughts are good.*
ašínwokcą *vt1*	*s/he has perverse thoughts about sb, smth*
Gá ašínwokcąbi įšnána én yągá cén.	*So they were having perverse thoughts about her as she sat there alone.*[7]
įyúkcą *vt2*	*s/he thinks, has an opinion about sb, smth*
Wáhįhąkta įnúkcą he?	*Do you think it will snow?*
Dóken įnúkcą?	*What do you think about it?*
įyúkcąkcą *vt2-redup*	*s/he thinks long and hard about sb, smth*
wíyukcą *vi2-abs*	*s/he thinks, ponders about things, forms his/her opinion about smth*
Žécen wíyukcą.	*That is the way he thinks.*
įknúkcą *vt3-pos*	*s/he thinks about his/her own*

---

7   Parks & DeMallie 2012b, 77:326.

ecį *vt1, vt3*
"Wanúȟ duwéȟ ú," ecį.

s/he thinks, wonders about smth
"Maybe there is someone coming,"
she thought.

epcá *vi1*

I think, it seems, apparently

žepcá *vi1*
Míš žepcá.

I think that, I thought that
I think alike.

gepcá *vi1*
Nįšnána gepcámį no.

I thought that, it seems like
I think you are alone.

ecákiyA *vt1*
Wíyą žé cądéšija ecáwakiya.

s/he considers, thinks sb is as such
I thought that woman was sad.

cet'ųknA *vt1*
Wóyaknage né cet'ųcikna.

s/he doubts, disbelieves sb, smth
I do not believe your story.

cet'ų'įc'iknA *vi3-refl*

s/he doubts him/herself

coná *vt1, n*
Cowánašįȟtįyą!
Dágu ehé nówa cowána!

s/he believes sb, smth; belief
I disbelieve it very much!
I believe everything you said!

coyá *vt1*
Wįcášta toką né coyáya he?

s/he believes in sb, smth
Do you believe in aliens?

wįjána *vt1*

s/he agrees with sb, smth; s/he believes
(in) sb, smth; s/he is confident in
sb, smth

wįjágicinabi *vi1-recip*

they agree with one another; they
believe in one another

wįjákena *vt1*

s/he considers sb to tell the truth,
considers smth to be true

wówįjaka *n*

belief

ogáȟnigA *vt1*
Owágaȟniga duká iwá'ešį.

s/he understands sb, smth
I understand it but I do not
speak it.

yapíja *vt2*

   Nína dąyą́ yapíja.

giksúyA *vt1-irr*

   Wanúȟ ųgíbišį cá.

   Miyéksuya he?

giksúyešį *vt1-irr*

   Ųspéhudana žé giksúyešį.

   Wanúȟ ųgíksuyabišį ca.̓

agíktųžA *vt1*

knašná *vt1-pos*

gaspéyA *vt1-caus*

   Gaspéyaya he?

otíʾįgA, otígA, otą́ʾįgA *part*

   Adé ú otíʾįga.

   Wįjákešį otíʾįga.

céwą, céwąna *encl*

   Wįjáka céwą!

   Cóȟ céwą.

céwąna:ga *encl*

   Céwąna:ga oká žécedušį.

wadáguʾįcʾina *vi3-refl*

dágukiyA *vt1*

   Né dágukiyešį.

---

s/he memorizes, mentions smth; s/he speaks highly of smth, sb

   He praises him highly.

s/he remembers sb, smth

   Maybe we will not remember about it.

   Do you remember me?

s/he forgets about sb, smth

   Do not forget the hatchet.

   We might not forget about it.

s/he forgets his/her own

s/he omits smth while speaking; s/he makes a mistake

s/he understands sb, smth

   Do you understand it?

it seems, I think, apparently

   It seems like my father is coming.

   I guess he is not telling the truth.

I wonder, I think

   I wonder if he is really honest about it!

   I wonder if it is true.

I wondered, I thought

   I thought it was him but it was not.

s/he feels, thinks greatly of him/herself

s/he thinks it is something

   He regards this as nothing.

ksábA *vs*
s/he is wise, intelligent, prudent

Hųgá žé ní:::na ksabé cá.
The chief was a reeeally wise man.[8]

įgáǧi *vs*
s/he is anxious, worried about smth

įgážąga *vs*
s/he is anxious, worried, bothered because of the lack of smth

Wóyude įmágaząga.
I am worried because I am short on food.

Iná dáguniȟ įgážągešį.
Mom is not lacking anything.

įníhą *vs*
s/he fears, is worried

Įníhą yįgá.
He sits in fear.

įníhąyA̧ *vt1-caus*
s/he/it makes sb worry

Dókiya yá hą́da įmą́nįhąyą.
When he goes away it makes me worry.

wakąkiyA *vt1-caus*
s/he considers sb, smth as holy

Ȟaȟátųwą cąnúpa né waką́kiyabi.
The Gros Ventres considered the pipe as holy.[9]

pe'óȟnoga *n, nprop*
idiot, person that is not smart; monster with a hole in the head

pat'á *n*
dumb, stupid person

įknúdą́šį *vi3-refl*
s/he disrespects, brags about him/herself; s/he is stupid, lazy

Wašíju né įknúdą́šį, nodéhą.
This Whiteman is disrespectful and greedy.

---

8   BigEagle 2017, 9.
9   Drummond 1976, "The Pipe of Peace."

Behaviour and Mental Disposition

šká *vt1, vi1*

Waštékta šká.
Nína šká.
Iyéyįkta wašká.
škášį *adv*
Škášį ųyígabis.
ħ'ą́ *vi1*
Dóken ųħ'ą́bįkta he?
oħ'ą́ *n*
Oħ'ą́ wašté.
oħ'áge *vs, n*

Sijáya omáħ'age.
oħ'ágesijA *vs*
oħ'ágewašte *vs*

s/he tries to do smth; s/he is busy;
s/he moves, behaves
   He is trying to be good.
   She is very busy.
   I'm trying to find it.
   calm, still, quiet
   Let us stay still.
s/he behaves; s/he does smth
   How will we do it?
action, behaviour, habit, manner
   Be nice.
s/he behaves, acts as such (as when
   joining a group); *character,*
   behaviour
   I have bad habits.
s/he behaves badly
s/he behaves well

ošté *adv*	*strangely*
wóštejA	*s/he/it is strange*
oštéȟ'age	*s/he/it is acting strange*
oštéšte	*strangely*
knužágA *vt1-pos*	*s/he mistreats, bullies his/her own, picks on his/her own* (as a child, sibling)
tawácį síjA *vs, n*	*s/he has a wicked mind; bad habits*
Wagágana žé tawácį síja.	*That old lady has a wicked mind.*
tawácį háskA *vs*	*s/he is patient*
tawácį núba *vs*	*s/he is undecided*
kuwá *vt1*	*s/he/it chases, hunts, goes after sb, smth; s/he treats, acts toward, cares for sb, smth*
Wanúȟ! Nikúwa cá.	*Beware! He might go after you.*
Wįcíjana né wakúwa.	*I care for this girl.*
gicúwa *vt1-pos*	*s/he treats, acts toward, cares for his/her own*
giknậ *vt1*	*s/he pampers, cuddles, caresses, sweet talks to sb*
įknúhA *vi3-refl*	*s/he keeps him/herself in a certain state; cares for him/herself*
Micįkši nidáguškinešį dąyậ įknúha céyaga.	*My son you are not a baby, you should take good care of yourself.*[10]
awáyagA *vt2*	*s/he cares, watches, looks after sb, smth*
Iná awámnaga.	*I care for mom.*
awáyages'a *n*	*guardian, bodyguard*
awágiciyagabi *vi1-recip*	*they watch, care for one another*

---

10   BigEagle 2019, 8.

awą́knagA *vt1-pos*
    Aknúštąbišį, awą́knaga bo!

s/he cares, watches over his/her own
    Do not lose your own (language),
      protect it you all!

awą́įc'įknagA *vi3-refl*
awągijiknagA *vt1-benef*

s/he cares for him/herself
s/he watches, cares for sb, smth for
    him/her

waktá *vi1*

s/he is expectant for sb or smth to
    happen; s/he/it is alert, careful,
    aware of smth

    Waktá mągá.
    Nína waktášį.

    I am sitting expecting it.
    He is very careless.

waktá ų́ *vi1*

s/he is expectant, anticipating smth,
    anxious, alert

waktáȟ *adv*
    Waktáȟ mągá.

on the look-out, expectantly
    I am on my guard.

waktáȟtįyĄ *vs*
waktášį *adv*
    Waktášį ecámų.

s/he is alert, is on his/her guard
carelessly
    I did it carelessly.

waktáya *adv*
    Wanágaš waktáya ománibi.

in anticipation, expectantly, cautiously
    Long ago they travelled cautiously.

yįgÁ, yągÁ *vi3*

s/he is sitting on, in smth; it is, it is
    located; s/he remains doing, does
    continously; s/he stays

    Adé waką́tąga maȟpíyam
      agą́n yągá.
    Napsų́ įȟnáye wiyákpaya yįgá.
    Iná mitą́kši įš gicí i'á mągá jé.

    My Holy Father who sits in the sky.
    The ring is shiny.
    I always sit down and discuss
      length with both my mom
      and aunt.

yįgÁ, yągÁ, hįgÁ, įgÁ *vi3-aux*
s/he remains doing, does continously; s/he stays

Įštímašį yįgá.
He is sleepless.

Ųwášį nągíkta.
You will stay still.

ecédu *vs*
s/he/it is like this; it happens as such; it is the right way

Míš emácedu!
I am like this too!

ecéya *vs*
s/he/it is in such disposition; s/he/it is affected by smth; it happens

Aké ecéya štén, dóken ecúkta cén?
If it happens again, how would he react?

įhÁ *vi1, vt1*
s/he laughs; s/he laughs at sb, smth

Duwéni įh'éšį.
None of them laughed.

Ųgíhabi no.
We laugh at it.

įhá'įc'iyA *vi3-refl*
s/he smiles

įhátA *vs*
s/he laughs hard

Mitákona įhát'emaya.
My friend made me laugh to death.

wówįhaga *vs*
s/he/it is funny

Nína wówįhaga!
It is very funny!

wayú'įhes'a *n*
joker, buffoon

įknú'įhA *vi3-refl*
s/he laughs at him/herself, about one's own behaviour

ktúžA *vs*
s/he is drunk

Waná aké nįktúža.
Now you are drunk again.

ktúžes'a
drunkard

ktúšya ú *vi1*
s/he is mentally ill

wįjána *vt1*
s/he agrees with sb, smth; s/he believes (in) sb, smth; s/he is confident in sb, smth

iyúškį *vi2*
Waʼáyazabi įmnúškį.

s/he has an interest in something
I'm interested in beading.

wawóyuškišį *vi2*
Wawómnuškišį.

s/he is not interested in anything
I'm not interested in anything.

opíʼįcʼiyA *vi3-refl*
Dąyą́ opíʼįcʼiya štén iyómagipi.

s/he behaves, occupies him/herself
If he behaves well I will be happy
about it.

gabį́ *vi1-aux*
Koška žé ecų́ gabį́.

s/he is reluctant, hates doing smth
This boy is lazy.

ksábA *vs*

s/he is wise, intelligent, prudent

ksamyágen *adv*

rather wisely, prudently

wasáza *vs*
Nína wanísaza!

s/he/it is ill-tempered, touchy
You are very touchy!

cígešį *vt1*
Úbi cígešį.

s/he objects against, refuses sb, smth
He refuses to come.

oʼį́cʼųnija *vt1*
Ecų́ maší duká oʼį́cʼųwanijac.

s/he refuses, resists
They asked me to do it but I refused.

wacą́ȟiye *vs*
Wacą́ȟįya wašte nuhá.

s/he is fortunate, has good luck
You have good luck.

síjeȟtįyĄ *vs*

s/he/it is the worst, wildest, meanest,
ugliest

wówašʼage *n*
Mastústa cén wówašʼage mnuhéšį.

energy, strength, power
I am tired, thus I do not have energy.

mnihĄ́ *vs*
Mitímnobi mnihą́bi.

s/he/it is strong, powerful
My older brothers are strong.

mnihą́šį *vs*
Wįcá žé mnihą́šį.

s/he/it is weak
This man is weak.

mnihé *vcont*
Mnihé aníya.

strong
You are getting strong.

mnihé'įc'iyA *vi3-refl*   s/he strengthens him/herself; s/he has
                              courage in him/herself
bagą́ *vt1*   s/he respects sb
   Wįcá žé bagą́bi céyaga.   That man should be respected.[11]
įknúdąšį *vi3-refl*   s/he disrespects, brags about
                              him/herself; s/he is stupid, lazy
   Wįcá gá įknúdąšį.   That man over there is lazy.
mocéǧ'a *vs*   s/he is greedy, cheeky, disrespectful
   Wįcá žé nína mocéǧ'a.   That man is very greedy.
ohóna *vt1*   s/he respects, honours sb
ohógicinabi *vi1-recip* they respect one another
   Wanágaš dąyą́ iyúha ohógicinabįkta.   Long ago they would all respect
                                          one another.
ótąna *adv*   straight, in a straight manner; in a
                             respectable way
   Ótąnaȟ máni wo!   Be a good, respectable person!
wa'áhopA *vi1-abs*   s/he shows respect for people, things
wa'áhopabi, wó'ahope *n* respect, observance for customs,
                             social rules
wóbagą *vs-abs*   s/he/it is respected
įksamyA, įksapyA *vt1*   s/he bothers, annoys sb
   Įksapciya he?   Am I annoying you?
   Šúga žé įksammaya.   The dog is bothering me.
ogíniya *vi1poss*   s/he sighs
céyA *vi1*   s/he cries
   Dágucen yacéya?   Why are you crying?
ceyés'a *n*   crybaby

---

11   Cumberland 2005, 325.

gacéyA *vt1* — s/he made sb cry by pushing, hitting
  Wagábe hį́kna wagáceya. — I swatted her and made her cry.
yacéyA *vt2* — s/he makes sb cry by speech
yucéyA *vt2* — s/he makes sb cry manually (pinching, cuddling too vigorously)
  Dóhąni mayánuceyešį no. — You never made me cry.
gahówayA *vt1* — s/he makes sb scream, cry by hitting him/her/it
  Nąbé awáhą wagáhowaya. — I stepped on her hand and made her scream.
nahówayayA *vt1-redup* — s/he makes sb squeal, cry in pain by stepping (on one's foot or tail)
įštámniğe *n* — tear (as in crying)
knaškíyą *vi1* — s/he is crazy, out of control, insane
  Né knaškíyą. — This one is out of control.
kúna *interj* — hurry up
  Kúna misúga! — Hurry up, young brother!
húȟni *vi1* — s/he rushes in
húȟniya *vt1-caus* — s/he hurries sb
  Iná ecágen húȟnimaya. — Mom always hurries me.
húȟniya, húȟniyena *adv* — hurriedly, in a hurry, in a rush
  Húȟniya wa'ú. — I came in a hurry.
  Húȟniyena wowádįkta. — I will eat in a hurry.
  Húȟniyena wowádįkta. — I will take a quick bite.
įnáȟni *vi1* — s/he hurries, is in a rush
  Há, įnáwaȟnįkta! — Yes, I will hurry!
įnáȟnigen *adv* — kind of in a rush; sort of hastily
įnáȟniyA *vt1-caus* — s/he rushes sb
  Misúga, įnáȟnimayešį. — Younger brother, do not rush me.

įnáȟniyą, įnáȟniyena *adv*   *hurriedly*

Įnáȟniyena tín hí.   *He arrived in the house in a hurry.*

10

Abilities and Talents

ogíhi *vt1-aux*
s/he can, is able to do smth

Wanágaš ecámų owágihi.
Long ago I was able to do it.

Wacó'ųbabi ogíhiši.
She cannot cook.

šką *vt1*
s/he tries to do smth; s/he is busy; s/he moves, behaves; s/he feels thus

Waštékta šką.
He is trying to be good.

Nína šką.
She is very busy.

wókcą *vi1*
s/he thinks, plans on doing smth

anó *vs*
s/he is able-bodied, as a younger person

Naháĥ anínoc.
You are still able-bodied.

ówecoga *vs*
s/he is talented

Žé ówecogac.
She is very talented.

máni *vi1*
s/he walks; s/he progresses, behaves as such in life; s/he accompanies, walks with sb

Cóĥtįyą mawáni.
I walk honestly.

škanwáyupiya *vt2*
s/he is skilled at playing games

ųspé *vs*
s/he learns, acquires a skill

Micíĥši óda ųspékta.
My son will learn a lot.

wayápi *vi2-abs*
Naȟ'ų oką́ eyį́kte žé wayápišį
jé'e sten.

s/he is skilled at speaking
He understands all right, but when
he tries to speak he cannot do it.[12]

yapíyagen *adv*
Yapíyagen žeyá.

in a verbally skillfull manner
He said that in a skillful manner.

yupí *vt2*

s/he does smth skillfully

wayúpi *vi2*
Šų́gatąga gá nína iyópsijabi wayúpi.

s/he is skilled, good at smth
That horse over there is a very
good jumper.

Dágu gáǧa hą́da nína wayúpi.

She is very skilled in whatever
she makes.

wayúpiyagen *adv*
Wayúpiyagen ecų́.

in a skillful manner
Do it in a skillful manner.

wawáyupi *vi1-abs*

s/he is skillful

yupíya *vs, adv*

it is valuable; well, in a skillful,
good manner, nicely

Amų́giya né dágu yupíyašį.
Yupíya wa'ų́.

This car is worthless.
I am doing well.

yupíyagen *adv*
Yupíyagen įknúza.

skillfully, handsomely
He dressed himself in fancy clothes.

įktų́skiyA, įtkų́skiyA *vt1-pos*

s/he finishes, completes his/her
own task

Waná įktų́swagiya.
Owáyawa įtkuswagiyac.

Now I am done with it.
I finished school.

įktų́syA, įtkų́syA *vt1-caus*
knaštá *vt1-pos*
Onówą né knaštá.

s/he finishes, completes smth
s/he finishes his/her own speech
He finished singing his song.

---

12   Cumberland 2005, 338.

76

knuštą *vt1-pos*

s/he finishes his/her own thing; s/he decides regarding his/her own thing

Wówaši waknúštą cén wakní.

I came home because I finished working.

wotkícuni *vi1*

s/he finishes eating

Wotkícuni áya.

He is finishing eating.

Wónwecųni.

I finished eating.

yaštą *vt2*

s/he stops talking about smth

Yaštą žehą, awícakidaga.

After he finished singing, he looked at them.[13]

tayúzA *vt2*

s/he controls sb, smth; s/he has the responsibility or right to do something

Hįknágu tayúza.

She controls her husband.

Ozúye ya'í cén duwéȟ Nakón-cažé cíga štén niyé tanúzįkta.

Because you went to war whoever wants a Nakoda name you will have the right (to give a name).

kuwápija *vs*

s/he/it is unmanageable

Súga tága žé kuwápijac.

That horse is unmanageable.

gaȟpíja *vs*

it is possible to make, to do

Dágu gaȟpíjagešį.

This thing is impossible to do.

wahógų *vi1*

s/he gives advice, dares

Micíkši wahówagų.

I gave advice to my son.

wahógųkiyA *vt1-caus*

s/he lectures, advises sb

Žéci yéšį wahógųkiya.

He advises him not to go over there.

įgíjiyutA *vt1-benef*

s/he tries, measures, tastes sb else's

Wožábi įmíjiyuta!

Try my gravy!

---

13 Parks & DeMallie 2012a, 85:507.

awáyagA *vt2*
Iná awą́mnaga.
Wábahta awáyagįkta.

s/he cares, watches, looks after sb, smth
I care for mom.
He will look after the sacred bundles.

awą́knagA *vt1-pos*
Aknúštąbįšį, awą́knaga bo!

s/he cares, watches over his/her own
Do not lose your own (language), *protect it you all!*

awą́'įc'įknagA *vi3-refl*
awą́giciyagabi *vi1-recip*
awą́gijiknagA *vt1-benef*

s/he cares for him/herself
they watch, care for one another
s/he watches, cares for sb, smth for him/her

11

Expressing Thoughts and Feelings

Speaking and Telling

hó *n*
  wįcóho
  Hó namáȟ'ų wo, wówacį no!
i'Á, iyÁ *vt1, vi1*

  Dóhąni én imá'ešį.
  Owáštena i'á.
i'ábi *n*
i'ékiyA *vt1-caus*
igíji'A *vt1-benef*
i'éšį *vi1, n*
Nakón'i'A, Nakón'iyA *vi1, vt1*

  Né duwé Nakón'i'a he?
  Gitézi né Nakón'i'abišį.

voice
  human voice
  Hear my voice, I am begging!
  s/he speaks, talks to sb, with sb;
    s/he speaks
  He never speaks to me.
  Speak slowly.
language
s/he makes sb speak
s/he speaks for, on behalf of sb
s/he is mute; mute person
s/he speaks Nakoda; s/he speaks
  Nakoda to sb
    Who speaks Nakoda?
    These kids do not speak Nakoda.

Wašín'i'A *vi1, vt1*

    Ecágen Wašín'i'abi.

    Dóhạni Wašín'ici'įktešį no!

iyéska *vi1, n*

    Iyéska mašíbi.

iyégijiska *vt1-benef*

    Mikúši iyéwejiska.

i'épina *n*

eyÁ *vt-irr*

    Aké eyá wo!

    Dóken epíkta he?

e'íc'iyA *vi3-refl*

egíya, ejíya *vt1-dat, vs-pass*

    Oȟ! Žé ewícayagiya.

    Dóken egíyabi he?

dágeyešį *vi1, interj*

    Dágeyešį! Dáguškina žé gídą̌ᷤ
    įštíma'.

oyágA *vt2*

    Ecéduȟ omnága.

wóyaga *vt2*

    Wóyaga cén ecų́.

ogíyagA *vt1-dat*

ogíjiyagA *vt1-benef*

    Omíjiyaga wo!

---

s/he speaks English; s/he speaks, talks to sb in English

    They always speak English.

    I will never talk to you in English!

s/he interprets, translates, converses; translator, interpreter

    They asked me to translate.

s/he interprets, translates for sb

    I translate for my grandmother.

chatterbox

s/he says smth

    Say it again!

    How could I say this?

s/he talks to him/herself

s/he tells sb smth; s/he/it is called (by a name)

    Oh! You told them that.

    How is he called?

s/he does not say anything; be quiet

    Shh! The baby is finally sleeping.

s/he announces, tells, talks about smth

    I tell it exactly the way it is.

s/he promises, tells, relates, declares smth publicly

    He promised it so he has to go through with it.

s/he tells smth to sb

s/he tells smth to sb; tells smth for sb else

    Tell me!

oknágA *vt1-pos* s/he tells his/her own (story, news); s/he confesses his/her own

Wówahtani oknágabi. They confess their sins.

o'íknagA *vi3-refl* s/he tells of him/herself; makes him/herself known

wóknagA *vi1-abs* s/he tells stories; s/he tells his/her own story

Waníyedu štén wó'uknagabįkte no. Next winter we will tell stories.

Anágihmą wóknaga. He is telling it secretly.

įwóknagA *vt1, n* s/he tells a story about smth; legend

Nağí įwóknaga. He is telling a vision.

Dágu įwóknagabi? What are they talking about?

awóknagA *vt1* s/he talks about, discusses smth

Hí ga'éca awóknagabi. He arrived and then they talked about it.

wógiknagA *vt1-dat* s/he tells sb a story

Įtúšį wómagiknagešį. Do not lie to me.

o'óknage *n* fable, tale

hugágą *vi1* s/he tells a fairy tale

Gábina hugágąbis'a. Old people used to tell fairy tales.

hugágijigą *vt1-benef* s/he tells sb a fairy tale

hugágąbi *n* fairy tale

ohúgagą *n* legend, fable

knašná *vt1-pos* s/he omits smth while speaking

i'éknašna *vi1* s/he had a slip of the tongue, misspoke

wíyuta *vi2* s/he talks in sign language, makes signs

wígiyuta *vt1-dat* s/he talks in sign language to sb, makes signs to sb

akínija *vt1* s/he debates, argues over smth

Ecágen akínijabi. They always argue about it.

akínijabi *n*
Akínijabi žé dą́yą́ knuštą́bi.

argument, dispute, quarrel
The argument was settled
peacefully.

wa'ákinija *vi1-abs*
Gicí wa'áwakinija.

s/he debates, argues over things
I am debating with him.

yukcą́ *vt2*
Dóken gicí yukcą́kta he?

s/he discusses smth
How will he discuss this thing
with him?

wahógų *vi1*

s/he gives advice, dares

hóyekiyA *vt1-dat*
Žéci hóyewįcawakiyįkta.

s/he sends a message to sb
I will send a message over there
to them.

wayápi *vi2-abs*

s/he is skilled at speaking

wįjákA *vi1, vs*
Cóȟ wįjáyaka?
Žé wįjáka.

s/he tells the truth; it is true
Are you telling the truth?
That is true.

cažéyadA *vt2*
Ųmá né ektáší cažémnada.

s/he calls sb's name
I said the wrong name.

wįjána *vt1*

s/he agrees with sb, smth; s/he believes
(in) sb, smth; s/he is confident in
sb, smth

yu'íškadA *vt2*

s/he teases, plays jokes on sb; s/he
touches sb sexually

įknádą *vi3-refl*

s/he brags about him/herself

įknúdą́šį *vi3-refl*

s/he disrespects, brags about him/
herself; s/he is stupid, lazy

wašté'įc'ina *vi3-refl*

s/he boasts about him/herself

yacéyA *vt2*

s/he makes sb cry by speech

yahókudu *vt2*

s/he denigrates sb

> Many verbs of speaking or verbs involving human voice
> are constructed with the instrumental prefix *ya-*.

yajúsina *vt2*   s/he belittles sb
  I'á hą́da wįcáyajusina.   *When she talks she belittles them.*

yapį́ja *vt2*   s/he memorizes, mentions smth; s/he
                                        speaks highly of smth, sb

ya'į́škade *n*   joke
wayá'įškadA *vi2-abs*   s/he teases, plays jokes on people
wayá'įškades'a *n*   joker, teaser
wayá'įškada síje *cp*   dirty joke
yasíjA *vt2*   s/he bad-mouths sb, ruins smth by
                                        speech
  Ecágen mayásija.   *She is always bad-mouthing me.*

wayásijA *vi2-abs*   s/he bad-mouths, speaks ill of things,
                                        people

cą́dé yasíjA *vt2*   s/he makes sb feel bad by speech
yašíkna *vt2*   s/he insults sb
ya'íyowaza *vi2*   s/he/it produces an echo (by speech
                                        or singing)

ya'į́hA *vt2*   s/he makes sb laugh by speech
ya'ónihą *vt2*   s/he congratulates, honours sb by
                                        speech; s/he brags about smth
  Wįcá žé nína ya'ónihąbi.   *They praise this man highly.*
  Adé mna'ónihą.   *I honour my dad.*
  Ecágen ya'ónihą eyá.   *He is always bragging about it.*

ya'ótą'į *vi2*   s/he announces smth, tells the news

Asking and Answering

he *part*
question marker

Dágu núda he?
What are you eating?

Né dágu he?
What is this?

ná *vt1*
s/he asks for smth

Dágu yaná?
What did you ask for?

giná *vt1-dat*
s/he asks smth of sb

Aǧúyabi magínabi.
They asked me for bread.

waná *vi1-abs*
s/he asks for things

įyúǧA, ~ įwúǧA *vt3*
s/he asks sb about smth

Niyé įnúǧa he?
Did you ask for it yourself?

Žé įwúȟ wahí.
I come to ask about that.

įc'íyuǧA *vi3-refl*
s/he asks him/herself about it

įgíjiyuǧA *vt1/3-benef*
s/he asks sb for him/her

Wįkóśke žé įcíjimuǧa.
I asked that girl for you.

wawíyuǧA *vi3-abs*
s/he asks questions, investigates

Né'įs i'ábi né'ųs, ecágen wawíyuǧa.
This one is talking and always asking questions.

okíyA *vt1*
s/he asks sb to do smth

Dágu teȟíga oníkiyįkta.
He will ask you to do difficult things.

ayúptA *vt2*
s/he answers sb

Amáyupta!
Answer me!

Magíbąc'ehą amnúpta.
When she called me, I answered.

a'íc'iyuptA *vi3-refl*
s/he answers a question s/he had

agíjiyuptA *vt1-benef*
s/he answers for him/her

wa'áyuptA *vi1-abs*
s/he answers

Duwé wa'áyuptįkta?
Who will answer?

wó'ayupte *n*
answer

Ordering and Thanking

ši *vt1-dit-aux*
s/he tells, asks, orders, commands sb

Íš uwáši.
I told her to come too.

Umáyaši he?
Are you telling me to come here?

yuháši *vt1*
s/he orders sb to carry smth

eyéši *vt1-dit*
s/he orders sb to say it

gaȟší *vt1-dit*
s/he orders sb to make it

iyógiši *vt1*
s/he sends sb away; s/he orders sb to stop doing smth

iyúgaši *vt1*
s/he orders sb to go to bed

knuháši *vt1-pos*
s/he orders his/her own to carry smth

piná *vt1*
s/he is thankful for smth

Nína dąyą́ pi'ų́nabic.
We are very thankful for it.

pináyA *vt1-caus*
s/he pleases sb, makes sb be grateful; s/he thanks sb

Micį́kši pinámaya.
My son pleased me.

Né wowádįkte né'įš pinámayaya.
For what I am about to eat, I thank you.

Pinámayaye no!
I thank you!

wópina *n*
thanks, gratitude

"Wópina!" epá.
"Thanks!" I said.

wópina k'ú *vt1*
s/he gives gratitude

Wópina tága cic'ú no.
I give you great thanks.

owópina *vs*
s/he is thankful, grateful

Nína owópina.
He is very thankful.

Forbidding, Objecting, Scolding, Promising, and Doubting

anápta *vt1*
Kizį́kta šką́ duká anáwaptac.

s/he stops, forbids sb to do smth
She tried to fight him but I
stopped her.

wa'ánaptA *vi1-abs*
gišíja *vt1*

s/he stops, blocks, forbids things
s/he forbids, stops, stops sb from
doing smth

Žé wagíšija.
Žé gišíja!

I forbid him.
Make him stop (as a naughty
child)!

ecų́kiyA *vt1-caus*

s/he makes sb do it; s/he allows smth,
sb to do smth

Žécen mikúši ecų́makiya.
cígešį *vt1*
Úbi cígešį.
iyópeyA *vt1*
Micį́kši iyówapeye no.
iyópegiciyabi *vi1-recip*
Ecágen misų́ga iyópegiciyabi.

My grandmother lets me do that.
s/he objects against, refuses sb, smth
He refuses to come.
s/he scolds, reproves sb
I scolded my son.
they quarrel, scold, attack one another
My younger brothers are always
quarrelling with one another.

wawíyopekiyA *vi1-abs*
gat'áyA *vt1*
Koškána né wagát'aya.
wahóyA, įwáhoyA *vt1-dit*
Ecámųkte wahówaya.
Mike wahómaya timánįkta.
yacó *vt2*
Waktá! Niyácokta.

s/he scolds people
s/he scolds, reprimands sb
I scolded this boy.
s/he promises sb to do smth
I promised to do it.
Mike promised me he will visit.
s/he sues, summons, takes sb to court
Beware! He will sue you.

Wįcášta yuzábi né gašgábi hį́k
  yacóbic.

*The man they arrested was jailed
  and put on trial.*

Wayáco žé yacóbi oȟ'ą́ko yuhá ca.

The judge had a speedy trial.

céyagešį *part*

should not, must not, cannot possibly

  Ú céyagešį.

He must not come.

  Cóȟ ecúbi céyagešį.

They cannot possibly have done that.

cet'ų́'įc'iknA *vi3-refl*

s/he doubts him/herself

cet'ų́knA *vt1*

s/he doubts, disbelieves sb, smth

  Wóyaknage né cet'ų́cikna.

I do not believe your story.

12

Making Evaluations

Making Positive Evaluations

dąyą́, dayą́ *vs, adv*
s/he/it is well, good, all right; well, properly

  Eyáš dąyą́.
    I guess he is good.

  Tawáci̧ dąyą́ši̧.
    He is mentally disabled.

  Dąyą́ wa'ų́.
    I am fine.

tawáci̧ dąyą́ *vs*
s/he is considerate

wašté *vs*
it is good, nice (event, temperature, object); s/he is pretty, handsome, nice

  Hąyákena waštéc!
    Good morning!

  Ağúyabi né waštémna.
    This bread smells good.

waštéšte *vs-redup*
they (objects) are good, nice

waštéya *adv*
nicely, in a good manner, well

  Mitáwaci̧ waštéya ehą́wa'i.
    I reach my mindset, goal with a good heart.

cažé wašté *vs*
s/he has a good reputation

  Wíyą né cažé wahtéši̧.
    This woman does not have a good reputation.

įcą́dewašte *vs*
                              s/he is pleased with smth, happy about smth

Hí ga'éca įcą́demawašte.   *When he came it made me happy.*

Waštémna *vs*   *s/he/it smells good*

Hokwá, wašténimna no!   *Oh, you smell good!*

Wašténa *vt1*   *s/he likes, loves sb, smth*

Šá žé miyé waštéwana.   *I, myself, like the colour red.*

Waštégina *vt1-dat*   *s/he enjoys, loves, is pleased with smth*

I'ábi waštégina.   *She enjoys talking.*

Nína wacíbi waštéwagina.   *I really like dancing.*

waštégicinabi *vi1-recip*   *they like, love one another*

Waną́gaš koškä waštéʼųgicinabi.   *Long ago a boy and I were in love.*

wašté'įc'ina *vi3-refl*   *s/he boasts about him/herself*

waštéjaga *vs*   *s/he is kind, good-natured, pleasant to live with*

owáštejaga *vimp*   *it is beautiful* (day)

owáyak *vcont*   *looking a certain way*

Nína wį́yą owáyak wašté.   *That is a very nice woman to look at.*

owáyak wašté *vs*   *s/he/it is beautiful to look at, is good-looking*

owáštenkina *adv*   *happily*

owášten-kiyA *vt1*   *s/he enjoys, is happy about sb, smth*

waštéhtįyA *vs*   *it is very good, the best, nicest*

Ecų́ žé waštéhtįyą.   *She did the very best.*

iyópiyA *vs*   *s/he is happy, pleased, merry*

iyógipi, ogípi *vs-dat*   *s/he is happy about sb, smth*

Iyónigipi he?   *Are you happy about it?*

Ą́ba iyógipi!   *Happy birthday!*

iyógipiyA *vt1-caus*   *s/he/it makes sb happy, satisfied*
  Wíyą žé iyógipiwaya.   *I made that woman happy.*
  Híc'ehą iyógipimaya.   *When she came she made me happy.*

wacį'iyogipi *vs*   *s/he feels happy*
  Ąbédu nén wacį'iyomagipi.   *I feel happy today.*

wįjágicinabi *vi1-recip*   *they agree with one another; they*
                                    believe in one another

wįjána *vt1*   *s/he agrees with sb, smth; s/he believes*
                                    (in) sb, smth; s/he is confident in
                                    sb, smth

įyúkcą *vt2*   *s/he thinks, has an opinion about*
                                    sb, smth

  Wáhįhąkta įnúkcą he?   *Do you think it will snow?*
  Dóken įnúkcą?   *What do you think about it?*

įgíknucą *vt1*   *s/he considers smth*

cądé yuką *vs*   *s/he is considerate*
  Cądé mayúką cén úšiwana.   *I pity him because I am considerate.*

wakąkiyA *vt1-caus*   *s/he considers sb, smth as holy*
  Nakódabi cąnúpa né wakąkiyabi.   *The Nakoda consider the pipe*
                                    as holy.

wįjákena *vt1*   *s/he considers sb to tell the truth;*
                                    s/he considers smth to be true

ecákiyA *vt1*   *s/he considers, thinks sb is as such*
  Wíyą žé cądéšija ecáwakiya.   *I thought that woman was sad.*

įkní *vt1*   *s/he notices, pays attention to sb/smth;*
                                    s/he investigates, looks into smth

gecį *vt1*   *s/he thought smth*
  Wíyą toká gecíbi.   *They thought she was a different*
                                    woman.

žécedu *adv*   in the correct way, thus, like that; it is
                                                   like that, it happened like that
  Žécedu ecų́.   He is doing it right.
  Wayáwawįcakiye eyé žéceduȟtįyą.   He said it exactly like the teacher.
žéceduȟ *adv*   exactly in that way
  Žéceduȟ ecúbįkta.   They will do it exactly in that way.
žéceȟ *adv*   exactly in that way
įyúškį *vt2*   s/he admires sb, smth
  Hokší įyúškį.   He adores the baby.
įgíjiyuškį *vt1/2-benef*   s/he admires sb, smth for sb else
ówecoga *vs*   s/he is talented
wóguga *vs*   s/he/it is beautiful, pretty
  Ąbédu wóguga.   It is a beautiful day.
  Wíyą žé wóguga.   That woman is beautiful, attractive.
pija *vs-aux*   it is easy, worth it, feasible, good to do,
                                                   able
  yuhápija   it is worth having
  ecúpija   it can be done, it is doable

Making Negative Evaluations

síjA *vs*   s/he/it is bad, hard, difficult, harmful,
                                                   unpleasant; s/he/it is ugly
  Yawábi síja.   It is hard to read.
  Šų́ga síja žé wąyága cén napá.   He ran away because he saw that
                                                   bad dog.
sijá akípa *vi1*   s/he encounters, is afflicted with bad
                                                   luck; it is bad luck
sijáyA *vi*   it is wrong
  Sijáyįkta otʃ'įga.   I think there is something wrong.

sijáya *adv*

    badly, poorly

    Sijáya eyá.

        He curses.

    Sijáya oȟáge no.

        He has bad habits.

síjehtįyĄ *vs*

    s/he/it is the worst, wildest, meanest, ugliest

    Búza ódabi wąží síjehtįyą.

        There are a lot of cats, but one is the wildest.

tawáci̜ síjA *vs, n*

    s/he has a wicked mind; bad habits

    Wagágana žé tawáci̜ síja.

        That old lady has a wicked mind.

owáyage síjA *vs*

    s/he/it is bad-looking, looks bad

wóginihąga *vs*

    s/he/it is fearsome, dangerous, ferocious

    Wakpá žé wóginihąga.

        The river is dangerous.

iyógipiši̜ *vs-dat*

    s/he is displeased about sb, smth

iyógipiši̜yA *vt1-caus*

    s/he offends sb

    Iyógipiši̜ciya he?

        Did I offend you?

iyógipiši̜yą *adv*

    feeling sad, displeased about smth

    Iyógipiši̜yą wa'ų́.

        I am feeling depressed.

i̜déšitkiyA *vt1-pos*

    s/he frowns his/her eyebrows; s/he looks discontented

waȟténaši̜ *vt1, vs*

    s/he hates, dislikes sb, smth (taste, task, person); s/he/it is worthless

    Wayáwabi waȟtéwanaši̜.

        I do not like to study.

    Wíyą žé waȟténaši̜.

        She dislikes that woman.

duwéniši̜ i̜c'ína *vi3-refl*

    s/he considers him/herself as nobody

teȟíyą *adv*

    with difficulty, poorly

    Teȟíyą yi̜gá.

        He is in critical shape.

ų́šiga *vs*

    s/he is poor, pitiful

    Ų́šigabi otí̜i̜geši̜.

        I do not think they are poor.

    Midáguyabi nína ų́šigabi.

        My relatives are very poor.

dogį́š *adv*   *poorly, weakly*

  dogį́š ų́   *s/he/it is weak from an illness*

  dogį́š yįgÁ   *s/he is dying, is on his/her*
                                               death bed

  dogį́šyagen   *poorly*

tawácį otóką *vs*   *s/he is strange*

žécedušį *vs, adv*   *it is incorrect; it is not in that way;*
                                               incorrectly

  Žécedušį ecų́.   *He is doing it incorrectly.*

13

Family and Friends

General Terms and Stages of Life

ti'óšpaye *n*	*group of relatives, extended family*
tiwáhe *n*	*family, household*
įknúš'aga *vs*	*she is pregnant*
Wíyą žé įknúš'aga.	*That woman is pregnant.*
wį'íknuš'age	*pregnant woman*
įknúš'akyA	*he makes her pregnant*
tų́ *vt1*	*she bears, delivers him/her*
Wįcáwatųga, iyómagipi.	*When I gave birth to them I was happy.*
tų́bi *vs*	*s/he is born*
Tahé nén matų́bi no!	*I am born here in Moose Mountains.*
cįjátų *vs*	*she gives birth*
Cįjátųga ecá, nų́babina wįcáyuha.	*She gave birth, she has twins.*
cįhį́ktuyA, ~ cįhį́tkuyA *vt1*	*s/he adopts a son*
cįhį́ktuna *n*	*human offspring*
togápa *n, vs*	*first-born child in a family; s/he is the oldest child of a family*

hokšítogapa *n*
Hokšítogapa wiyódahąm žecí
iyódąga.

first-born child in a family
The first-born son sits over to
the south.

ohágapa *n, vs*

youngest born child in a family; s/he is
the youngest born child in a family

Hokšína ohágapa.

He is the youngest boy.

bibína, ~ bébena *n*
Bibína yuhá ų́s iyómagipi.
Dágeyešį! Dáguškina žé gídą̆h
įštíma.̓

baby
I am happy because she had a baby.

Shh! The baby is finally sleeping.

dáguškina *n, vs*
Dáguškina yužáža!
Dáguškina žé waná wį́da.

baby, infant, child; s/he/it is a baby
Bathe the baby!
The baby is now crawling.

tezíȟnina *n*

baby with the umbilical cord severed;
little boy

wamnónįja *n*
Wamnónįja žemáca.

orphan
I'm an orphan.

cįjá *n*
Cįjábi dóna nuhá he?

child; one's child; cub
How many children do you have?

cįjátų *vi1*

she gives birth (human and animal)

cįjáyA *vt1*
Jan cįjáwaya.
Cįjá'ųyą̨bikte no!

s/he adopts a child
I adopted Jan as a child.
We will have him as our own child.

cįjódA *vs-coll*
Wanágaš mikúši cįjódac'ehą.

s/he has many children
Long ago my grandmother had a
lot of kids.

wįcį́jana *n, vs*
Wįcį́jana né asą́bi k'ú.
Wįcį́jana gá búza wąží k'úbi.
wįcį́janana

girl; she is a girl
Give this girl milk.
They gave that girl a cat.
little girl

gitézi *n*
  Gitézi óda wįcáyuha.
  Gitézi né nakón'i'ábišį.
  Gitézina hahábina.
hokší *cont*
  Hokší įyúškį.
  Máza hokší
hokšína *n*
  Hokšína gá tába né táwa.
  Hokšína žé nežémna.
  hokšína wąyágabi
  hokšína wąyágabi tíbi
  hokšínana
koškà *n, vs*
  Koškà né ptéjena.
  Naháĥ koníška, miyéš waná
    magána.
koškáškana, koškánana *n-redup, vs*
  Komáškaškanahą žéhą wéksuya.

wįkóške *n*
  Waná wįkóškehąkta.
wįkóškeškena, wįkóškenana
  n-redup, vs
hųgágebi *n-pl*
  Hųgágebi né'įš snokkíciyabįkta.

įšnána ú *vi1, n*
  Misúga įšnána ú.
  Įšnána úkta.

boy, lad, kid, brat
  She has a bunch of brats.
  These kids don't speak Nakoda.
  Kids are lively.
child, baby; boy
  He adores the baby.
  Iron boy
boy (between 7 and 13 years old)
  That boy over there owns this ball.
  That boy smells like urine.
  child care
  daycare centre
  small boy
young man; he is a young man
  This young man is short.
  You are still a young man, as for
    myself I am old now.
teenage boy; he is a teenage boy
  I remember when I was a teenage
    boy.

teenage girl, young lady
  Now she is becoming a young lady.
teenage girl; she is a teenage girl

parents
  The parents too would know each
    other.
s/he is alone, is a bachelor; bachelor
  My younger brother is a bachelor.
  He will be alone.

omówahįtų *n* — co-parent-in-law

wíyą, wį- *n* — woman; she is a woman

    Wíyą žé wóguga. — That woman is beautiful, attractive.

    Wíyą žé įknúšaga. — That woman is pregnant.

wįcá *n, vs* — man; he is a man

    Koškábi nówa tiyúwągabi. — All of the young men took the lodge down.

    Ogícize nén wįcášta wąží ta'óbi. — A man was wounded in this war.

    Wįmáca no. — I'm a man, warrior.

wįcáȟtįyąna, wįcáȟtįyą *n, vs* — elderly man, senior; he is an elderly man, senior

gábina *n-pl* — elders, old people

    Gábina hugágąbis'a. — Old people used to tell fairy tales.

    Gábina óhą ecágen yįgá. — He always sits among the elders.

    Gábina háda wacítųši cen. — When you get old you become forgetful.

    Gábina anáwįcağoptąm! — Listen to the elders!

watápe *n* — buffalo hunter, hunter; elderly man, ancestor

    Watápe žemáca no. — I am a hunter.

    Watápe hékta wóknagabis'a. — Long ago the ancestors used to tell stories.

watápe wíyą *cp* — elderly woman

wagágana, wagága *n-redup* — elderly woman; my wife

    Wagágana žé tawáci síja. — That old lady has a wicked mind.

wįtáge *n* — old woman

wįwázija *n* — widow

wįcáwazija *n* — widower

timágini *vt1-pos*

Dóhą mitúgaši timáyaginįkta?

ní *vi1*
Atkúgu, húgu įš nahą́ȟ níbi.

Duwéni níšį.
Búza né nahą́ȟ ní.
niyá *vs, n*
Niyášį iyáya.
niyá *vi1-caus*

Tóga nųm niwáya.
niyáhą ų́ *vi1*

Né téhą niyáhą ya'ų́kta!
Duwéni niyáhą ųbišį.
t'Á *vs*
Šų́gatąga t'á ginį́ja.
Ȟtánihą t'į́kta.
wot'Á

s/he visits his/her relative, sb else's
relatives
When will you visit my
grandfather?
s/he lives
His father and his mother too are
still alive.
No one survived.
The cat is still living.
s/he/it breathes, is alive; breath of life
He is starting to choke.
s/he/it makes sb live; s/he spares,
allows sb to live
I spared the two enemies.
s/he is living (a certain length of
time)
You will be living for a long time!
No one is alive.
s/he/it dies, is dead
The horse almost died.
She would have died yesterday.
s/he/it dies in the distance

Kinship Terms

EGO + 2 generations

	my	your	our	his/her
grandfather	mitúgaši (reference, address) ųká (address)	nitúgaši	ųgítukąkišitku <mitugášibi>	tugą́šicu tugą́šitku
grandmother	mikúši (reference, address) ųjí (address)	nikúši	ųgíkušitku	kušítku

EGO + 1 generation

	my	your	our	his/her
father	adé (address) miyáde ~ mi'áde ~ mi'átkugu (reference)	niyáde	miyádebi ~ aktúgu'ųyabi ~ atkúgu'ųyabi	atkúgu~ atkúgubi
mother	iná (address) mihų́, mihų́gu (reference)	nihų́ nihų́gu nihų́bi	inábi ~ ųgínabi ~ hų́gu'ųyabi	hųgúbi
father's brother	adéna	niyádena ~ niyádebi		
father's sister and mother's brother's wife	mitų́wi	nitų́wi	tųwícuyąbi	tųwícu

mother's brother and father's sister's husband	minékši	ninékši	nekšíjuyąbi	nekšícu
mother's sister and father's brother's wife	inána	ni'inána(bi)	ųgínanabi	
mother's sister's husband and father's sister's husband	adéna	niyádéna ~ niyádebi		
father-in-law	mitúga ~ mitúgą	nitúgą		tugágu
mother-in-law	mikų́	nikų́	ųgíkųbi	kųgú

EGO is male

	my	your	our	his/her
older brother and older male parallel cousin	micína	nicína		cįcúna
older sister and older female parallel cousin	mitágena	nitágena	ųgítagenabi	tákuna
younger brother and younger male parallel cousin	misúgagu ~ misúga	nisúgagu ~ nisúga		sųgágu

younger sister and younger female parallel cousin	mitą́kši	nitą́kši		tąkšį́co
female cross-cousin	mihágaši	nihágaši ~ nihągašibi	mihągašibi	hągášico ~ hągašicobi
male cross-cousin	mitą́hąši	nitą́hąši ~ nitąhąšibi	mitąhąšibi	tahą́ši ~ tąhąšibi
wife	mitáwįju	nitáwįju	<ųgítawįjubi>	tawįju
brother-in-law	mitą́hą	nitą́hą		tą̨há
sister-in-law	mihágo	nihágo		hągágu

EGO is female

	my	your	our	his/her
older brother	mitímno	nitímno	ųgítimno(gu)bi	timnógu
older sister and older female parallel cousin	micų́n(a)	nicų́n(a)		cų́gųna
younger brother and younger male parallel cousin	misúga	nisúga		sųgágu
younger sister and younger female parallel cousin	mitága ~ mitą́	nitą́		tągágu

male cross-cousin	mišíc̓eši	nišíc̓eši ~ nišic̓ešibi	u̧gíšic̓esibi	šic̓éšicu ~ šic̓etko ~ šic̓etkobi
female cross-cousin	mišícepą̨ši	nišícepą̨ši		šicépą̨ši
husband	mihį́kna	nihį́kna	u̧gíhį̧knągubi	hį̧knágu
co-wife	mitéya			
brother-in-law	mišíc̓e	nišíc̓e		šic̓étku
sister-in-law	mišíjepą̨	nišíjepą̨		šijépą̨gu

EGO – 1 generation

	my	your	our	his/her
son	micį́kši	nicį́kši	<u̧gícį̧kši>	cį́hį̧tgu
daughter	micúkši	nicúkši	u̧gícu̧kši	cúwį̧tku
nephew	mitú̧ška	nitú̧ška		tu̧šká
niece (male speaker)	mitúžą̨	nitúžą̨		tu̧žą́co

EGO – 2 generations

	my	your	our	his/her
grandchild	mitákoža	nitákoža	u̧gítakožabi ~ u̧gítagožakpagu	takóžakpagu

Other Terms

	my	your	our	his/her
child	micį́jena	nicį́jena	micijabi	cijena
male friend of a man	mitákona	nitákona	u̧gítakonagu	takónagu
female friend of a man	mišį́	nišį́	u̧gíšitku	šį̧tkúya

14

Social Relations

Greeting, Visiting, and Inviting

háu
    Háu koná! Dóken ya'ú?
hą́
    Hą́, dąyą́ wącímnaga.
ą́ba wašté
    Ą́ba wašté yuhá bo!
hąyákena wašté
pinámayaya
    Miyéco žé pinámayaya.
wópina k'ú
    Wópina tą́ga cic'ú no.
ú *vi1*

    Waná nén wa'ų́.

hello, hi (yes) (man speaking)
    Hello friend! How are you?
hello, hi (yes) (woman speaking)
    Hello, it's good to see you.
it's a nice day; good day
    You all have a nice day!
good morning
I thank you
    Thank you for inviting me.
s/he gives gratitude
    I give you great thanks.
*s/he/it is, lives, exists; s/he stays, lives
somewhere; s/he feels, exists, is in a
certain way*
    Now I live here.

Ȟaȟátųwą óm ųk'ų́bis'a.	We used to live with the Gros Ventres.
Dóken ya'ų́? — Dą̜yą́ wa'ų́.	How are you? — I am fine.
egíya, ejíya *vt1-dat, vs-pass*	s/he tells sb smth; s/he/it is called (by a name)
Oȟ! Žé ew̜ícayagiya.	Oh! You told them that.
Dóken egíyabi he?	How is he called?
Dóken eníjiyabi he? — John emágiyabi.	How are you called? — I am called John.
koná *n*	friend; male friend (man speaking)
Háu koná!	Hello friend!
-ší̜- *root*	female friend (woman speaking)
miší̜	my friend
niší̜	your friend
ší̜tku	her friend
konáyA *vt1*	s/he has sb as a friend
Nínaȟ konáwayeši̜.	I am not really friends with him.
gicó *vt1-dat*	s/he invites sb
Miyéco žé pinámayaya.	Thank you for inviting me.
Íciyuhana cicóbi.	I invite you all.
gicícobi *vi1-recip, n*	they invite one another; gathering
i̜gíco *vt1*	s/he invites sb (as for a meal)
Wón i̜w̜ícawecobi̜ktac.	I will invite them to eat.
timáni *vi1*	s/he visits
Micí̜kši taw̜íju gicí timáni úbi̜kta.	My son and his wife are coming to visit.
timágini *vt1-pos*	s/he visits his/her relative, or sb else's relative
Dóhą̜ mitúgaši timáyagini̜kta?	When will you visit my grandfather?

apápa *vt1*
Ti'óba apápa.
Duwé apápa he?

s/he knocks lightly on smth
He is knocking lightly on the door.
Who is knocking on the door?

iyódągA *vi2*
Iyódąga íš nągáhą wóda wo!

s/he sits down
Sit down now and eat!

omníjiye *n*
Omníjiye žén cažé wak'ú.

meeting, gathering
I voted there in the meeting.

akípa *vt1*

Dąyą́ magína acícipa.

s/he meets sb; s/he encounters, experiences smth
I am pleased to meet you.

wa'ákipa *vi1-abs*
agícicipabi *vi1-recip*
ogíjihįyą *vt1-benef*
Né mnéšį cén omíjihįyą.

s/he meets sb, people
they meet one another
s/he regrets smth, is sorry about smth
I am sorry I did not go.

Positive Social Behaviour

kóya, kówa *adv*
Íš kóya úkta.

along, with, accompanying, and
He is coming along too.

máni *vi1*

Inína mawánįkte no.
Cóȟtįyą mawáni.
Óm mawáni.

s/he walks; s/he progresses, behaves as such in life; s/he accompanies, walks with sb
I will walk quietly.
I walk honestly.
I walk with them.

aknáda *vt1*
gicíja *vt1*

Wíyą žé wécija.

s/he accompanies sb singing
s/he is with sb (as a friend or spouse); s/he accompanies sb
I am with that woman.

cądéwašteyA *vt1-caus* — s/he satisfies sb

iyógipiyA *vt1-caus* — s/he/it makes sb happy, satisfied

Híc'ehą iyógipimaya. — When she came she made me happy.

įcądewašte *vs* — s/he is pleased with smth; happy about smth

pináyA *vt1-caus* — s/he pleases sb, makes sb be grateful; s/he thanks sb

Micį́kši pinámaya. — My son pleased me.

Pinámayaye no! — I thank you!

ógiyA *vt1-dat* — s/he helps sb

Dóken ócijiyįkta? — How can I help you?

Ówįcagiyabi cį́ga. — She wants to help people.

Dágucen ócijiyįkteší? — Why can't I help you?

ógiciyabi *vi1-recip* — they help each other

Owá ógiciyabi. — They all cooperate.

ógiyabi *n* — helper

wacį́ *n, v3-aux* — mind, plan, goodwill; s/he plans, intends to do smth

Ecú́ wacą́mi. — I plan to do it.

awácį *vt3* — s/he feels, thinks about smth, has smth on the mind; it is a purpose

Bigána awácįhą zuyéyabi. — They were intending to go to war against the Piegans.

oȟ'ą́ *n* — action, behaviour, habit, manner

Oȟ'ą́ wašté. — Be nice.

oȟ'ą́ge *vs, n* — s/he behaves, acts as such; character, behaviour

Sijáya omáȟ'ąge. — I have bad habits.

okóna *adv* — friendly

okónayÁ *vt1-caus* — s/he is friendly with sb

okónagiciyabi *vi1-recip, n* — they are friendly, associate with one another; society, union, association

Okónagiciyabi opá. — He joins the union.

ópA *vt1* — s/he is part of smth, joins, qualifies for smth (games, contest)

Micį́kši ópa ogíhišį. — My son cannot qualify.

Agícida owápįkte no! — I will join the army!

ahópA *vt1* — s/he respects, honours, reveres sb, smth

Makóce ahóyapa bo! — You all respect the land!

ahópe'įc'iyA *vi3-refl* — s/he has self-respect, honours him/herself

Wakáyą ahópe'įc'iya. — He honours, blesses himself spiritually.

ahógipA *vt1-pos* — s/he has a deep, religious respect for his/her own

wa'áhopA *vi1-abs* — s/he shows respect for people, things

wa'áhopabi *n* — respect

wó'ahope *n* — respect, observance for customs, social rules

bagą́ *vt1* — s/he respects sb

wóbagą *vs-abs* — s/he/it is respected

ótąna *adv* — straight, in a straight manner, in a respectable way

Ótąnaȟ máni wo! — Walk in the straightest way possible!

yu'ónihą *vt2* — s/he honours, respects, defers to him/her/it

Dóhąni mitáwįju ahówagipešį. — I never disrespected my wife.

ahótą'į *vt1* — s/he respects, praises sb

Iná ahówatą'į. — I respect mom.

ohóna *vt1* — s/he respects, honours sb

ohógicinabi *vıı-recip*
Wanágaš dąyą́ iyúha
ohógicinabįkta.

they respect one another
Long ago they would all respect
one another.

Negative Social Attitude

síjA *vs*

Dágu síja awácį.
Wagágana tawácį síja.

šikná *vıı*

Waktá šiwákna!
Šikná stéya no.

šiknákiyA *vtı-caus*
šiknáyA *vtı-caus*
šiknáya *adv*

Šiknáya i'ábi.

šiknáyagen *adv*

Šiknáyagen ų́.

knąyÁ *vtı*

Dóhąni mąknáyešį.
Wįcáwaknąyįkte no.

knąyákiyA

waknáyÁ *vıı*
aknáya *n*
oknáye wašté *vs*
wacį́tųšį *vıı*

Mitágoža wacį́tųšį.

waknáyÁ *vıı*

s/he/it is bad, hard, difficult, harmful,
unpleasant; s/he/it is ugly
He is tormented.
She is an old, wicked lady.
s/he/it is mad, angry
Beware, I am angry!
He is angry it seems.
s/he is mad at sb
s/he makes sb mad
angrily
They talk angrily.
kind of angry
She is feeling kind of angry.
s/he fools sb
He never fooled me.
I will trick them.
s/he fools, tricks sb
s/he fools people
fool
s/he is easy to fool, gullible
s/he is crazy, foolish
My grandson is crazy.
s/he fools people

wa'íc'icağa *vi3-refl*
Žé níš waníc'icağašį.

it is his/her fault
It was not your fault.

įknúdąšį *vi3-refl*

s/he disrespects, brags about him/
herself; s/he is stupid, lazy

pat'á *n*
tawácį ecédušį *vs*
wįktógağA, wįtkótkogağA *vi1, n*

Owá wįktó'ųgağabi.

wįktóktoyagen *adv*
Wįtkótkoyagen ų́.

zakté *vs*
Nína nizákte.

zaktébi *n*

a'į́hąbi įc'íya *vi3-refl*

iyópeyA *vt1*
Micį́kši iyówapeya no.

iyópegiciyabi *vi1-recip*
Ecágen misų́ga iyópegiciyabi.

akínįja *vt1*

akínįjabi *n*
Akínįjabi žé dąyą́ knuštą́bi.

wa'ákinįja *vi1-abs*

iyógipišį *vs-dat*

dumb, stupid person
s/he is stupid
s/he makes a fool out of him/herself;
fool dancer, clown
We all made a fool of ourselves.

crazily, foolishly
He behaves crazily.

s/he is mischievous
You are really mischievous.

person who fools around, who is
mischievous

s/he makes a fool, laughing stock of
him/herself

s/he scolds, reproves sb
I scolded my son.

they quarrel, scold, attack one another
My younger brothers are always
quarrelling with one another.

s/he disputes, wrangles, fights, argues
over smth

argument, dispute, quarrel
The argument was settled peacefully.

s/he disputes, wrangles, fights, argues
about things

s/he is displeased about sb, smth

111

iyógipišįyA *vt1-caus* — s/he offends sb
  Iyógipišįciya he? — *Did I offend you?*

iyógipišįyą *adv* — *feeling sad, displeased about smth*
  Iyógipišįyą wa'ų́. — *I am feeling depressed.*

įštéjA *vs* — s/he is bashful, shy, easily embarrassed, ashamed

įštéješį *adv* — *shamelessly*
  Įštéješį i'á. — *She spoke shamelessly.*

įštén *vcont* — *embarrassing*

įštén įc'íyA *vi3-refl* — s/he makes a fool of, embarrasses him/herself

įštényA *vt1-caus* — s/he embarrasses, shames sb
  Misúgabi įšténwįcawaye no! — *I shamed my younger brothers!*

wo'įštéjaga *vs* — s/he/it is shameful

wó'įštenyagen *adv* — *shamefully*

įstústA *vs* — s/he is bored, fed up
  Šką́šį mągá cén įmą́stusta. — *I am bored by sitting still.*

įciknuni *vs* — s/he is confused
  Į́š wamą́kašką oyáde įciknuni áya. — *The animal nation is getting confused.*

kténa *vt1* — s/he beats sb (in a game)
  Mayáktena no! — *You beat me!*

kténas'a *n* — *winner*

oknáye wašté *vs* — s/he is easy to fool
  Žé oknáye wašté. — *That one is easy to fool.*

woksÁ *vt1* — s/he breaks his/her word; s/he betrays sb

Relationships of Possession

yuhÁ *vt2*
s/he has, possesses smth; s/he carries sb, smth; she gave birth to a child; s/he holds smth (meeting, ceremony); s/he keeps, looks after, treats sb

Dágu nuhá?
What do you have?

Wóyude óda ųyúhabi.
We have a lot of food.

Gakí yuhá éknąga.
Carry it and put it over there.

Cįjátųga ecá, núbabina wįcáyuha.
She gave birth, she has twins.

Dąyá mayánuha.
You treated me well.

knuhÁ *vt1-pos*
s/he has his/her own, carries, keeps smth with him/her

Wįcíjana gá búza wąží knuhá.
That girl over there has one cat with her.

wayúhA *vi2-abs*
s/he has things

Wamnúhe gápešį.
I did not say I had it all.

wóyuha *n*
belongings, one's things

gíjiyuhA *vt1/2-benef*
s/he has, keeps, carries smth for sb

Gíjiyuha maní.
He walks carrying it for her.

yuhákiyA *vt1-caus*
s/he makes sb have, carry, keep smth his/her; s/he owns it, it is his/her own

táwa *pro, vs*
Cuwíknąga nitáwa wašté no.
Your coat is nice.

Mitáwa žé júsina.
Mine is small.

Duwé né táwa?
Who owns this?

aktášį *vt1*
s/he rejects, does not want, disowns sb

Wįcá žé aktášį.
She does not want that man.

įktóm įciyope yá *vt2*
s/he exchanges, returns, takes an article back

ok'ú *vt1*

Iná amógįyą omák'u.
Ok'úšį kó.

*s/he lends smth to sb; s/he shares
smth with sb*
Mom lent me the car.
He did not even share.

15

Education and Schooling

School and School Material

yawá *vt2* — s/he counts smth; s/he reads smth
  Yawá bo. — All of you count.
  Waʼówabi waką́ yawá. — He is reading the Bible.
  Wówįhága mnawá cén įwáħa. — I am laughing because I read something funny.

giyáwa *vt1-dat* — s/he reads smth to sb
įknáwa *vi3-refl* — s/he counts him/herself in
wayáwa *vi2-abs* — s/he counts things; s/he reads things, has the ability to read; s/he studies, goes to school, is a student
  Wayáwabi waħtéwanašį. — I do not like studying.
  Wayáwa gicúni híbi štén. — They will come when school finishes.

gíjiyawa *vt1-benef* — s/he reads smth for sb; s/he counts smth for sb
  Waʼóyabi cíjimnawakta. — I will read the book for you.

wayáwabi *n* schooling, studying, school (as a learning process)

wayáwa tágaȟtįyą *cp* university

wayáwa wįcášta *cp* student

wayáwa wókmA *vi1-abs* s/he writes, does his/her homework

Hąyákeji wayáwa wókma žé waná ecúbis'a. They should write that homework for tomorrow.

wayáwawįcakiye, school teacher
~ **wayáwawįcakiya** *n*

tída wayáwa *np* home school; day school

wayáwa wįcášta *np* student

owayáwa įtácą *cp* school principal

owáyawa, wayáwa tíbi *n, cp* school (the building), school house

Ábawaką gicúni štén, owáyawa mnįkta. On Monday, I will go to school.

Wayáwa tíbi dóhąn inánįkta he? When will you go to school?

Wįkóške nená wayáwa tíbi aktágabi. These girls are running to school.

owáyawa otókšu *cp* school bus

owáyawatąga, high school
owáyawa wągáduwa *n, np*

ektá úbi owáyawa *ph* boarding school

o'įštįmąbi owáyawa *np* boarding school

okmÁ *vt1* s/he writes, draws smth; paints, sketches sb, smth

Né šá okmá. Colour it in red.

Wanągaš i'ábi né okmábišį. Long ago they did not write the language.

Wa'óyabi wąží wašíju i'ábi oyákma oyágihi? Are you able to write a letter in English?

116

Basic mathematical operations are expressed in the following
way: *štén* 'if, when' is also used to refer to a future event, but
means 'equal, results in' in mathematical operations; *aké* 'again'
means 'plus' (addition); *énagu* 'you take it' means 'take away'
(substraction); *cogą́n* 'in the middle' means 'divided by' (division).
Lastly, the suffix -*ȟ* (intensifier) means 'times' (multiplication).

Addition (+): number ***aké*** number ***štén*** number
+ =

Substraction (–): number, number ***énagu štén*** number
– =

Multiplication (×): number***ȟ*** number ***štén*** number
× =

Division (÷): number ***cogą́n*** number ***štén*** number
÷ =

Here are a few examples:

Dóba **aké** nų́ba **štén** šákpe.	*Four plus two equals six.*
Dóba, nų́ba **enágu štén** nų́ba.	*Four minus two equals two.*
Dobáȟ nų́ba **štén** šaknóǧą.	*Four times two equals eight.*
Dóba **cogą́n** nų́ba **štén** nų́ba.	*Four divided by two equals two.*

okmábi *n*	*colour, mark, written production, writing process*
Dukté okmábi waštéyana?	*What colour do you like?*
įwá'okma, įwó'okma, įwókma *n*	*pen, pencil, chalk, any writing instrument*

okmátoto *n-pl*	*crayons*
wókmes'a, ~ **wa'ókmas'a** *n*	*artist*
wa'ókmabi *n*	*letter, written word, drawing*
wo'asnigiye *n*	*vacation*
gağóbi *n*	*mark*
ogíhi *vt1-aux*	*s/he can, is able to do smth; s/he succeeds*
gitézi *n*	*boy, lad, kid, brat*
įbážužu *n*	*eraser*
wa'ámnezA *vi1-abs, n*	*s/he examines, scrutinizes, studies things; examiner*
ųspé *vs*	*s/he learns, acquires a skill*
Micį́kši óda ųspékta.	*My son will learn a lot.*
ųspé'įc'iyA *vi3-refl*	*s/he learns smth on his/her own*
Utábi ųspémįc'iya.	*I taught myself how to shoot.*
wa'ų́spe *vi1-abs*	*s/he is learned, knowledgeable*
wó'ųspe *n*	*lesson*
ųspékiyA *vt1-caus*	*s/he teaches smth to sb*
Né duwé ųspénijiya he?	*Do you have someone to teach you?*
Owága onéžišį žécen ųspéwakiya.	*I teach him not to pee in bed.*
Dóken ecúbi ųspémąkiya.	*Teach me how to do it.*
wa'ų́spekiyA, wó'ųspekiyA *vt1-abs-caus, n*	*s/he teaches sb things; teacher*
wa'ų́spekiyes'a *n*	*teacher*
Wa'ų́spekiyes'a eyé žéceduhtįyą.	*He said it exactly like the teacher.*
wa'ų́spewįcakiya *n*	*teacher* (male)
wa'ų́spewįyąkiya *n*	*teacher* (female)
wasnókkiyA *vt1-caus*	*s/he teaches smth to sb*
į'ų́ *vt1-dit*	*s/he paints, rubs, applies smth on it*

i'útų *vt1*
  Miyé i'úwatų.
  Tíbi žé i'úwatų.
i'útų iwókma *cp*
nah'ú *vt1*

  Nacíh'ų no.
  Iná nawáh'ų ecámųkta duká!
anáǧoptą *vt1*
  Adé anáwaǧoptąšį.
  I'á štén anáǧoptą wo.
wa'ánaǧoptą *vi1-abs*
  Wa'ánaǧoptą wa'í.
  Škášį wa'ánaǧoptą yįgábi.
wa'ánagijiǧoptą *vt1-benef*
wįcó'i'abi *n*
wįcó'i'e *n*
Nakón-wįcó'i'e *n*
wįcá ógiyes'a *cp*
wócažeyada *n*
iyéska *vi1*
  Wa'ówabi ųs iyéskabi.
iyéska, iyéskabi *n*
  Wįcá gá iyéskabi žéca.

iyégijiska *vt1-benef*
  Mikúši iyéwejiska.
  Wašíjubi iyéwįcagijiska.
iyáwehtįyą, owókma wąyágabi *n, cp*

s/he paints smth
  I painted it myself.
  I painted the house.
crayon, paintbrush
s/he hears, listens to sb, smth;
  s/he obeys sb
  I hear you.
  I should have listened to mom!
s/he listens to sb, smth
  I did not listen to dad.
  When he talks you listen to him.
s/he listens to things
  I went there to listen.
  They were sitting still and listening.
s/he listens to what sb has to say
language, word; letter (correspondence)
language, word
Nakoda language, word
mentor
words of a song
s/he interprets, translates, converses
  They translate using a book.
interpreter, translator; announcer
  That man over there is an
    interpreter.
s/he interprets, translates for sb
  I translate for my grandmother.
  He translates for the White people.
computer

ijázo *vt1, n*	*s/he draws a line on smth; line; yardstick, ruler*
Wa'óyabi žén ijázo okmá.	*He drew a line in the book.*
įyútA, iyútA *vt2*	*s/he tests, tries, measures smth (food, drink, clothes, task)*
Waȟpé né įyúta.	*Try this tea.*
į'íyute *n*	*ruler*

Shapes and Colours

omnétų *n, vs*	*square; it is square*
o'ípa dóba *cp*	*square*
o'ípa mįmą́ *cp*	*circle*
o'ípa yámni *cp*	*triangle*
ȟóda *vs*	*s/he/it is grey*
Bill tašų́ge ȟóda gaȟká áyac.	*Bill was leading his grey horse.*
ȟon	*grey condition*
ȟonȟóda, ~ ȟotȟóda	*they are grey*
ȟonyÁ	*s/he paints, colours, dyes sb, smth in grey*
ȟonkíjiyA	*s/he paints, colours sb, smth in grey for sb*
ȟonkíyA	*s/he paints, colours, dyes his/her own grey*
ȟon'íc'iyA	*s/he paints him/herself in grey*
tó *vs*	*s/he/it is blue, green*
Įštá tó	*he has blue eyes*
toyÁ	*s/he colours, paints, dyes smth blue*
togíjiyA	*s/he paints sb, smth in blue for sb*

120

Iyécįgayena mitáwa tomíjiya duká šáyabi wacígac.	*He painted my car blue but I wanted it red.*
togíyA	*s/he colours, paints, dyes his/her own blue*
to'íc'iyA	*s/he paints him/herself in blue*
toyéna	*blue, green condition*
tóna *vs*	*s/he/it is light blue*
tónahtįyĄ	*s/he/it is very light blue*
totóna	*s/he/it is light blue*
tosą *vs*	*s/he/it is light blue*
tósabA *vs*	*s/he/it is dark blue, almost black*
tošá, tóhtįyĄ *vs*	*s/he/it is purple*
pežíto *n, vs*	*bluejoint grass; s/he/it is blue-green, green*
šá *vs*	*s/he/it is red*
šašá	*they are red*
Pąǧí šašá žená éyagu.	*Take those red potatoes.*
šagíjiyA	*s/he paints, colours sb, smth in red for sb*
šagíyA	*s/he reddens, paints, colours, dyes his/her own in red*
ša'íc'iyA	*s/he reddens, paints him/herself in red*
šayéna	*red condition*
šayÁ	*red condition*
šágeja	*s/he/it is kind of red*
ša'í'ų	*s/he paints, applies red paint on sb, smth*
ošá	*it is red inside*

ošágiyA	*s/he paints his/her own red inside*
ošáša	*they are red inside*
-nuda *vs*	*s/he/it is red, scarlet* (in compounds only)
matónuda	*cinnamon-coloured black bear*
paȟnúda	*turkey*
sábA *vs, n*	*s/he/it is black; pitch, tar*
samyÁ	*s/he blackens sb, smth; paints, colours, dyes smth in black*
sapsábA	*s/he/it is black spotted, black here and there*
Įdé né sapsába.	*He has black spots on his face.*
sap'íc'iyA	*s/he blackens, paints him/herself in black*
sapyá	*blackly, darkly*
sábeȟtįyĄ	*s/he/it is pitch black*
są́ *vs*	*it is beige, faded, off-white*
skána, ská *vs*	*s/he/it is white*
skaská	*they are white*
skaskána	*s/he/it is pure white*
skayÁ	*s/he whitens sb, smth; s/he paints, colours, dyes smth in white*
skagíjiyA	*s/he paints, colours sb, smth in white for sb*
skagíyA	*s/he whitens, paints, colours, dyes his/her own in white*
ska'íc'iyA	*s/he whitens, paints him/herself in white*
skayéna	*white condition*

ǧí *vs*	*s/he/it is light yellow*
ǧiǧí	*they are light brown*
ǧiyÁ	*s/he paints, colours, dyes smth in brown*
ǧigíjiyA	*s/he paints, colours sb, smth in brown for sb*
ǧigíyA	*s/he paints, colours, dyes his/her own brown*
ǧi'íc'iyA	*s/he paints him/herself in brown*
ǧiyéna	*brown condition*
ǧíȟtiyÁ	*s/he/it is deep yellow*
zí *vs*	*s/he/it is golden, dark yellow, tan, brown*
zizí	*they are golden, dark yellow, tan, brown (inanimate plural)*
Zí žé nitáwa.	*Yours is brown.*
ziyÁ	*s/he paints, colours, dyes smth in yellow*
zigíjiyA	*s/he paints, colours sb, smth in yellow for sb*
zigíyA	*s/he paints, colours, dyes his/her own yellow*
zi'íc'iyA	*s/he paints him/herself in yellow, brown, blond*
ziyéna	*yellow condition*
zísabA *vs*	*it is dark brown*

16

Professions and Trades

wówaši n	job, work, occupation; workplace; servant, worker
wayáco n	court judge
wayáco wįcá cp	judge (male)
wayáco wíyą cp	judge (female)
wa'ákihe wįcášta cp	lawyer
adéyabi n	reservation agent, Indian agent
tugášina, ~ tugášina n	Grandfather; creator; president
wócegiya wįcášta cp	church minister
šinásaba wašíjuwaką cp	Catholic priest
šinásaba wįcáwaką cp	Catholic priest
pežúda wįcášta cp	medicine man; doctor
pežúda wíyą cp	nurse
pežúda wįcák'u cp	pharmacist
wamákašką nįktéwįcakiyes'a cp	veterinarian
wa'ánowes'a n	chanting doctor
hí wįcáyušnoges'a cp	dentist
ocágugaǧa n	road builder
wíkni ok'és'a cp	driller

wíkni ok'ábi *cp*	*drilling*
ók'e wįcášta *cp*	*miner*
iyéska *vi1, n*	*s/he interprets, translates, converses; translator, interpreter*
Wįcą́ gá iyéskabi žéca.	*That man over there is an interpreter.*
wayáwawįcakiye, ~	*school teacher*
wayáwawįcakiya *n*	
Wayáwawįcakiye eyé žéceduhtįyą.	*He said it exactly like the teacher.*
basíbi *n*	*driver* (of people)
wįcágasaksaga *n*	*driver* (of cattle)
wįcágahaba *n*	*driver*
wa'ówabi gáǧe *cp*	*agency clerk*
owókma en wówašį *ph*	*clerk*
yužúžu wacíbi *cp*	*stripper*
yužúžu wíyą *cp*	*female stripper*
wóhena *n*	*cook*
wacó'ųbe *n*	*baker*
wówįcak'us'a *n*	*waiter*
hokší awáyages'a *cp*	*babysitter*
agícida *n*	*warrior, soldier, police; army*
Agícida žéca.	*He is a soldier.*
Agícida míco.	*The police called me.*
Agícida owápįkte no!	*I will join the army!*
agícida įtą́ca, ocą́gu agícida *cp*	*police officer*
ocą́gu wa'áyawąge *cp*	*highway patrol officer*
ahcómaza *n*	*police constable in a Nakoda reservation*
ceškámaza *n*	*council, alliance; police officer*

cuwíknąga šašábi *cp-pl*	*Royal Canadian Mounted Police, mounties*
ókneša *n*	*Royal Canadian Mounted Police, mounties*
įtácą *n, vs*	*leader, boss; s/he is the boss*
ógiyes'a *n*	*servant, assistant*
Adé Wakątąga ógiyes'a	*the Lord's servant*
wįcá ógiyes'a	*mentor*
onágasni *n*	*firefighter*
onákuwes'a *n*	*prairie or forest firefighter*
wókšus'a *n*	*farmer, gardener*
Wókšu wįcášta žé asąbi yusní.	*The farmer is milking it.*
wa'įcaȟye *n*	*farmer, agriculturalist*
wįcá ógiyes'a *cp*	*mentor*
wįcá pagášna, pahá wįcágijašna *cp*	*barber*
wįcábağe *n*	*announcer*
wa'ókmas'a *n*	*writer, author, painter, scribe*
wa'ówabi wįcágijahis'a *cp*	*postal worker*
wanįktekiyes'a *n*	*doctor*
pte'áwąyage, na'ųkce *n*	*cowboy*
pteyúhA *vi2, n*	*s/he is a rancher; rancher*
ptekúwa *n*	*cowboy, cowpuncher; bronc rider; rancher*
moȟták okmábi *cp*	*typewriter; telegraph*
wótą'į wįcášta *cp*	*journalist*
gįyá ųs'a *cp*	*airborne pilot*
tigáğes'a *n*	*house builder*
tiyúžaža wįcášta *cp*	*janitor*
cągážibe, ~ cągážiba *n*	*carpenter*

wįcášta *n*

    Ába waká štén wįcášta
    onowabįkta no!

    wįcášta owáyawa
    cą́ą́gan yįgábi wįcášta

hųgá *n, vi1*

    Hųgá gaȟníȟabi.
    Hųgá žé mnacókta.

hųkwíyą *n*

Wazíya *nprop*

man, adult male; person (of both
sexes), *people*
On Sunday the people are going
to sing!
student
chairperson
chief, king; he is a chief
They chose a chief.
I will sue the chief.
queen; queen in playing cards
Santa Claus

17

Agriculture, Gardening, and Ranching

Working the Land and the Forest

yuptÁ *vt2*
  Íyą žé mnuptá.
  Miyé mnuptákte no.

ayúptA *vt2*
mąkáyuptA *vi2*
  Mąkáyupte yá.

įmą́kayupte *n*
cą́íkpaza *vt3-pos*
  Mikúši owókšubi én ú.

okšú *vt1*
  Miyéh owákšu.

wókšu *vi1-abs*
wókšus'a *n*
ogíjikšu *vt1-benef*
  Iná owéjikšu.

ogíkšu *vt1-pos*

s/he breaks, turns over, plows smth
  I turned the rock over.
  I will plow it myself.

s/he plows smth (field, garden)
s/he plows a field
  He is going to plow the field.

plow
s/he fences his/her own field, garden
  My grandmother is in the garden.

s/he plants smth (seed, plant, crop)
  I planted it by myself specifically.

s/he plants things (garden, crops)
farmer, gardener
s/he plants smth (plants, garden) *for sb*
  I plant it for my mother.

s/he plants his/her own (garden)

owókšubi *n*
Owókšubi žén ų́.

įmą́ka gaksá *n*

mą̨káyuǧe *n*
įtímahen *adv-post*

omą́ȟkaǧe *n*
Omą́ȟkaǧe žén íyą nówa
duktékte yą̨gá.
įcą́ǧA *vs*
Waȟpé įcą́ǧa.
įgíjicaǧA *vs-benef*
wa'į́caǧA *vi1-abs*
kpasnádA *vt1-pos*

yukmí *vt2*

Mnukmí ámna.
oná *n*
onágasni
onáyA
agánA *vt1-dit*

Waȟpé awáganešį.
ganána *vt1*
Sú wagánana.

garden, planted area
She is over there in the garden.
farming disk (circular blade on
• a harrow)
harrow
inside of, within an area, enclosure,
pasture, field
field
The rocks are scattered here and
there in the field.[14]
s/he/it grows up
The flowers are growing.
it (plant, cereal, fruit) grows for him/her
it (crops, plants) grows
s/he pushes, plants his/her own
straight into the ground
s/he pulls out plants from the ground;
weeds smth
I am weeding.
prairie fire
firefighter
s/he sets the prairie on fire
s/he pours liquid on sb, smth; spreads,
sprinkles smth on it
I did not water the plants.
s/he sows, scatters with the hand
I'm sowing seeds.

---

14   Cumberland 2005, 253.

ahínapA *vi*
    Waȟcá žé ahínapa.
    Naháȟ ahínapešį.
gašná *vt1*

    Íš síyutabi dóba gašná.
peží *n*
    Peží žé acú.
pežíšeja *n*
pežíto *n, vs*

pežígabuza *n*
pežíȟoda *n*
pežískuya *n*
peží'įjašta *n*
peží'įkpa, peží įcápe *n, cp*
peží įyúǧe, peží ogáǧe *cp*
peží paȟtábi *cp*
peží įjašna hí *ph*
kpahį *vt1*
wakpáhį *vi1-abs*
makóce *n*
    Makóce né ahópa wo!
    Makócedahą bahí.
mąká, ~ maká *n*
    Mąká agán bapsų́.
    Ȟogá žé mąká k'á.

it (plant) *sprouts*
    The flower sprouted.
    It did not sprout yet.
s/he cuts smth short with a tool (hair, grass); *mows the lawn*
    It cuts a four feet swath [of wheat].[15]
grass, hay
    The grass is covered with dew.
straw
bluejoint grass; s/he/it is blue-green, green
dried hay
sagebrush
sweetgrass
lawnmower
hayfork
rake
hay bale
mowing sickle
s/he harvests smth
s/he harvests grain, cereals
land, territory, earth, ground; homeland
    Respect the land!
    He picked it up from the ground.
earth, soil, ground, dust, dirt, mud
    He spilled it on the ground.
    The badger is digging dirt.

---

15   Drummond 1976.

mąkán *adv*	on the ground, earth
Mąkán yųgá.	He lies down on the ground.
mąkámahen *adv*	underground; under the ground; below the surface of the earth
mąkámnuna *n*	dust
makóce įkúwa, wádapa *cp, n*	tractor
makóce mnaská *cp*	prairie, flat land
ocą'įyukse, ocánakseyabi *n*	sawmill

Horses and Cattle

šúgatąga *n*	horse
šúgatągana *n*	little horse
šųgána *n*	old horse
šųkmnóga *n*	stallion
šųkháhana *n*	spirited, lively horse
šųk'íkceya *n*	cayuse, horse or pony of little value
šųkskúsku *n*	mangy horse
šųksídeksa *n*	bobtail horse
šųktúske *n*	stunt horse
šųkwówaši *n*	work horse
šųk'ókuwasije *n*	bronc
šųkpámnina *n*	bucking horse
šųkwícahtįyaną *n*	old stallion
šųkyúhųhųza *n*	pacer
šųkhíša *n*	bay horse, reddish horse
šųkhíto *n*	blueish-grey horse
šųkhítokneška *n*	straight-eyed horse, blue roan horse
šųkhízi *n*	sorrel horse
šųkknékneǧa *n*	pinto horse

šųknídeska *n*	*Appaloosa*
šųknúni *n*	*wild horse*
šųksába, šúgasaba *n*	*black horse*
šųkská *n*	*white horse*
šųkzí *n*	*buckskin horse; sorrel horse*
šųk'ášpąyĄ *vi1*	*s/he brands horses*
šųkhį́hpąyĄ *vs*	*s/he falls from a horse*
šųkhótųtų, hotútų *vi1*	*it (horse) neighs; it (wolf, coyote, dog) howls*
šųk'íkiyA *vi1*	*s/he gallops a horse*
šųk'íkoyakyA *vi1*	*s/he harnesses a horse, ties a horse to a wagon*
šųkkúwa *vi1*	*s/he chases, handles, pursues horses*
miník'u *vt1*	*s/he waters an animal*
mnik'ábi *n*	*water well*
šųkmínik'u *vi1*	*s/he waters horses*
šųk'ówode *n*	*place where horses feed*
šųksíhamaza, šųkšágemaza *n*	*horseshoe*
šųktí *n*	*stable, barn*
Duwé šųktí mokúka.	*Someone shot and made holes in the barn.*
įwátape *n*	*horse used in buffalo hunting*
agáŋyigA, ~ agáŋyągA *vi3*	*s/he rides a horse*
Koškábi nówa šųk'ágąnyąk tiwókšą wįnówąbis'a.	*All of the young men used to ride horseback around the camp, singing love songs.[16]*
Šųkská agáŋmąga.	*I ride a white horse.*

---

16   Parks & DeMallie 2002, 5.

šųk'áktakkiyA *vt1-caus*	*s/he rides a horse, makes a horse run*
įyúdįda *n*	*reins*
ak'į́ *n*	*saddle*
ak'į́ha *n*	*saddlebag*
ak'į́maheda *n*	*saddle blanket*
ak'į́pasu *n*	*saddle horn*
ak'į́ šúgatąga *cp*	*pack horse*
ak'į́gijitų *vt1-benef*	*s/he saddles a horse for him/her*
ak'į́sų *n*	*saddle pad*
ak'į́tųga *vt1*	*s/he saddles a horse, harnesses a dog*
wak'į́ táwa *vi3*	*it (horse) is saddled*
Šúgatąga wak'į́ táwa.	*The horse is saddled.*
gadónawąga *vi1*	*it (horse) gallops*
gadónawąkkiyA *vt1-caus*	*s/he makes a horse gallop*
hugáškA *vt1*	*s/he ties its leg; hobbles a horse*
nawą́kwąga *vi1-redup*	*it (horse) trots*
ašpáyą *vt1*	*s/he brands a horse, cattle*
pté *n*	*buffalo (generic term); buffalo cow; domestic cow*
Hékta nahą́ĥ pté óda žehą́.	*There was still a lot of buffalo in the past.*
ptewíyena *n*	*buffalo cow, domestic cow*
ptewánųwą *n*	*cattle, domestic cow*
Ptewánųwą įjápsįdena ús awįcawagu.	*I brought the cows back home with the whip.*
ptehéhąska *n*	*Texas longhorn*
pte'áwąyage, na'úkce *n*	*cowboy*
pteyúhA *vi2, n*	*s/he is a rancher; rancher*
ocábaza *n*	*pasture*
Ocábaza éwįcawaknąga.	*I put them in the pasture.*

ocágaške *n* — enclosure
kiyúȟa *vi1* — it (animal) breeds, copulates
  Šųkwíyena žé kiyúȟa. — That mare is breeding.

Hunting, Fishing, and Trapping

kuwá *vt1* — s/he/it chases, hunts, goes after sb, smth
  Wanúȟ! Nikúwa cá. — Beware! He might go after you.
  Sųkpé wakúwa. — He hunts muskrat.
  capkúwa — s/he hunts beaver
hokúwa *vi1* — s/he fishes
  Hokúwa wa'óyabi opétųbįkta. — They must buy a fishing permit.
  Ába né nína wašté cén hokúwa ųyábi. — It is a very nice day today, thus we will go fishing.
ho'įcuwa, ~ ho'įkuwa *n* — fishhook; fishing pole and line
kudé *vt1* — s/he shoots at sb, smth
  Žé wakúde. — I shot that.
  Paǧúdatąga kudé yá. — He goes shooting at geese.
įkúde *n* — weapon, something one shoots with (bow, crossbow, gun)
wakúde *vi1-abs* — s/he shoots things; hunts
wakúdebi *n* — shooting, hunting
cótąga *n* — gun
  cótągawahukeza — bayonet
  cótąktąga — cannon
cúú *interj* — imitation of the sound of a bullet
įšákpe *num, n* — sixth; pistol, handgun
įwáyage *n* — gunsight
įyókšu *n* — cartridge; shotgun

oné *vt₁*
> s/he looks for smth; hunts

  Owánįkta né.
> I will look for it.

  Wíbazoką ųgónes.
> Let us go search for saskatoon berries.

ogíne *vt₁-pos*
> s/he looks for his/her own

  Hokšína gá húgu ogíne.
> That boy is looking for his mom.

ogíjine *vt₁-benef*
> s/he hunts for sb

  Mikúši owéjine.
> I hunt for my grandmother.

wóne *vi₁-abs*
> s/he hunts, looks for things

owícanebi *n*
> hunter

tapÁ *vt₁*
> s/he follows, pursues sb, smth

  maštítapA
> s/he follows, pursues, tracks rabbit

watápA *vi₁-abs*
> s/he follows, pursues; s/he hunts buffalo

  Watápe yá.
> He is gone hunting.

watápe *n*
> buffalo hunter, hunter; elderly man, ancestor

  Watápe žemáca no.
> I am a hunter.

  Miyéȟ watápe žemáca.
> I am a real hunter.

įwátape *n*
> horse used in buffalo hunting

iyáme í *vi₁*
> s/he went hunting

  Íyąȟe óhą iyáme í.
> He went hunting up there in the mountain.

iyáme yÁ *vi₂*
> s/he goes hunting

  Wįcábi žé'įš dóki iyáme yábis'a há'ųka.
> As for the men they usually went hunting.

  Aké iyáme yábi.
> They go hunting again.

  iyáme kní
> s/he returns from hunting

wáknibi *n*
> game, meat brought back from a hunt

oyé *n* — track, animal tracks

    Táȟtįna oyé óda. — There a lot of deer tracks.

    táȟca oyé — deer tracks

    maštín oyé — hare tracks

    pte'óye — buffalo tracks

    šųk'óye — horse, dog tracks

    ziktán oyé — bird tracks

    bis'óye — mouse, gopher tracks

    oyébi — tracks

oyé otápA *vt1* — s/he follows sb's tracks

ó *vt1* — s/he shoots and wounds sb, smth; kills sb, smth

    Wahį́kpe ų́s ma'óbi. — I was shot with an arrow.

gíji'o *vt1-benef* — s/he shoots and hits sb, smth for him/her; s/he kills sb, smth for him/her

    Táȟca žé míji'o. — He shot that deer for me.

ta'ó *vt1* — s/he/it wounds sb, smth

    Žé watá'oga. — I sort of wounded it.

    Šúga žé ta'ó. — He wounded that dog.

    ta'óbi — wound

utÁ *vi1* — s/he fires, shoots, discharges a weapon

    Utábi ųspémįc'iya. — I taught myself how to shoot.

    utábi — sound of a shotgun

a'útA *vt1* — s/he shoots at sb, smth

    Ahágeȟ a'ú'ųtabi. — We shot the last one.

    Šúga táwa žé a'úwata. — I shot at his dog.

    a'úgijitA — s/he shoots at sb, smth for him/her

wanáse *vi1-abs* — s/he goes on a buffalo hunt

> Many verbs of shooting, colliding, hitting with an impact
> are constructed with the instrumental prefix *mo-*.

mo- *pref*

by an impact from a distance (by shooting, hitting with a projectile, poking with a stick); *by colliding into smth with a vehicle; by blowing on smth; by the action of the wind, rain*

mohókšu ·   *s/he takes smth apart by shooting*

mohóyA   *s/he makes smth howl, cry* (dog) *by shooting*

mohų́shųza   *s/he makes smth swing* (branch) *by shooting*

mohúšte   *s/he makes smth* (animal) *lame by shooting*

moȟcína   *s/he frays smth* (cloth, blanket) *by shooting*

moȟnógA   *s/he makes a hole in smth by shooting; punches a hole with a projectile*

moȟpÁ   *s/he knocks sb, smth down by shooting*

mokógA   *s/he makes a tapping sound by hitting with a projectile, or a stick on smth; s/he plays pool*

mokpą́   *s/he shatters smth into pieces by shooting*

mokúkA   *s/he shoots and makes holes in smth*

momnáska	*s/he flattens smth by shooting, colliding, or running over it*
momnéja	*s/he shoots smth* (birds, pot) *into pieces*
mopóbA	*s/he explodes, bursts smth by shooting*
mopsága	*s/he shoots smth hanging from a branch and it falls*
moptáyА̨	*s/he knocks smth over by shooting*
mosíjA	*s/he ruins smth by shooting*
mosnéjA	*s/he splits smth open by shooting or colliding into it*
mošná	*s/he makes smth ring by shooting*
mošnА̨	*s/he shoots and misses smth*
mošpúšpu	*s/he breaks smth into pieces by shooting*
mosódA *vt1*	*s/he shoots smth, sb down; s/he uses all of the bullets on sb, smth*
Bízena nówa mowį́cawasoda.	*I shot all of the gophers.*
mosón	*shooting smth, sb down*
mosónyA	*s/he has smth, sb killed by shooting*
wamósodA	*s/he shoots down, kills all the game*
t'Á *vs*	*s/he/it dies, is dead*
Šų́gatąga t'á ginį́ja.	*The horse almost died.*
gat'Á	*s/he kills, knocks sb by striking with a club*
mot'Á	*s/he kills, stuns smth by shooting*
kté *vt1*	*s/he/it kills sb, smth*
Tá wążí ktébi.	*They killed a moose.*

gikté	*s/he kills sb, smth for him/her;*
	s/he kills his/her own
wakmúges'a *n*	*trapper*
yahtákyA *vt1-caus*	*s/he traps*
įyáȟtage, įyáȟtakiya *n*	*trap*
cąkníyaȟpe *n*	*deadfall*
Žé cąkníyaȟpe kuwá.	*He went to check his traps.*

18

Banking, Money, and Commercial Transactions

mázaska n	money; dollar
Mázaska nuhá? — Hiyá, mnuhéšį.	Do you have money? — No, I do not have any.
Mázaska óda mak'úbi.	They gave me a lot of money.
Mázaska dóna yacígabi he?	How much money will you want?
Mázaska dóba owágini.	I earned four dollars.
mázaska wąží cp	one dollar; loonie
mázaša n	penny, cent; copper
mázaska éknągA vt1-dat	s/he bets on sb, smth; s/he puts money on sb, smth
mas- cont	iron, metal; money
maskážA vi1	s/he earns, makes money
maskámna vi1	s/he earns money
Maskámna cén wacą́hiya.	He was lucky to win this money.
maskásodA vi1	s/he wastes money
masknúsodA vt1-pos	s/he spends his/her own money

mask'ú *vt1-dat* — s/he gives money to sb
  Wócįs'a žé mask'ú. — *Give money to the beggar.*
mastúga *vs* — s/he is rich, wealthy
  Wówašibas mastúga jé. — *Because he works he has a lot of money.*

mastúbiga *n-pl* — wealthy, rich people
masyúhA *vi2* — s/he has money
  Wanágaš masyúhabįšį. — *Long ago they did not have money.*
masyúheja *vs* — s/he has money; s/he is wealthy
masyúhešį *vi2* — s/he does not have money; s/he is poor
masyúsodA *vi2* — s/he spends money
gábina maswįcak'ubi *cp* — old-age pension
mas'įškadA *vt1* — s/he gambles money
mas'ónodA *vi1* — s/he borrows money
  Mas'ómijinoda. — *He borrowed money for me.*
mas'ówąyaga, mas'óyuħpe, mázaska tíbi, mázaska tí *n, cp* — bank, financial institution
gaktú *vt1, vi2* — s/he slices meat for drying; s/he earns money

gašpábi okíse *cp* — 10 cents, dime
gašpábi *n* — 25 cents, quarter
wa'ókmabi, wa'ówabi *n* — debt, bill, credit
wa'ówabitoto *n* — paper money
wa'ówabiska *n* — bank cheque
ĺ'įyopeya *n* — worth, amount
gažúžu *vt1* — s/he pays smth off (debt); pays for smth
  Iyé gažúžubi. — *They are paying for it themselves.*
  Ecágen ųgážužubi. — *We always pay for it.*
gíjažužu *vt1-benef* — s/he pays for smth for sb
  Wįkóškebi wįcáwejažužu. — *I paid for the young ladies.*

knažúžu *vt1-pos*
  jjážužu *n*
  Įjážužu waná gicíga.
opétų *vt1*
  Hųská né duktén opéyatų he?
  Hokúwa wa'óyabi opétųbįkta.
opégijitų *vt1-benef*
  Wa'óyabi opémijitų.
  Šųkcíjana wążí opégijitų.
opégitų *vt1-dat*
opégitų tíbi *cp*
wópetų *vi1-abs, n*
  Dohą́n štén wópetų nį́kta?
  Wįcíjana žé wópetų yéšį.
ok'ú *vt1*

  Iná amógįyą omák'u.
ok'úbi *n*
yupíyašį *vs*
  Amúgiya né dágu yupíyašį.
wa'ókmA, ~ **wókmA** *vi1-abs*

  Nína wa'ówakma.

s/he pays for his/her own
  fare, paycheque
  She wants her paycheque now.
s/he buys, purchases smth
  Where did you buy these pants?
  They must buy a fishing permit.
s/he buys smth for sb
  Buy me a book.
  She bought a puppy for her.
s/he buys smth from sb
trading post
s/he shops/buys things; merchant
  When are you going shopping?
  The little girl did not go shopping.
s/he lends smth to sb; s/he shares smth
  with sb
  Mom lent me the car.
loan
it is not valuable
  This car is worthless.
s/he writes things; s/he has debts, has
  credit in a store
  I have a lot of debts.

19

Leisure and Sports

škádA *vi1, vt2*

   Tągán škáda wo!

   Mitákona gicí waškáda.

škatkíyA *vt1-caus*

   Mihų̇́ tągán škatmą́kiya.

aškáda *vt1*

oškádA *vi1, n*

oškáde *n*

oškáde tíbi *cp*

wayá'i̧škadA *vi2-abs*

i̧hÁ *vi1, vt1*

wówi̧haga *vs*

   Nína wówi̧haga!

   Wówi̧haga mnawá cén i̧wáha.

ya'i̧hA *vt2*

yu'i̧hA *vt2*

s/he plays; s/he plays a musical instrument

   Play outside!

   I play with my friend.

s/he lets sb play

   Mom lets me play outside.

s/he plays on smth

s/he plays inside of smth; playground

picnic; festival; arena

gymnasium

s/he teases, plays jokes on people

s/he laughs; s/he laughs at sb, smth

s/he/it is funny

   It is very funny!

   I am laughing because I read something funny.

s/he makes sb laugh by speech

s/he makes sb laugh (by speaking, tickling, goofing around)

įhát'A *vs*	*s/he laughs hard*
įhát'at'A *vs-redup*	*s/he laughs loudly*
įhát'at'ana *n-redup*	*laughters*
įhát'eyA *vt1-caus*	*s/he/it makes sb laugh to death*
Mitákona įhát'emaya.	*My friend made me laugh to death.*
owábazo *n*	*circus*
owábazoti, wabázobi tibi *n, cp*	*theatre*
wįcįde škášką k'iyabi *ph*	*movie theatre*
waškáškąyabi *n*	*movie, movies, cinema*
Waškáškąyabi ektá iyáyabi.	*They went to the movies.*
owákma *n*	*photograph*
wįcįde okma *vt1*	*s/he takes a picture of, photographs sb*
wįcįde okmábi *cp*	*photograph*
wįcįde owábi, wįcįdowabi *cp, n*	*picture, painting, photograph*
Né wicįdowabi né mayágina ca.	*This is the picture you asked me for.*
įdé okmá, įdókma *vt1*	*s/he photographs, takes a picture of sb*
wįcįde éyagu *vt2, n*	*s/he photographs, takes a picture of sb;*
	s/he takes footage of sb; camera
wįcįde éyagu wįcášta *ph*	*cameraman*
yuhótų *vt2*	*s/he makes smth sound manually;*
	s/he plays a musical instrument with
	the hands
bahótų *vt1*	*s/he makes a sound by pushing on*
	smth; s/he plays a music instrument
	(trumpet, accordion)
cahkáhomni *vi1*	*s/he spins an ice top*
cah'íjahomni *n*	*game of tops played on ice*
ecúbina *n*	*game, any kind of contest*
ecúna *n, vi3*	*game; s/he gambles*

Mitákona, ecúnašį!   *My friend, do not gamble!*

Iná gicí ecúna.   *She gambles with my mom.*

hába ecúbina *cp*   *moccasin game*

kiȟpé ecúbi *vt3-pl*   *they wrestle*

kiȟpé ecúbina *cp*   *wrestling match*

kténa *vt1*   *s/he cheats, beats sb* (in a game)

mokógA *vt1*   *s/he makes a tapping sound by hitting with a projectile or a stick on smth; s/he plays pool*

mokógabi *n*   *pool game*

nąbé škádabi, nąbé ecúbina, nąm'écųbina *cp, n*   *hand game*

na'íc'ikmįkmąbi, nakmíkmąbi *n*   *bicycle*

ki'íyągA *vi1*   *s/he races*

ki'íyągena, kíyągena *n, vi2*   *race; s/he races*

Ųkíyągenas!   *Let us race!*

Hokšíbina gáki ki'íyągenabi no.   *The boys are racing over there.*

wa'óyabi ecúbina *cp*   *deck of cards*

hųkwíyą *n*   *queen; queen in playing cards*

įȟpékiyA *vt1-dat*   *s/he throws smth at sb; s/he deals the cards; s/he leaves smth for sb*

ohíyA *vt1*   *s/he wins smth* (game, contest, battle)

Owáhiya!   *Bingo!*

Ohíya štén nína waštékta.   *If he wins something it will be very good.*

ópA *vt1*   *s/he is part of smth; s/he joins, qualifies for smth* (games, contest)

Micíkši ópa ogíhišį.   *My son cannot qualify.*

škanwáyupiya *vt2*   *s/he is skilled at playing games*

kį'į́ *vt1*	*s/he throws smth at sb; s/he stones sb*
kį'íyegiciyA *vi1-recip*	*they throw smth to one another*
kį'íyeyA *vt1*	*s/he throws, casts, propels smth*
Tába žé kį'íyeya.	*Throw the ball.*
tába *n*	*ball*
Tába bapóba.	*He exploded the ball.*
Tába žé kį'íyeya.	*Throw the ball.*
tába yukába *cp*	*baseball glove*
tábana *n*	*small ball*
tábapabi *n*	*baseball bat*
tapkápsijektena *n*	*ball game*
tapnápsijabi *n*	*football*
togáhe įnážįbi *cp*	*first base player*
cá ų́s apábi *ph*	*bat (baseball bat, hockey stick)*
įtágapsija *n*	*baseball bat*
tamkápsija nąbį́kpa *n*	*baseball glove*
tamkápsijabi *n*	*baseball, softball*
tamškádA, ~ tapškádA *vi1*	*s/he plays baseball, ball*
tapškádabi, ~ tamškádabi *n*	*baseball*
tapškádabi wapáha *cp*	*baseball cap, helmet*
tamyúkaba įtą́cą *cp*	*baseball coach*
otámškadabi *n*	*baseball diamond*
yukám-nažį *n*	*catcher*
gazógic'ų *vi-irr*	*s/he skates, plays hockey*
Éstena gazógic'ų mnį́kte no.	*I will go play hockey soon.*
Hokšíbina né iyúha gazógic'ųbi.	*All of the boys play hockey.*
Gazógic'ų akín yįgá.	*He is watching the hockey game.*
gazógic'ų skádA *vi1*	*s/he plays hockey*
cahkázo ecúbina *cp*	*hockey team, game*
Cahkázo ecúbina owápa.	*I am part of a hockey team.*

kąsú ecúbina *cp*	*dice*
ya'íškade *n*	*joke*
wayá'iškadA *vi2-abs*	*s/he teases, plays jokes on people*
wayá'iškada síje *cp*	*dirty joke*
wayá'iškades'a *n*	*joker, teaser*
wayú'įhes'a *n*	*joker, buffoon*
yu'íškadA *vt2*	*s/he teases, plays jokes on sb;*
	s/he plays with sb sexually
wópaȟtA *vi1-abs*	*s/he watches people, things, a game*
Wópaȟte ųyás.	*Let us go watch.*
wópaȟte *n*	*onlooker*
wópaȟtes'a *n*	*spectator*

20

Dances and Ceremonies

Dances and Songs

wací *vi1, n*
s/he dances; dance

Dóhąn wa'úcibįkta?
When will we dance?

Wanágaš wacíbi né ecén.
Long ago they danced like this.

wacíbi *n*
dance

agícida wacíbi
soldier dance

amíknąga wacíbi
crow belt dance

cąyúmįmą owáci
hoop dance

cąyúmįmą yuhá wací
hoop dancer

ceȟkúwabi
chase the pot dance

gahómni wacíbi
round dance, courting dance

gasáksak wacíbi
whipping dance

hąwácibi
night dance

įšką́ wacíbi
lustful dance

knoknók wací
fancy dance

ktų́š wacíbi
tea dance, drunken dance

mağážu wacíbi
rain dance

maštín wacíbi	*rabbit dance*
mató wacíbi	*bear dance*
mįméya wacíbi	*round dance*
napéšį wacíbi	*no retreat dance*
Omáha wacíbi	*Omaha dance*
pağų́da wacíbi	*duck dance*
pehą́ğina wací	*sandhill crane dance*
peží amíknąk wacíbi	*grass dance*
šiyó wací	*chicken dance*
šųkwácibi	*horse dance*
tijáȟ wacíbi	*medicine lodge dance, Sundance*
tatą́k wacíbi	*buffalo dance*
tącówaci, tącó wacíbi	*naked dance*
tokána wacíbi, tokána owáci	*fox dance*
ų́knak wacíbi	*travelling dance*
wagícic'u wacíbi	*giveaway dance*
wakté wacíbi	*scalp dance, victory dance*
wamní įpíyaga wacíbi	*eagle belt dance*
wamní wacíbi	*eagle dance*
wanáği wacíbi	*ghost dance; northern lights, aurora borealis*
wįktógağe wacíbi, wįktógağa wacíbi	*clown dance, fool dance*
wį'įȟpeye wací	*wife throw-away dance*
wacíkiyA *vt1-caus*	*s/he makes sb dance*
Né mį́š imáduka cen wacíciciyabic.	*It was just me — I was hungry so I made you dance.*
wacís'a *n*	*dancer*
Micų́kši wacís'a yuką́.	*My daughter is a dancer.*
owáci *vi1, n*	*s/he dances inside of it (building, hoop); dance*

owácibi *n* — dance hall, dance arbour

įwáci *n* — dance outfit

įwágici *vt1-dat* — s/he dances over, on account of smth

cąwáką *n* — Sundance tree, centre pole; wood cross

cą́ gahómni *np* — stick used in a round dance

wací įknų́za *vi1* — s/he is dressed in regalia

wací okónagiciye *np* — dance committee

   Hącogądu žehą́ wacíbi žedáhą wakní. — I came home from the dance at midnight.

   Huhúžubina wacíbi yuká. — There is a dance in Regina.

wacíbi ecų́binas'a *np* — dance contestant

wacíbi įknúza *cp* — costume

wó'įye *n* — cloth offering used in Sundances

nową́ *vi1* — s/he/it sings

   Tijáȟ wanówą. — I sang Sundance songs.

   Dóhąda yanówąbįkta? — At what time will you sing?

gíjinową *vt1-benef* — s/he sings for sb; sings in his/her honour

   Adé wéjinowąkte no. — I will sing in honour of my father.

ginówą *vi1-refl* — s/he sings to him/herself

   "Bahá ektá yągá hįk gínowąsa" gáya. — "He used to sit on a hill and sing to himself," he said.

anówą *vt1* — s/he sings over sb (as a cure)

wįnówą, wį'į́nową *vi1, n* — he sings a love song; love song

   Koškábi nówa šųk'ágąnyąk tiwókšą wįnówąbis'a. — All of the young men used to ride horseback around the camp, singing love songs.

įnówą *vt1* — s/he sings about smth

onówą *n* — song

   Duwé onówą snokyá? — Who knows these songs?

   hąnówąbi — night song

hųgóȟ'ą onówą	*giveaway song*
įcinową	*brave song*
Nakón-nowąbi	*Nakoda song*
ogícuni onówą	*closing song*
ticówaknąga onówą	*flag song*
watápabi onówą	*buffalo hunter song*
wįgųnową, ~ wį'įnową	*love song*
wópina onówą	*grateful song*
wótijaǧa anówąbi	*Sundance singing*
zuyé onówą	*war song*
zuyéska onówą	*soldier song*
ȟ'oká *viı, n*	*s/he sings with a drum group; s/he beats the drum in a powwow or dance; singer*
ȟ'oká yįgábi *cp*	*drum singer, member of a drum group*
ahíyayA *viı, viı/2*	*s/he sings a song*
Koškábi nówa ahíyayabi.	*The young men were all singing.*
Duká nągų tokąką ahíyayes'a.	*He used to sing different songs.*
wócažeyada *n*	*words of a song, lyrics*

Ceremonies

ecųbi *n*	*ceremony*
cégiyA *vt1-dat*	*s/he blesses sb, smth; s/he supplicates, prays to sb*
Adé! Cémągiya!	*Father! Bless me!*
Adé wakątąga cécigiya, hó namáȟ'ų wo!	*Holy Father, I pray to you. Hear my voice!*
įcégiyA *vt1-dit*	*s/he prays to sb for smth*

wacégiyA *vi1-abs*
Iyúhana wacégiyabi.
Ųšigiya nawážį hįkna wacéwagiye no.
Ecén įš wacéwagiye no.
wacégiyabi *n*
wócegiya *n*
Wócegiya íbi.
wócegiya óhą ų́ *vi1*
wócegiya wįcášta *cp*
wócegiye *n*
Wócegiye én ağúyabiwaką yúdabi.

įnį́ *vi1*

įnį́bi *n*
Įnį́bi én iyódągabi.

Įnį́bi wagáğįkta.
Įnį́bi wagáğa štén, miní óda wacíga.

įnį́bi ecúbi *cp*
įníbi gáğabi *n*
įnígağA *vi1*
įnį́ tíbi *cp*
įníyuktą *n*
wakáȟ'ąbi *n*

s/he prays
They pray in a mass.
I stand humbly and I pray.
That is the way I pray.
prayer, ceremony
Medicine Ceremony; church service
They went to the church service.
s/he/it is Christian
church minister
religion, spirituality; prayer
They take communion bread in (Christian) religion.
s/he does a Sweat Lodge Ceremony, goes into a sweat lodge
sweat lodge (structure or ceremony)
They are sitting here in the sweat lodge.
I will make a sweat lodge.
When I make a sweat lodge, I want a lot of water.
Sweat Lodge Ceremony
sweat lodge
s/he builds a sweat lodge
sweat lodge
sweat lodge
Medicine Ceremony in which medicine people demonstrate their medicine power

waktóknaga ecúbi *cp*

ceremony in which warriors tell their war exploits in a public setting in order to inspire the people, especially the young

acáštųbi ecúbi *ph* — *Naming Ceremony*

cąnúba oȟpáǧa ecúbi *ph* — *Pipe-lifting Ceremony*

gisníwįcayabi ecúbi *cp* — *Healing Ceremony*

hąhébi wanáǧi wówįcak'ubi *ph* — *Feed the Night Spirits Ceremony*

įwážikte *n* — *First Kill Ceremony*

mayáwašiju wowįcak'ųbi *ph* — *Feed the Little People Ceremony*

pežúda éyagu ecúbi *ph* — *Medicine Ceremony*

šųkcíjana wóhąbi ecúbi *ph* — *Puppy Soup Ceremony*

wahíkiyabi *n*

Yuwipi Ceremony, Tie-up Ceremony, Calling of the Spirits Ceremony; Shaking Tent Ceremony; radio (object); radio broadcast

wahíkiyabi ecúbi *cp*

Yuwipi Ceremony, Tie-up Ceremony, Calling of the Spirits Ceremony; Shaking Tent Ceremony

wakpámni ecúbi, wįcák'ubi ecúbi *cp* — *Giveaway Ceremony*

wįktóktoga i'Á *vi1* — *s/he speaks backward as in a Clown Ceremony*

wó'ecų *n* — *work, occupation, ceremony*

Wó'ecų žé wįcák'ubi. — *They gave them those ceremonies.*

wótijaǧa, tijáǧabi n — *medicine lodge, Sundance arbour*

tíbi tága *cp* — *Sundance arbour; big lodge*

Tíbi tága nážikiya bo! Wahóȟpi įkóyaga. — *You all erect the big lodge! The nest will be attached.*

tijáǧabi *n* — *Sundance arbour*

tijáȟ *cont*
    tijáȟ wacíbi
    Tijáȟ wanówą.
tijáȟ wacíbi *np*
cąbásnade *n*
cuwícapabi *n*
įcápepena *n-redup*
cąwáką *n*
cążáda *n*
iyážo *n*
iyážo k'įbi *n*

Sundance
Sundance
I sang Sundance songs.
Sundance
Sundance brush fence
piercing during a Sundance
piercing skewer
Sundance tree, centre pole; wood cross
fork in a sacred tree
whistle, eagle bone whistle
whistle carrier

21

Spirituality and Culture

Spirituality

waką *vs, adv* — s/he/it is holy, spiritually powerful; s/he/it is mysterious, magical; in holy manner

Miní waką niyá wašté ųk'úbįkte no! — Sacred water give us good health!

Nakónwįcóȟage waką no. — The Nakoda way of life is holy.

océti waką — microwave oven

ocágu waką — Canada/USA border; medicine line

wakáȟ'ą *vi1* — s/he performs conjuring, demonstrates his/her power

wakáȟ'ąbi *n* — conjuring; Conjuring Ceremony

Nągáhą né wótijağa ecúbi háda wakáȟ'ąbi ejíyabi. — Today when they do a Sundance they call it a Conjuring Ceremony.

waką awókcą *cp* — spirituality

waką í *vi1* — s/he went for a vision quest

waką iyódągA *vi1* — s/he fasts

waką iyódągabi *n* — fast

wakáȟ'ą *vi1*	*s/he conjures*
wakáką *vs-redup*	*s/he/it is kind of holy, very holy*
wakąkiyA *vt1-caus*	*s/he considers sb, smth as holy*
wakąsija, ~ wakąšija *n, vs*	*evil-spirited being; s/he/it is evil-spirited*
Wakątąga *n*	*Great Spirit, Mystery* (traditional);
	God, Lord, Holy Father (Christian)
Adé, wakątąga wakmúȟa waką	*Father, Creator, give me the holy*
mak'ú no.	*rattle.*
Wakątąga cįhį́ktu, *nprop*	*Jesus Christ*
Wakątąga cįhį́tku,	*Jesus*
Wakątąga hokšítogapa	
Wakątąga cįhį́ktu ųktébi *ph*	*Good Friday*
wakątąga cįhį́tku yuhábi ą́ba *ph*	*Christmas*
wakáya *adv*	*in a holy way, spiritually correct way*
Wakáyą wąyága.	*It* (spirit) *watches over him.*
Dágu wakáyą ecúšį.	*He did not do it in a holy way.*
Wakáyą iyódąga.	*She is fasting.*
wįcáwaką *n*	*Holy man*
Wįcáwaką žéca.	*He is a Holy man.*
Iná waką *nprop, cp*	*Holy Mary; expert, person with a*
	holy gift
įwáką *vi1, n*	*s/he is an expert*
Gamúbi įwáką.	*He is a drum expert.*
miníwaką *n*	*Holy water; whisky*
Miníwaką yaǧóba.	*He is sipping a whisky.*
ptepá *n*	*buffalo skull*
wa'ázinyA *vi1-abs*	*s/he smudges things ritually*
wa'ážutųbi *n*	*regalia, decorated outfit*
wábaha *n*	*eagle staff, banner*

Iná maká *nprop*
   Iná maká pinámayaye no,
   Nakónwįcóh̃'age waką́ no!
Nakón'iyabi, Nakón'i'e *n*
   Nakón'i'abi dóken eyábi he?
   Nakóni'abi ecúgųbįkte no!
Nakón'įc'ina *vi3-refl*
Nakón-nowąbi *n*
Nakón-wįcóh̃'age *n*
   Nakónwįcóh̃'age waką́ no.
Nakón-wįcó'i'e *n*
makóce įdóba *cp*
waką́ awókcą *cp*
okónagiciye *n*
wócegiya *n*
   Wócegiya íbi.
wócegiya óhą ų́ *vi1*
wócegiya wįcášta *cp*
wócegiye *n*
   Wócegiye én ağúyabiwaką yúdabi.

wó'įye *n*
   Wó'įye mitáwa žé ahómįjitą́'į.
ahótą'į *vt1*
   Iná ahówatą́'į.
ahógijitą'į *vt1-benef*
   Wó'įye mitáwa žé ahómįjitą́'į.
   Mitúgaši, mikúši, wóyude nén
   éknebi žé ahómįjitą'į!

Mother Earth
   Thank you Mother Earth, for the
    holy Nakoda way of life!
Nakoda language
   How is it said in Nakoda?
   We will use the Nakoda language!
s/he behaves like a Nakoda
Nakoda song
Nakoda custom, tradition, way of life
   The Nakoda way of life is holy.
Nakoda language, word
fourth dimension; fourth spiritual realm
spirituality
society
Medicine Ceremony; church service
   They went to the church service.
s/he/it is Christian
church minister
religion, spirituality; prayer
   They take communion bread in
    (Christian) religion.

cloth offering used in Sundances
   He blessed my sacred cloth.
s/he respects, praises sb
   I respect mom.
s/he blesses smth for sb
   He blessed my sacred cloth for me.
   Grandfather, grandmother, bless
    the food that is placed here for me!

ahópA *vt1*
Makóce ahóyapa bo!

ahógipA *vt1-pos*

Dóhąni mitáwįju ahówagipešį.
ahópe'įc'iyA *vi3-refl*

Wakáyą ahópe'įc'iya.

wakmúha, ~ wakmúha *n*
Wakmúha né minékši gága.
wábahta, ~ wóbahte *n*
Wábahta awáyagįkta.
wópiyena *n*
įwágaška *n*
įwágaškeca, owį́cagaške, įwáhiye *n*
nağóhązi *n*
cąnúba *n, vi1*
Cąnúba ųgíjukta!
Šiyónide cąnúba táwa žé gicí
cąnúbabįkta.

cąnúba įbáhage *cp*
cąnúba įhúcą *cp*
Cąnúba ohpáğa ecúbi *ph*
cąnúbaha *n*
įjú *vi1*
Įwájušį no.
Cąnúba ųgíjukta.
įgíju *vt1-dat, vt1-pos*

s/he respects, honours, reveres sb
You all respect the land!
s/he has a deep, religious respect for
his/her own
I never disrespected my wife.
s/he has self-respect, honours him/
herself
He honours, blesses himself
spiritually.
gourd rattle
My maternal uncle made this rattle.
sacred bundle
He will look after the sacred bundles.
medicine bundle
bundle
love medicine
spirit bundle; spirit shadow light
pipe; s/he smokes pipe
Let us two smoke the pipe.
They will smoke with Pheasant
Rump's pipe.
pipe tamper
pipe stem
Pipe Ceremony
pipe pouch
s/he smokes
I do not smoke.
Let us two smoke the pipe.
s/he smokes for sb; s/he smokes his/her
own thing

162

knegíyA *vt1*	*s/he makes an offering* (food, cloth); *s/he blesses smth*
Duwé knegíyįkta?	*Who will do the blessings?*
knegíyabi, kneyábi *n*	*offering*
tóyude kneyábi	*food offering*
hųgóh'abi *n*	*giveaway*
hųgóh'ą	*s/he does a giveaway, birthday*
wakpámni ecúbi *cp*	*Giveaway Ceremony party*

War Culture

zuyÁ *vi1, adv*	*s/he goes on the war path; going on the war path*
zuyé í	*s/he went to war*
zuyé yÁ	*s/he goes to war*
zuyé onówą	*war song*
zuyéyabi *n*	*war party*
zuyéska *n*	*soldier*
zuyéska onówą	*soldier song*
zuyés'a *n*	*warrior*
zuyés'a tíbi *cp*	*warrior lodge society*
ozúye'is'a *n*	*war veteran*
ozúye'i *vi1*	*s/he went to war*
Ozúye dáhą kní.	*He came back from war.*
agícida *n*	*warrior, soldier, police, army; military uniform*
Agícida owápįkte no!	*I will join the army!*
Agícida žéca.	*He is a soldier.*
Agícida míco.	*The police called me.*

agícida įtáca, ocágu agícida *cp*	*police officer*
agícida oȟ'áge *cp*	*war deeds*
agícida wacíbi *cp*	*soldier dance*
agícida wi'óti *cp*	*warrior lodge*
agícida wi'óti hųgá *np*	*chief of the warrior lodge*
agícida wíwin'ųbi *cp*	*soldier division*
ohídiga ecų́ *cp*	*war deeds*
wįcóȟ'ą *n*	*deed, act of bravery*
gicízA *vt1-dat*	*s/he fights with sb*
Ecágen gicíza.	*He always fights with him.*
gicízabi *vi1-recip, n*	*they fight one another; fight, fighting*
Gicízabi wamnúpi.	*I am skilled at fighting.*
Wá ųs gicízabi škádabi cén.	*They are doing a snowball fight.*
gicízabišį *n*	*peace, ceasefire*
ogíciza, ogícizabi, ~ ogícize *n*	*war, battle*
Ogíciza gicúnįkta wacégiyabi.	*They pray for the war to stop.*
Ogícize nén wįcášta wąží ta'óbi.	*A man was wounded in this war.*
ogíciza mniwáda *cp*	*battleship*
ogícize maká agą́n wáda *ph*	*tank*
ogícize tága *cp*	*First World War*
ogícize tága įnúba *cp*	*Second World War*
įdáziba *n*	*bow*
wą́ *n*	*arrow*
wąhį́ *n*	*arrowhead*
wąhį́kpe, ~ wąhį́kpa *n*	*flint, flint arrowhead; arrow*
wąhį́kpekpena *n-redup*	*little bow and arrows used by children*
wążú *n*	*quiver*
wahácąga *n*	*shield*
įyáge *n*	*feather on an arrow, fletching*

wahúkeza, ~ wahúkeza *n*	*spear*
wahúkeza įdáziba	*bow spear*
įjáťe *n*	*war club*
cótąga *n*	*gun*
cótągawahukeza	*bayonet*
cótąktąga	*cannon*
cúú *interj*	imitation of the sound of a bullet
įšákpe *num, n*	*sixth; pistol, handgun*
įwáyage *n*	*gunsight*
sú *n*	*seed, pellet; bullet*
wábaha *n*	*eagle staff, banner*
wótawa *n*	*medicine bundle; war charm*
wįcápaha *n*	*human scalp*
wįcápaha šiná *cp*	*scalp robe*
wakté wacíbi *cp*	*scalp dance, victory dance*
máza wanáp'į *cp*	*medal*
yuwéšnega *n*	*war trophy*
wayúza *n*	*slave, captive*
cą'íjaskabi *n*	*trenches*
owąk'a'i *n*	*war chief, leader of a war party*
ébazo *vt1*	*s/he points his/her finger, gun at sb, smth*
pahá éyagu, wįcápaha éyagu *vt2*	*s/he scalps sb, an enemy*
atákpe *vt1*	*s/he attacks sb*
Bigána atáwįc'ųkpabi.	*We attacked the Piegan.*
tóga *n*	*enemy*
Tógabi owá nazámpadahą híbi.	*All of the enemies arrived from behind.*
tógayA *vt1-caus*	*s/he has sb as an enemy*
tógagiciyabi *vi1-recip*	*they are enemies, at war against one another*

tóktamakoce *n*	*enemy territory*
tokkté *vi1*	*s/he kills enemies*
dų̨wÁ́ *vi1*	*s/he opens his/her eyes*
dų̨wé hí	*s/he arrives scouting*
dų̨wé'i	*s/he went scouting*
dų̨wé'u	*s/he comes scouting*
dų̨wéyA	*s/he goes scouting*
dų̨wé'is'a *n*	*scout*
iyóhi *vt1*	*s/he reaches smth; s/he counts a coup*
	(touches the enemy in battle)
nadą́ í *vi1*	*s/he went on a raid, to war*
anádą *vt1*	*s/he raids an enemy*
Nakóda tíbi žéci awį́canadą̨bi.	*They raided the Nakoda.*
onákoda *n*	*peace*
Onákoda gáǧa.	*He made peace with her.*
Onákoda gaȟwį́cakiya.	*He made them make peace.*
onákodagiciyabi *vi1-recip*	*they are in peace with one another*
wasé gitų́ *vt1-pos*	*s/he wears paint, war paint*

22

Communication

Written Comunication

okmÁ *vt1* — s/he writes, draws smth; s/he paints, sketches sb, smth

Wanágaš i'ábi né okmábišį. — Long ago they did not write the language.

okmábi *n* — colour, mark, written production, writing process

Okmábi žé John ecų́. — John did the writing.

wa'ókmA, ~ wókmA *vi1-abs* — s/he writes things; s/he has debts, has credit in a store

Hąyákeji wayáwa wókma žé waná ecų́bis'a. — They should write that homework for tomorrow.

wa'ókmabi *n* — letter, written word, drawing

Wa'ókmabi wabážužu. — I erased the words.

wa'ókmas'a *n* — writer, author, painter, scribe

wa'óyabi, ~ wa'ówabi, ~ wóyabi *n* — paper, letter, book, newspaper

Wa'óyabi bakšíja. — Fold the paper.

Iná wa'óyabi hiyúwakiya. | I send a letter to mom.
Wa'óyabi ayáskaba yįgá. | He is infatuated with the newspaper.

wa'ówabi smúna *cp* — newspaper
wa'ówabi owópetų *cp* — newsstand, magazine store; a stationery store

wa'óyabi waką́ *cp* — Bible, legal document; mail; email
cąwópiye wa'ówabi *cp* — mailbox
wa'ówabi wįcágijahis'a *cp* — postal worker
wa'óyabi oyúȟpe, ~ wa'ówabi oyúȟpe *cp* — post office

įnáȟni wa'ówabi *cp* — post card
įnáȟni mas'ápabi *cp* — telegram
įnáȟniyena wa'ówabi *cp* — telegram
wįcó'i'abi *n* — language, word; letter
wótą'į wįcášta *cp* — journalist
yeyÁ *vt1-caus, vi-aux* — s/he sends sb, smth away; propel

Dágu nówa yewáya. | I send everything away.

iyéyA *vt1* — s/he sends smth (mail), sb there from here (away from speaker)

Wa'óyabi iyéwaya. | I sent the mail.

yegíciyabi *vi1-recip* — they send smth to one another
yegíjiciyA *vt1-benef* — s/he sends sb, smth away for sb
hóyekiyA *vt1-dat* — s/he sends a message to sb

Žéci hóyewįcawakiyįkta! | I will send a message over there to them.

įyáskamye, ~ į'áyaskamye *n, cp* — stamp, tape, something that is glued on
wa'óyabi įyáskamya —
iyóȟpeya *vt2* — s/he mails a letter
wahóya *vi1-abs* — s/he orders things by mail

Wa'óyabi žé wahówayįkta. | I'm going to order that book by mail.

wótą'į *n*	*news; announcements*
ya'ótą'į *vi2*	*s/he/it spread news; proclaims, advertises smth*
yu'ótą'į *vt2*	*s/he/it announces smth, spreads the news*
wótą'į wa'óyabi *cp*	*newspaper*
įhúgą *vi1*	*s/he announces publicly, announces by calling out*
i'éska *vi1*	*announcer; speaker*
i'éwįcašta *n*	*councillor; announcer*

Making a Telephone Call

mas'ápA *vi1, n*	*s/he makes a telephone call; telephone, telephone call*

Waná hinága! Togáhe mas'áwapįkta.   *Wait now! First I will make a telephone call.*

mas'ápabi *n*	*telegraph, telephone*
mas'ágicipabi *vi1-recip*	*they telephone one another*
mas'ágijipA *vt1-benef*	*s/he telephones sb on behalf of him/her*
mas'ágipA *vt1-dat*	*s/he telephones sb*
Mas'ámayagipa he?	*Did you phone me?*
Duwé mas'ámagipa?	*Who is calling me?*
mas'ó'i'abi *n*	*telephone*
omás'ape, ~ omás'apa *n*	*telegraph, telephone office*
otkéya *vti1-caus*	*s/he hangs up the phone*

Radio and Televisual Communication

owánaȟ'ųbi, okná i'ábi yuzábi, okná i'ékiyabi, i'ábi yuzé *n, cp*	*radio*

i'ékiyabi *n*	*speaker; radio*
wahíkiyabi *n*	*Yuwipi Ceremony, Tie-up Ceremony, Calling of the Spirits Ceremony; shaking tent; radio (object); radio broadcast*
yukúda *vt2*	*s/he reduces in volume, turns smth down*
yušpá *vt2*	*s/he turns smth on (radio, television)*
natága *vt1*	*s/he turns smth off (radio, television)*
įyáwehtįyą, owókma wąyágabi *n, cp*	*computer*
iwábazo *n*	*television*
wabázobi tíbi *cp*	*theatre, movie house*
waškášką́yąbi *n*	*movie, motion picture*
wįcį́de škášką k'iyabi *ph*	*movie theatre*
įdé okmá, įdókma *vi1, vt1*	*s/he takes a picture, photograph; s/he takes a picture of, photographs sb*
įdé į'ókma *cp*	*camera*
wįcį́de okmá *vt1*	*s/he takes a picture of, photographs sb*
wįcídowa, wįcį́dowabi *n*	*picture; photograph*
wįcį́de okmábi, wįcį́dokmabi *cp, n*	*picture; painting*
wįcį́de éyagu *vt2, n*	*s/he photographs, takes a picture of sb; s/he takes footage of sb; camera*
Wįcį́de émayagu.	*She took a picture of me.*
wįcį́de éyagu wįcášta *ph*	*cameraman*
wįcį́de oyábi *cp*	*picture, painting, photograph*
Wįcį́de oyábi óda yuhá.	*She has a lot of pictures.*
wįcį́de okmábi éyagus'a, ų́ wįcį́de okmábi *ph*	*camera*

23

Nationalities and Settlements

Indigenous Groups and Nakoda Bands

Bigána *nprop*
Piegan people, person of Piegan descent

Bízebina *nprop*
Gopher people (Nakoda band living near Maple Creek, SK)

Cągúsam wįcášta *nprop*
American citizen

Cą́he wįcášta *nprop*
Wood Mountain people (band of Nakoda, SK); Carry The Kettle people

Cą́hnada *nprop*
Strong Wood people (band of Nakoda)

Cąknúhabi wįcášta *nprop*
They Carry Their Own Wood people (band of Nakoda)

Cątúwąbi *nprop*
Forest Villagers or Wood Villagers people

Céǧa K'ína wįcášta *nprop*
Carry The Kettle people (band of Nakoda living in Carry The Kettle, SK)

Húdeša, Húdešana, Húdešabina *nprop*
Red Bottom people (band of Nakoda living in Fort Peck, MT)

Huhúmasmibi *nprop*
They Clean Bones people

Ȟaȟátuwą *nprop*	*Gros Ventres, Atsina people; person of Gros Ventres, Atsina descent*
Ȟébina *nprop*	*Rock Mountain people* (band of Stoney living in Morley, AB)
Ȟénatųwąbina *nprop*	*Mountain Village people* (band of Nakoda living in the Little Rocky Mountains and Fort Belknap, MT)
Ȟewáktųkta *nprop*	*Hidatsa people; person of Hidatsa descent*
I'ášijana, I'ášija, ~ I'ásija, *nprop*	*person of Dakota, Chippewa, Saulteaux descent*
Inína ųbi *nprop*	*Quiet people* (band of Nakoda that lived near Cypress Hills, SK)
Įdúgaȟ wįcášta *nprop*	*White Bear people*
Įháktųwą *nprop*	*Yankton Dakota people; person of Yankton Dakota descent*
Įháktųwąna *nprop*	*Yanktonai Dakota people, person of Yanktonai Dakota descent; generic for a Sioux person* (Lakota and Dakota)
Íyaȟe wįcášta *nprop*	*Stoney Nakoda people; person of Stoney Nakoda descent*
Lakóta *nprop*	*Lakota people; person of Lakota descent*
Maȟpíyato *nprop*	*Arapaho people; person of Arapaho descent*
Mínahąska *nprop*	*American citizen*
Miníšatųwąbi *nprop*	*Red River people* (band of Nakoda)
Miníšoše šųkcébi wįcášta *nprop*	*Missouri Dog Penis people*
Oknána *nprop*	*Oglala Lakota people*

Osníbi wįcášta *nprop*	*Cold Band people* (Fort Belknap, MT, and Mosquito, SK)
Pámnaska *nprop*	*Flathead tribe; person of Flathead descent*
Panána, ~ Panáne *nprop*	*Arikara, Pawnee tribe; person of Arikara, Pawnee descent*
Póǧe oȟnóga, Póȟnoga *nprop*	*Nez Perce people; person of Nez Perce descent*
Pteǧábina *nprop*	*Swamp people* (band of Stoney)
Sakná *nprop*	*person of Métis descent, mixed blood*
Sihábi *nprop*	*Foot people* (band of Nakoda)
Sihásaba *nprop*	*Blackfoot people; person of Blackfoot descent*
Snohéna wįcášta *nprop*	*Shoshone people; person of Shoshone descent*
Šahíya *nprop*	*Cree people* (generic term); *person of Cree descent*
Šahíya wašíju *nprop*	*Métis; Gros Ventres, Atsina people; person of Gros Ventres, Atsina descent*
Šahíyena *nprop*	*Cheyenne people; person of Cheyenne descent*
Šahíyeskąbi *nprop*	*Piapot Cree people; person of Piapot Cree descent*
Šųkcébina wįcášta *nprop*	*Dog Penis people* (band of Nakoda)
Tamínabina *nprop*	*They Have Sharp Knives people* (band of Nakoda)
Tanídebina *nprop*	*Buffalo Hip people* (band of Nakoda)
Téhąn Nakóda *nprop*	*Stoney Nakoda people; person of Stoney Nakoda descent*
Tóga *nprop*	*Blackfoot; anyone who is not Nakoda*

Toką́bi *nprop*	*Strangers people*
Wadópaȟnatųwa *nprop*	*Fort Belknap people*
Wadópena, Wadópana *nprop*	*Paddler people* (band of Nakoda living in Fort Peck, MT, and Pheasant Rump, SK)
Waką́hežabina *nprop*	*Little Girls people* (band of Nakoda living in Fort Peck, MT)
Wakpá wįcašta *nprop*	*Fort Belknap Agency people*
Wašį́ azínyabina *nprop*	*Fat Smoker people* (band of Nakoda, SK)
Wazíȟe wįcášta *nprop*	*Carry The Kettle people* (band of Nakoda living in Carry The Kettle, SK)
Wazíya wįcášta *nprop*	*Northern people living in Fort Belknap, MT, and Mosquito, SK*
Wé wįcáštanprop	*tribe of Blood* (Kainai); *person of Blood descent*

Non-Indigenous Groups

Gisų́na *n*	*person of Asian descent*
Hásaba *nprop*	*person of African or Afro-American descent*
Hásaba wíyą *cp*	*woman of African or Afro-American descent*
Haskána, Haská *nprop*	*person of European or Euro-Canadian descent; Whiteman*
Iyášija, ~ Iyásija	*French, German, Ukrainian, or Russian descent*
Įštámaškida *nprop*	*Japanese*

Sna'ót'e *nprop*	*half-breed, Whiteman*
Šéba *n*	*Black person*
Špe'óna, Špe'úna *nprop*	*person of Mexican or Spanish descent*
Wašíju *n, vs*	*minor spirit, deity; European people, person of European descent, Caucasian, Whiteman; s/he is of European descent*
Wašíjusaba *cp*	*person of African or Afro-American descent*

Placenames

A'íkpoǧą oyúze *ngeo*	*Sweet Grass Hills* (MT)
Cába hé *ngeo*	*Beaver Hills* (AB; located east of Edmonton)
Cába wakpá *ngeo*	*Beaver Creek* (SK)
Cagúsam *ngeo*	*United States of America; Canada*
Capúga-Matópa-Hústaga *ngeo*	*Mosquito Grizzly Bear's Head Lean Man First Nation reserve* (SK)
Cąsúska wakpá *ngeo*	*Maple Creek* (SK)
Cąšúška wakpá *ngeo*	*Poplar* (MT)
Cąwám *ngeo*	*Canada*
Cą́he *ngeo*	*Wood Mountain* (SK)
Cahní wakpá *ngeo*	*Powder River* (MT)
Cahní oǧáǧe *ngeo*	*Dodson* (MT)
Céǧa K'ína *nprop, ngeo*	*Carry The Kettle* (Chief of the Nakoda people from 1891 to 1923); *Carry The Kettle First Nation reservation* (SK)

Gaȟé núba *ngeo*	*Zurich* (MT)
Hásaba makóce *ngeo*	*Africa*
Huhúžubina *ngeo*	*Regina* (SK)
Hókuwa O'įnažį *ngeo*	*Fort Qu'Appelle* (SK)
Húgabaha *ngeo*	*Chief Mountain* (MT)
Húgajuk'ana *ngeo*	*Little Chief Canyon* (MT)
Ȟépa, Taȟé *ngeo*	*Moose Mountain* (SK)
Ȟuȟútųwą óyage *ngeo*	*Hays* (MT) .
Iyásija makóce *ngeo*	*France, Germany, Ukraine*
Įdeša ti'óda, Agásąm ti'óda *ngeo*	*Harlem* (MT)
Įǧúǧa wídana *ngeo*	*Snake Butte* (MT)
Įštágitų tí *ngeo*	*Indian Head* (SK)
Íyaȟe tága *ngeo*	*Rocky Mountains*
Íyaȟe wídana *ngeo*	*Little Rockies* (MT)
Kį'íbi *ngeo*	*Sintaluta* (SK)
Ktųsyą *ngeo*	*Wolseley* (SK)
Maká otíbi *ngeo*	*Fort Benton* (MT)
Makáska gaȟópa *ngeo*	*Mission Canyon* (MT)
Matóska *nprop, ngeo*	*White Bear* (Nakoda Chief and signatory of Treaty 4, 1875); *White Bear First Nation reserve* (SK)
Máza Ok'á *ngeo*	*Zortman* (MT)
Minínuzahą *ngeo*	*Swift Current River; Swift Current* (SK)
Miníša *ngeo*	*Red River* (MB, ND, MN)
Miníšoše wakpá *ngeo*	*Missouri River*
Miníwaką *ngeo*	*Manitou Beach* (SK)
Mniwáži *ngeo*	*Lake Superior*
Ogíciza wakpá *ngeo*	*Battleford River* (SK)
Oǧúǧa wídana *ngeo*	*Snake Butte* (MT)
Owácegiya są'ímna *ngeo*	*Pink Church* (MT)

Owókpamni tí *ngeo*	*Fort Belknap Agency* (MT)
O'íyuweǧa, ~ Oyúweǧa *ngeo*	*Malta* (MT)
Pežískuya bahá *ngeo*	*Malta* (MT)
Ptéǧa búza *ngeo*	*Dry Lake* (MT)
Sakná ti'óda *ngeo*	*Lewiston* (MT)
Šiyó *ngeo*	*Sheho* (SK)
Šiyónide *nprop, ngeo*	*Pheasant's Rump* (Nakoda Chief and signatory of Treaty 4, 1876); *Pheasant Rump Nakota Nation reservation* (SK)
Šiyóša *ngeo*	*Red Pheasant Cree Nation reservation* (SK)
Šuknúni bahá *ngeo*	*Wild Horse Butte* (MT)
Šuktógeja o'ípa, Tabéȟ'a wakpá *ngeo*	*Wolf Point* (MT)
Tácehubana *ngeo*	*Moose Jaw* (SK)
Tacéži wakpá *ngeo*	*Tongue River* (MT)
Tiská Óda *ngeo*	*Chinook* (MT)
Titáǧa *ngeo*	*Edmonton* (AB)
Toktí, Agáda, Tugí wakpá *ngeo*	*Hays* (MT)
Tugíska wakpá *ngeo*	*Musselshell River* (MT)
Tugášina makóce *ngeo*	*United States of America*
Úšiya máni *nprop, ngeo*	*Ocean Man* (Nakoda chief); *Ocean Man First Nation reservation* (SK)
Waȟníca wakpá *ngeo*	*Poplar* (MT)
Waká tíbi *ngeo*	*St. Paul's Mission* (MT)
Wakpá juk'ána, Asábi wakpá *ngeo*	*Milk River* (MT)
Wakpé núzahą *ngeo*	*Swift Current River* (SK)
Wanábe *ngeo*	*Bearpaw Mountain* (MT)
Wasé oyúze *ngeo*	*red ochre collecting place*
Wasé wakpá *ngeo*	*Lodge Pole* (MT)

Wašíjusaba makóce *ngeo*	*Africa*
Wazíȟe *ngeo*	*Cypress Hills* (sk)
Wį́bazoką wakpá *ngeo*	*Saskatoon* (sk)
Wį̨cápaȟe *ngeo*	*Skeleton Hill or Skull Mountain*
	(burial site near Sintaluta, sk, and
	one of the former names for Carry
	The Kettle First Nation reservation)
Wį̨cášta wakpá *ngeo*	*Peoples Creek, Dodson Creek* (mt)
Wį̨cį́spayazą *ngeo*	*Calgary* (ab)
Wómnapta *ngeo*	*Montmartre* (sk)

24

Geography and Landscape

Land

mąká, ~ maká *n*	*earth, soil, ground, dust, dirt, mud*
Ȟogá žé mąká kʼá.	*The badger is digging dirt.*
Mąká né sábehtįyą.	*The mud is pitch black.*
makágąn, mąkán *adv*	*on the ground, on earth*
Makágąn iyódąga.	*He sits on the ground.*
mąkámahen *adv*	*underground; under the ground; below the surface of the earth*
makámahen, ~ maką́mahen *n*	Saskatoon: Saskatchewan Indian Cultural Center; *den, basement*
mąkámnuna *n*	*dust*
makáhasaba *n*	*coal*
makáto *n*	*clay*
makóȟnoga *n*	*cave*
makómnaya *n*	*prairie, flat land*
makóšija *n*	*badlands*

makówaja *adv*	*all over the world*
mąkóškąšką, makóce škąšką	*earthquake*
n-redup	
makóškiška *n, vs*	*rough, bumpy road; it is a rough,*
	bumpy road
Ocągu okná yéšį, žé makóškiška.	*Do not go through that road,*
	it is rough.
makóce *n*	*land, territory, earth, ground; homeland*
Makóce né ahópa wo!	*Respect the land!*
Makóce wóguga.	*That is a beautiful landscape.*
makóce mnaská *cp*	*prairie, flat land*
makóce owáštejaga *cp*	*heaven*
maštámakoce *n*	*desert, land to the south*
wiwína *vi*	*it is swampy*
Makóce né wíwina.	*This land is swampy.*
bahá *n*	*hill, mound*
Bahá sám žéci wa'í.	*I went over the hill.*
bahádahą *adv*	*from the hill*
bahágąn *adv*	*on a mound, hilltop*
Bahágąn yągá wįhámne cá.	*He is sitting on a hill having dreams.*
bahátakiya *adv*	*toward the hill*
Bahátakiya maníšį.	*He did not walk toward the hill.*
abáha, abáhana *n*	*knoll, small hill, mound*
áȟunąptą *adv*	*hillside*
a'íbazija *n*	*row of hills*
cą *n*	*tree, wood, stick*
Cą iyáni.	*Climb up the tree.*
cąȟúnąptą *n*	*wooded hillside*
Cąȟúnąptą én yągá.	*She sat on a wooded hillside.*

cą'ókšą, ~ cąwókšą *adv*
  Cą'ókšą mawáni.

cąwóhą, ~ cą'óhą *adv*
  Gadám cąwóhą yá wo.

cąwóhocągu *n*

cąwóšma *n*

cówaja *n*

ȟé *n*
  Ȟé nén matúbi no.

ȟeyátakiya *adv*

įȟé *n*

íyąhe, ~ íyaȟe *n*
  Íyąhe wągámneȟ íbi.

gaȟé *n*

gaȟópa *n*

mayá *n*

mayá'oȟnoǧa *n*

mayátąga *n*

omnáwitąga *n*

otį́da *n*

wóšma *n, vs*

hebíya *adv*
  Hebíya įnáži̧.

ȟoškíškina *n*

įpá *n*

naȟ'ámya *adv*
  Naȟ'ámya mągés'a.

įtímahen *adv-post*

around the bush, forest
  I walk around the forest.

in a wooded area, in the bush, forest
  Go over there in the woods.

trail in the woods

dense bush, forest

forest

mountain, mountain ridge
  I was born here in the mountains.

toward the hill

mountain, gravel

mountain, stony hill
  They went to the highest mountain.

ravine, coulee, cut bank; mountain, hill

canyon, ravine, valley, gully

cliff, bluff

hole in a rock

mountain

large flat area, large prairie

clearing, opening without trees, prairies

brush, thick bush; it is dense, tightly packed

halfway up a hill
  He stopped halfway up the hill.

sandy, hilly terrain

head of smth (mountain, hill)

on the hillside
  I habitually sit on the hillside.

inside of, within an area, enclosure, pasture, field

omnáyA *vimp*	*it is flat*
omnáyena *n*	*small flat area*
omnáwitąga *n*	*large flat area, large prairie*
owókšubi *n*	*garden, planted area*
opáya *adv*	*through, along, following the course of;*
	in, through a valley, coulee
Ocągu žé opáya yá.	*Follow the road.*
Opáya hokún ma'únibi.	*We walked down the valley.*
osmága *n*	*coulee; crease*
omáȟkaǧe *n*	*field*

Cardinal Directions

wazíyam *adv*	*in, to the north*
Wagíyą sába wazíyam žéci iyódągabi.	*The Black Thunderbirds sit over in the north.*
wazíyada *adv*	*north; in, to the north*
wazíyada wí hinápagiya *ph*	*northeast*
wihíyayešį *n*	*north*
Wihíyayešį ecíyadahą éduwą.	*He looked toward the north.*
wazíyatakiya, wazíyakiya *adv*	*northward, toward the north*
wiyódahą *n*	*south; noon, midday*
wiyódahą ektá	*to the south*
wiyódahą wódabi	*dinner*
wiyódahą sám	*afternoon*
wiyódahąm *adv*	*in, to the south*
Hokšítogapa wiyódahąm žéci iyódąga.	*The first-born son sits over to the south.*
wiyódahątakiya *adv*	*southward, toward the south*

182

wiyóhąbam *adv* — in, to the east
Kúši wanáǧi oyáde wiyóhąbam žéci iyódąga. — The Grandmother spirit nation sits over in the east.

wíhinąpa *n* — east

wíhinąpatakiya *adv* — eastward, toward the east

wiyóȟpeya, ~ wiyóȟpaye *n* — west; sunset

wiyóȟpeyada *adv* — at, in the west

wiyóȟpeyam *adv* — in, to the west
Wagíyą šá wiyóȟpeyam žecí iyódągabi. — The Red Thunderbirds sit over there in the west.

wiyóȟpeyatakiya *adv* — westward, toward the west

tadé'uya *n* — cardinal directions, world quarters

tadé'uya dóba *cp* — four cardinal directions

Water

miní *n* — water
Miní mnéza. — It is pure water.
Miní waką nína niyá wašté ųk'úbįkte no! — Very sacred water, give us good health!

mnísni *n* — cold water

mniwája *n* — sea, ocean
"Mniwája agásampadahą ųhíbic›éhą," eyá. — "We came from across the ocean," she said.

mnigákna, ~ mnijákna *adv* — beside the water, at the shore

mnihúde *n* — shore

miní iyáya *cp* — flood

mnihíyeyA *vimp* — there is a flood

miníbaha *n* — wave

miníbahahatąga *n*	*big swells or waves*
miní ahínąpe *vi*	*it is a spring*
mnip'ó *n*	*steam coming up from water when the water is cold*
mníkada *n*	*warm springs*
mniwája húda *n*	*seacoast*
minĩȟaȟa, miníhįȟpaya *n*	*waterfall*
minítąga *n*	*lake*
minítąktąga	*lakes*
buzáda *adv*	*on the shore, away from the water*
Buzáda škádabis'a.	*They always play on the shore.*
buzádakiya	*toward the shore*
wída *n*	*island*
wídana	*small island*
wídaya	*like an island*
makóce wídaya *cp*	*strait*
cogánwida *n*	*island in the middle of a lake*
wakpá *n*	*river*
Wakpá juk'ána iyáyabi.	*They went through the narrow river.*
wakpána *n*	*creek*
wakpá gáǧabi *cp*	*irrigation ditch*
wakpádahą *adv*	*from the river*
Wį́bazoką wakpádahą hí.	*He arrived from Saskatoon River.*
įyúweǧa *n*	*crossing place on a river, creek*
mné *n*	*lake (archaic)*
ptéǧa *n*	*slough, lake*
Ptéǧa žé búza.	*The slough is dry.*
Ptéǧa ópta mná.	*I went across the lake.*
pteptéǧana	*little sloughs*

miní natága *cp*　　　　*dam*

wiwí *n*　　　　*swamp, marsh; quicksand*

wiwína *vi*　　　　*it is swampy*

Makóce né wíwina.　　　　*This land is swampy.*

25

Weather, Natural Phenomena, and Substances

Weather

ošíjejA *vimp*
Ošíjejįšį no.
Ošíjeja tagą́n hą́da, timáhen
waʼų́ jé.

apšíjejA *vimp*

opšíja gamóta *vimp*
gaʼóšijejA *vimp*
osní *vimp*
Osní áya.
Tągą́n osní he?

osnísni *vimp-redup*
Waní ų́ gáki hą́da osnísnisʼa.

there is a storm; it is stormy weather
It is not stormy.
Whenever there is a storm outside I always stay inside.

it is a stormy day; a day with bad weather

there is a dust storm
it is a wind storm
it is cold weather
It is getting cold.
Is it cold outside?

it is very cold weather
He wintered over there and it was usually very cold.

ogásni *vs, n* it is a draft of air; draft of air

ti'ógasni *vimp* there is a draft of cold air in a house

cusní *vimp* it is chilly weather

Tągán cusní. It is chilly outside.

maštá *vimp* it is hot weather

Ába né nína maštá. It is very hot today.

Ába né maštáḣtįyįkta gáyabi. They say today will be the warmest day.

maštá káda, makáda *vimp* it is hot weather

kádA *vimp* it is hot (weather, food, objects), *spicy*

Ába káda. It is a hot day.

onínida *vimp* it is hot and humid; sweltering

knaptá *vimp* it (weather) *cleared up*

Mağážu né knaptá. The rain cleared up.

gasódA *vi, vt₁* it (sky) *cleared up; s/he massacres, wipes out sb*

a'óhązi *vimp, n* it is cloudy, overcast; shade

Hąwí tą'íšį a'óhązi no! The sun is not visible, it is overcast!

knaptá *vimp* it (weather) *cleared up*

Mağážu né knaptá. The rain cleared up.

maḣpíya *n* sky, heaven; cloud

Adé wakątąga maḣpíyam agą́n yągá. Father Great Spirit who sits in the sky.

Adé'ųyabi maḣpíya ektá nągá. Our Father who art in heaven.

maḣpíyakta *adv* to the clouds

maḣpíyam *adv* in the sky

Adé wakątąga maḣpíyam agą́n yągá. My Holy Father who sits in the sky.

maḣpíyato *n* blue sky

amáȟpiya *vimp, n* — it is cloudy; cloud

Ába né amáȟpiyašį. — It is not cloudy today.

Amáȟpiya óda. — There are a lot of clouds.

amáȟpiya naȟnéjA *vimp* — there is a cloudburst, a sudden heavy rainfall

ganúsnuza *vimp* — it is breezy

ganúsnuzagen *adv* — with a breeze

Ganúsnuzagen hą́. — It remains breezy.

ganų́za *vimp* — it is windy; wind

Nína ganų́za. — It is very windy.

Ganų́za žé yušnóga. — The wind uprooted it.

ganų́za tą́ga, ~ **ganų́zatą̨ga** *vimp, n* — it is a gale wind; gale wind, tornado

maštá ganų́za *vimp* — it is a hot wind, like a Chinook wind

tadé *n* — wind

Tadé né ų́s ihá maȟpúȟpu. — My lips are chapped because of the wind.

tadéya — with the wind

tadéyąba, ~ **tadé'ąba** *vimp* — it is a windy day

tadé'omni *n* — tornado

tadé'omni tą́ga *cp* — whirlwind

tadéwam *adv* — facing the wind

Owá tadéwam ma'ų́nibi. — We all walked facing the wind.

uyÁ *vimp* — the wind blows this way

Tadó uyé né, cą́ né yuksá. — The wind blew this way and broke the tree.

waspą́ *n* — Chinook wind

wi'ómni *n* — twister wind, whirlwind, dust devil

įjámna *vimp* — there is a blizzard, drifting snow

Mąká agán įjámna. — It drifts on the ground.

hokún įjámna *vimp*
there is a ground blizzard, drifting snow on the ground

taníya *n*
his/her/its breath; breath, air, oxygen, atmosphere

Taníya žé dókiyo iyáya tą́į́šį.
The air dissipates in all directions.

mağážu *n, vs*
rain; it rains

Mağážu né knaptá.
The rain cleared up.

Mağážuktešį no.
It is not going to rain.

amáğažu *vs*
it rains on smth

mağážu įkmúga,
~**mağážu kmúga** *cp*
rainbow

mağážu wаką́ *vimp*
it is a hot summer drizzle

ot'į́ *vimp, n*
it is thundering; thunder

Ową́hįkna hį́kta né, ot'į́cuna cén.
Lightnings came about and it kept on thundering.

ot'į́hįkna
there is a sudden thunder clap

ot'į́ *apA´*
it is a thunderclap

owádawąga *vi*
there are flashes of lightning; it is an electric storm

wá *n, vs*
snow; s/he/it is snowy

Nína wá gaȟmóga.
The snow is blowing away hard.

Wá yupšų́ka.
He made it into a snowball.

Makóce én dóhąni wášį.
The land that is never snowy.

wáhįhĄ *vimp*
it snows

Wáhįhįkte no.
It will snow.

Tągán éduwą wáhįhą.
Look outside it is snowing.

wáhįȟpa *vimp*
it is a snowfall

Nína wáhįȟpa.
It is a very heavy snowfall.

wamnúmnu *vi*
there are fine snow particles blowing

waską́ *n*
melting snow

wašmá *vimp*
   Dókiya nówa wašmá.

wašmú *n*
wasú *n*
wasú hįhá *vimp*
wasúsmuna *n*
spą́ *vs*
totóba *vs*
ogáȟnoga *vs*
   Tągán ogáȟnoga.
   Tągán wa'ų́ cén mağážu cén
     omágaȟnoga.

cáğa *n*
   Cáğa agázeze hą́.
cuȟéwąga *vimp, n*
acúȟewąga *vs*

   Dágu nówa acúȟewąga.
cuȟpą́ *vimp, n*
   Hąyákena hą́da nína cuȟpą́.
štúda *vs*

it is deep snow
   The snow is deep everywhere.
melted snow
hail
it is hailing
small hail stone, sleet
it is damp
it is damp, wet
s/he/it is soaked in water; it is wet
   It is wet outside.
   I was outside and it rained so I
     am wet.
ice
   The icicles are hanging down.
there is hoar frost; hoar frost
it is frosted, covered with frost; there is
   hoar frost
   Everything is covered with hoar frost.
it is a heavy dew; dew
   In the morning there is a lot of dew
it is thawed, defrosted, soft

Celestial Phenomena

wįcáȟpi *n*
hąwí, wí *n*
   "Hąwí océti stéya," eyábis'a.

   Hąwí tą'į́šį a'óhązi no!

star
moon; sun; month
   "The moon is like a stove," they say
     usually.
   The sun is not visible, it is overcast!

hąwí bapsų́	*wet moon, Cheshire moon*
hąwí cogą́du, hąwí okíse	*half moon*
hąwí ožúna	*full moon*
hąwí togáhe oyášpe	*quarter moon*
wí yašpábi	*last quarter of the moon*
hąwí ų́šį	*it is a period with no moon; it is a night without a moon*
hąwísaba, hąwí sába iyáya	*lunar eclipse*
hąwácibi	*women's dance, night dance, moon dance*
hąwíyąba	*moonlight*
hąwí hįnápa	*sunrise*
tįšnága, ~ **tešnága** *n*	*22° halo, circular halo around the sun on cold winter days*
penyúza *n*	*sun dog, parhelion*
tešnága yušnóga *cp*	*sun dog on top of the sun*
tįšnága bašnóga *cp*	*half halo around the sun, especially in March*
ot'į́ *vimp, n*	*it is thundering; thunder*
ot'į́ apÁ *vimp*	*it is a thunderclap*
wanáǧi wacíbi np	*northern lights; aurora borealis; ghost dance*
caȟ'ówade *n*	*northern lights*
makówaja *adv*	*all over the world*
tadé'uya *n*	*cardinal directions, world quarters*
maȟpíya *n*	*sky, heavens; cloud*
maȟpíyakta	*to the clouds*
maȟpíyam	*in the sky*
naǧí makóce *cp*	*heaven*
makóce owáštejaga *cp*	*heaven*

Substances

mąká, ~ maká *n*
   Mąká agą́n bapsų́.
   Mąká né sábehtįyą.
mąkázi, wiyáska *n*
makáhasaba *n*
cą́ *n*
   Ganų́za cén cą́ gahų́hųza.

   Cą'ímaksa žé cą́ agámpadahą yįgá.
   Cą́ niyúha wabánažį.
wį́kni *n*
   Mató wį́kni snagíya.
íyą *n*
   Íyą wąmnága žehą́ hį́k nawápsija.
wasúsmuna *n*
įhé *n*
cahóda *n*
   Cahóda awágahikta.
   cahóda į́ógana
cuhé, pedį́hpaya *n*
wasé *n*
   Wasé ų́s ša'į́c'iya.

   wasé gitų́
   waséǧina
máza *n*
   mázaša
   mázaskazi

earth, soil, ground, dust, dirt, mud
   He spilled it on the ground.
   The mud is pitch black.
sand
coal
tree, wood, stick
   Because it is windy the trees are shaking.
   The saw is sitting on the wood.
   I put all of the sticks up.
fat, grease; gas, oil
   He rubs his with bear grease.
stone
   I saw a stone and I kicked it.
small hail stone, sleet
mountain, gravel, pebbles
ashes; coal
   I will cover it with ashes.
   pile of ashes
ashes
clay, ochre, paint of any colour
   He painted his face with red ochre.
   s/he wears paint, war paint
   yellow paint
iron, metal; money
   penny, cent; copper
   gold

mázaskana	*silver*
mą́za sú	*lead* (metal)
taníya *n*	*his/her/its breath; breath, air, oxygen,*
	atmosphere
miní *n*	*water*
Miní dágunišį.	*It contains no water.*
Miní žé cehúba žén ehą́'i.	*The water reached his chin.*
Miní ų́s dąyą́ gažáža.	*Rinse it well with water.*
miní sudá *cp*	*alcohol*
péda *n*	*fire, match*
pedáȟa	*ember, charcoal, spark*
pedį́ȟpaya	*ashes*
pen- *cont*	*fire*
penkákna	*near the fire*
penkáyena	*near the fire*
pencóna	*without a fire*
pensníya	*without a fire*
pen'ókšą	*around a fire*
įktų́, ~ įtkų́ *n*	*s/he/it is lit, in flames; house in flames;*
	arson
cetíbi *n*	*fireplace*

26

Fauna and Flora

Domesticated Animals

wahú núba *cp*	*two-legged creature or the two-leggeds*
wahú dóba *cp*	*four-legged creature or the four-leggeds*
búza *n*	*cat*
bus- *cont*	*cat, feline*
bustága	*bobcat*
bus'óye	*cat, feline tracks*
bušcíjana, búzina *n*	*kitten*
šúga *n*	*dog*
Šúga wapábi.	*The dogs are barking.*
šųk- *cont*	*dog, horse, sheep, canine*
šųkcíjana	*puppy*
šųksába	*black horse*
šųkhéyuke cijá	*lamb*
šųkhéwąga	*sheep*
šųkhéyuke, šųkhéyuką	*sheep*

šųkšóšona, šųkšóšo	*donkey, mule*
šošóbina	*donkey, mule*
šúga įdé pšųká, šųkpátąga *ph, n*	*bulldog*
ąbáhotųna, ąbáhotų *n*	*chicken*
ąbáhotųna cįjána *cp*	*chick*
ąbáhotųnamnoga *n*	*rooster*
ąbáhotųwįyena *n*	*hen*
šiyó *n*	*prairie chicken, pheasant, grouse;*
	domestic chicken
gugúša *n*	*pig*
Gugúša šįtų gá wįcá žé táwa.	*The man owns that fat pig over there.*
gugúša cįjána	*piglet*
gugúšamnoga	*hog*
gugúšana	*piglet, little pig*
gugúšawįyena	*swine*
pté *n*	*buffalo* (generic term); *buffalo cow;*
	domestic cow
ptecíjana	*calf*
ptewánųwą	*cattle, domestic cow*
ptewíyena	*buffalo cow, domestic cow*
ptewówaši	*ox*
ptemnóga	*bull*
cįjána *n*	*calf, offspring, cub*
įyústo *n*	*pet*

Wild Animals

bízena *n*	*gopher, ground squirrel*
bízena tága *cp*	*groundhog*

bis- *cont, vcont*	*rodent (gopher, prairie dog, mouse, rat); squealing*
bistága	*prairie dog*
bisbístąga	*rat*
bisknékneǧa	*spotted gopher, thirteen-lined ground squirrel*
bispízA *vi₁-redup*	*s/he/it squeals*
bispízena *n-redup*	*mouse*
įtúpsipsijana *n*	*kangaroo mouse*
cába *n*	*beaver*
cąkáhuknekneǧa *n-redup*	*striped gopher*
cąkáhuknekneǧana *n-redup*	*striped chipmunk*
tašnáheja *n*	*striped gopher*
tašnáheja ȟóda *cp*	*grey squirrel*
cąyúpina, cą'áninina *n*	*squirrel*
sųkpé *n*	*muskrat*
wahį́heya, waȟé'ąǧa *n*	*mole*
pahį́ *n*	*porcupine; porcupine quill*
wíyašpuna *n*	*shrew*
įkmų́ *n*	*lynx*
įkmúna	*bobcat*
įkmų́tąga	*mountain lion*
mató *n*	*black bear (only in compounds and personal names)*
matónuda	*cinnamon-coloured black bear*
matósaba	*black bear*
waȟ'ą́kšija *n*	*bear (generic)*
wamą́kamani *n*	*bear*
wamą́kašką *n*	*creature, animal; bear*
wacúwiska, waǧį́ *n*	*grizzly*

šųk- *cont*
    dog, horse, sheep, canine

  šúgašana, šųkšána
    red fox

  šųktógeja, šųktógena, šųktóga
    wolf

  šųkháskusku
    mangy dog, coyote, wolf; stray dog

  šųkcúk'ana
    coyote

tokána *n*
    grey fox; swift fox

mnáza, wį́kcena *n*
    wolverine

ȟogá, o'į́knuhena *n*
    badger

  Ȟogá žé mąká k'á.
    The badger is digging dirt.

škejá *n*
    fisher

ptą́ *n*
    otter

į́kusana *n*
    mink

įtúgasą *n*
    weasel

  įtúgasąskana
    white weasel (winter time)

  įtúgasązina
    brown weasel (summer time)

mągá, šijéją *n*
    skunk

wįcą́ *n*
    raccoon

įštásabA *vs, n*
    s/he has a black eye; raccoon

sįdésaba *n*
    black-tailed deer

heȟága, ~ heȟáge *n*
    elk

héžada *n*
    two-year-old deer

ųpá *n*
    elk cow

sįdégoskoza *n*
    mule deer

sįdéšana, šúgašana, šųkšána *n*
    red fox

tá *n*
    moose

  Tá bahágąn nážį.
    The moose is standing on top of a hill.

ta- *n*
    ruminant (generic meaning; moose, deer, elk, buffalo, pronghorn)

  táwįyena
    moose cow

tatága	*buffalo bull*
táȟca	*deer*
táȟcamnoga	*stag*
táȟcawįyena	*doe*
taȟcíjana, táȟtíjana	*deer* (generic); *herd of deer;*
	white-tailed deer
tatógana	*pronghorn*
hékiška, kíška *n*	*bighorn sheep, mountain goat*
héškoba *n*	*bighorn sheep*
įkú hą́ska *cp*	*mountain goat*
pté *n*	*buffalo* (generic term); *buffalo cow;*
	domestic cow
Pté páda.	*He is butchering a cow.*
ptemnóga	*bull*
ptewíyena	*buffalo cow, domestic cow*
maštíja *n*	*rabbit*
maštín, maštį́ *cont*	*rabbit*
maštíjatąga	*jackrabbit*
maštín wįyéna	*rabbit doe*
ȟubá wagíknągagana *cp*	*bat*
tahúhąska *n*	*giraffe*
wa'ų́cana, įyúnena *n*	*monkey*
pasúhąska *n*	*elephant*

Reptiles and Fish

snohéna *n*	*snake* (generic); *garter snake*
Snohéna wanį́jabi.	*There are no snakes.*
minísnohena	*watersnake*
snohéna kneknéǧana	*garter snake, water snake*

sįdéȟna, wó'ošija *n*	*rattlesnake*
wą́ *n*	*bullsnake*
wahį́kpekpena *n*	*blue racer* (snake)
patkážųda, paknážųtka *n*	*hog-nosed snake*
aknéška, aknéškana *n*	*lizard, salamander*
ḳeyá *n*	*snapping turtle*
patką́šana, ~ patkášina *n*	*slough turtle*
hoǧą́ *n*	*fish*
Ȟogą́ nína tága.	*This fish is very large.*
Hoǧą́ žé huhú ožúna.	*That fish is bony.*
hoǧą́ǧąna *n-redup*	*minnow*
hoǧą́tąga	*whale*
ho- *cont*	*fish*
hopsų́psųna *n*	*shiner*
hopépe *n*	*perch, pike*
homnáska *n*	*goldeye fish*
hopútįhį yuką́ *cp*	*catfish*
wawą́ga *n*	*whale*

Birds

ziktána, ~ zitkána, ziktán *n, cont*	*bird*
Ziktábina né cąwą́gądůȟ wahóȟpi gą́ǧabi.	*Those birds made a nest way up there in the tree.*
Ziktán wakúwa.	*I am chasing birds.*
ziktána wakmų́ȟa, ~ zitkána wakmų́ȟa	*hummingbird*
ziktásaba, ~ zitkásaba	*blackbird*
ziktáto, zitkánato, ~ zitkáto	*bluebird, bluejay*
ziktáǧina, ~ zitkáǧina	*goldfinch*

maǧá *n*	*duck, goose, swan* (generic)
paǧų́da *n*	*duck*
paǧų́dasaba	*American black duck*
paǧų́datąga	*goose*
paǧų́datąga skána	*snow goose*
paǧų́ɳ *cont*	*duck*
Paǧų́ɳ kuwé iyáya.	*He went duck hunting.*
paǧų́ɳcija	*duckling*
sihásaba *n*	*Canada goose*
sihúšaša, tahúto *n*	*mallard duck*
pasú agástaga, paȟní agástaga, póǧe	
agástaga, paȟnúda, tahúša *cp, n*	*turkey*
juwį́jijina, sihújijina *n*	*killdeer*
juwį́na *n*	*sandpiper*
amnóto, amnótona *n*	*teal, blue-winged duck*
peháǧina *n*	*sandhill crane*
wakpógiyą, žós'a *n*	*kingfisher*
hoká *n*	*heron*
mnip'ú, mnip'úhu *n*	*bittern*
mnóza *n*	*pelican*
wamní *n*	*golden eagle* (also as a generic term)
Wamní giyáyą én ahí.	*The eagles came flying in.*
wamní šagé	*eagle claw*
wamníkneška *n*	*spotted eagle*
anų́kasą *n*	*bald eagle*
ȟuyá *n*	*eagle*
á'ana *n*	*crow*
Á'ana ódabi.	*There are a lot of crows.*
bíško *n*	*nighthawk*
cąšká *n*	*hawk, chicken hawk*

cedą́ *n*	*hawk*
hejá *n*	*buzzard; turkey vulture*
Hejá agáwįȟ ų́.	*The turkey vulture is circling.*
kągí *n*	*raven*
ųkcékiǧa *n*	*magpie*
įȟát'at'ana *n-redup*	*magpie (its laughter)*
cątkúša, makúša *n*	*American robin*
gísabana, waníyedu ų́bis'a *n, ph*	*chickadee*
giyáyąno *n*	*mourning dove*
sįdéžada *n*	*sparrow; swallow*
ųbížade *n*	*barn swallow*
įjápsįpsįdana *n*	*swallow*
tašiyapopobena *n*	*meadowlark*
wapáǧi, įyágeǧi, peǧí *n*	*yellow-hooded blackbird*
wa'ámnoša *n*	*red-winged blackbird*
hįhą́ *n*	*owl; dove*
hįhą́ oȟnóga otís'a	*burrowing owl*
hįhą́ tága	*great grey owl*
hįhą́hąna	*pygmy owl*
hįhą́wapapana	*short-eared owl*
hįhą́są	*snowy owl*
tįknámųmųna *n*	*partridge, grouse*
šiyó *n*	*prairie chicken, pheasant, grouse;*
	domestic chicken
šiyójusina	*quail*
šiyótąga	*greater sage-grouse, sage hen*
caȟpą́, šiyágo *n*	*mud hen, American coot*
wasnásnąheja *n-redup*	*kingbird; catbird*
cągádodona *n*	*woodpecker*
cayágagana *n*	*wren*

cuwíǧi *n*	*scissor-billed curlew*
ȟmuyáhena *n*	*hummingbird*
zųzúja *n*	*flicker*
ųbí *n*	*tail of bird*
šagé *n*	*nail, hoof, claw*
pasú *n*	*beak; tip of the nose*
wíkta, ~ wítka *n*	*egg*
wítka há *cp*	*egg shell*
ȟubáhu *n*	*wing*
giyÁ *vi1*	*s/he/it flies*
ogíyÁ *vi1*	*s/he/it soars, flies about*
yuȟnáda *vt2*	*s/he claws, grabs sb, smth with the claws, nails*
wíyaga *n*	*feather*
šų, wíyaga šų *n, cp*	*longest feathers on the wing*
wó'įšte *n*	*eagle feather, plume, down feathers*
įyáge *n*	*feather on an arrow, fletching*
wacíhe *n*	*feather, plume tied up in the hair*
wahóȟpi *n*	*nest*
wahóȟpiya *n*	*rookery*
šųpá *vi1, n*	*it (bird) moults; moulting bird*
kpakpí *vi1*	*it (egg) hatches*

Shellfish

tugí *n*	*shell; seashell, pearl*
tugígina *n*	*snail*
tugískana *n*	*white shell*
tugítoto *n*	*clam shell*

šiptó *n*	*abalone shell*
modúdu *n*	*crab*
weyádą *n*	*leech; bloodsucker*
tųsná *n*	*leech; snail* (out of shell)
wamnúȟ'aȟ'ana *n*	*cowry shell, snail shell*

Insects and Other Critters

wamnúška *n*	*insect* (generic), *ant, bug, worm*
wamnúška hįšmą́šmą	*caterpillar*
wamnúška mnaská	*bedbug*
wamnúška nįdémnaska	*maple bug, box elder bug*
wamnúška pašáša	*red-headed ant*
wamnúška sapsábina	*cricket*
wamnúškaša	*flea*
wamnúška bağétibina	*ants*
cąwámnuška	*wood tick*
capúga *n*	*mosquito*
cąyéğa *n*	*firefly*
tažúška *n*	*deerfly*
tažúškatąga *n*	*horsefly*
tuȟmáğa *n*	*bee*
tuȟmą́ȟtąga *n*	*wasp; bumblebee*
tuȟmą́ȟti *n*	*beehive; bumblebee nest*
wóga, ~ wóğa *n*	*grasshopper*
tatók'ana *n*	*butterfly*
gimą́mąna, ~ gimą́miną *n*	*butterfly, moth*
honáğina, honáği *n*	*fly, housefly*
honáğina cįjábi	*maggots*
honáğinatotobi	*bluebottle fly*

cábabana *n*	*water beetle*
cąšká wamnímnina *cp*	*small, fast-flying hawk*
ȟeȟágana, ȟeȟágągana *n*	*spider*
ȟeȟágągana wakmúga,	*cobweb*
wosúsųbina *cp, n*	
hé'a, héya *n*	*louse, lice*
héyamnaȟ'ana *n*	*small louse after hatching*
susméja *n*	*dragonfly*
tabéȟ'a, tabéȟ'ana, ~ tabáȟ'a *n*	*frog*
tąníjana *n*	*gnat, sandfly*
taskákpa, tamnáska *n*	*wood tick*
hemnáska, hamnáskana *n*	*bedbug*
ųkcébakmįkma *n*	*stink bug, tumble bug*
hipépena *n*	*ant*

Mysterious and Divine Creatures

acąšį *n*	*evil fairy*
anúk'įde *n*	*two-faced devil*
ecábišį *n*	*invisible spirit, ghost*
ȟuȟúna *n*	*ghost, monster*
mayáwašiju, mayášiju *n*	*little people, cave people*
Mayáwašiju wowícak'úbi	*Feed the Little People Ceremony*
mnowága *n*	*water monster*
paǧúdapa nap'į́, wįcáȟpi cíja *nprop*	*Star Child*
pe'óȟnoga *n, nprop*	*idiot, person that is not smart; monster with a hole in the head*
ptešíȟ'ą *n*	*buffalo monster*
snohéna tága *n*	*big snake*

šiȟ'ą *n*	*beast*
tašúge wagíyą *cp*	*thunder horse*
wagíyą *n*	*thunderbird*
Wagíyą hotútųbi.	*The thunderbirds are making their cry.*
Wagíyą híbi cén.	*The thunderbirds have arrived.*
wagíyą hotúbi *ph*	*it thunders; thunderbirds*
waȟúbagoza, ȟubáhugoza *n*	*thunderbird*
wanáǧi *n*	*spirit, soul, ghost*
wįcášta toká *n*	*alien*
Tokábi né cowįcaya.	*He believes in aliens.*
Wįcášta toká né coyáya he?	*Do you believe in aliens?*

Trees and Plants

cá *n*	*tree; wood; stick*
Cá wanįja.	*There are no trees.*
Cá jónana k'ú wo.	*Bring a little bit of wood.*
Cá né škóba.	*This stick is bent.*
cąwágan	*up in a tree*
cábaǧe *n*	*pile of wood*
cąhábi n	*tree sap*
cąhúde *n*	*tree stump, base of a tree*
cąȟóda n	*ash tree*
cąpá, cą *n, cont*	*chokecherry, pin cherry*
cąpáhu *n*	*cherry tree*
cąpájuk'a *n*	*pin cherry*
cąpásusuna *n-redup*	*pepper*
Cąpásusuna yuká he?	*Is there pepper?*

cą́pépena *n-redup* — thistle, prickly plant

cą́páksa *n* — stump

cąsága *n* — twig

    Cąsága wążí wabáksa. — *I broke a twig.*

cąságena *n* — *water willow*

cąská *n* — *white poplar*

cąsúda *n* — *ash tree; hardwood*

cąšáša, cąšášana *n-redup* — *red willow*

cą́šeja *n* — *dead tree*

cąšį́ *n* — *resin, gum; chewing gum; rubber*

cąškóba *n* — *curved tree, stick*

cąšúška *n* — *box elder*

cą́teja, cątóto *n* — *green wood*

cąwába *n* — *evergreen tree, pine*

cąwába cąšį́ *cp* — *pine resin*

cąwídaga *n* — *grove of trees*

cąwóhą, ~ cą́óhą *adv* — *in a wooded area, in the bush, forest*

    Gadám cąwóhą yá wo. — *Go over there in the woods.*

cąwóhocągu *n* — *trail in the woods*

cąwóšma *n* — *dense bush; forest*

coǧą́žįja *n* — *diamond willow*

cų́taga *n* — *thicket*

waȟpé *n* — *leaf; tea*

    Duwé waȟpé cįgá? — *Who wants tea?*

    Waȟpé né įyúta. — *Taste this tea.*

waȟpé cąní *cp* — *kinnikinnick*

waȟpé ce'ága *cp* — *peppermint*

waȟpéȟpena *n-redup* — *flower* (with leaves)

waȟpésaba *n* — *black tea*

waȟpéto *n* — *green tea*

peží *n*	*grass, hay*
Peží žé acú.	*The grass is covered with dew.*
peží įcápe *cp*	*hayfork*
peží įyúǧe, peží ogáǧe *cp*	*rake*
peží pahtábi *cp*	*hay bale*
peží wįtkó *cp*	*marijuana, cannabis*
Peží wįtkó įjúbi ogíhibi.	*They are permitted to smoke weed.*
pežígabuza *n*	*dried hay*
pežíhoda *n*	*sagebrush*
pežískuya, wacáǧa, *n*	*sweetgrass*
pežíšeja *n*	*straw*
pežíto *n, vs*	*bluejoint grass; s/he/it is blue-green, green*
pežúda *n*	*medicinal plant; medicine in general*
Pežúda né mnihą́.	*This medicine is powerful.*
pežúdasaba *n*	*blackroot, Culver's root*
waštémna *vs, n*	*s/he/it smells good; horsemint*
abá'e, abáye *n*	*larb (psychoactive plant often mixed with red willow bark and used in ceremonies)*
hucą́saba *n*	*black root*
húda, hutką́ *n*	*root*
psá *n*	*cattail root*
sųkpétawode *n*	*bitterroot*
wahcá *n*	*flower, blossom*
Wahcá né ómna.	*Smell this flower.*
wahcáǧi *n*	*dandelion*
wahníca, wahcíca *n*	*white poplar; cottonwood*
wapépe *n*	*thistle*

gamúbi *n*	*drum; cattail stem and fuzz*
wazícą *n*	*pine tree*
hįcą *n*	*cattail*
hįcą́hu *n*	*cattail stalk*
hįktą́ *n*	*cattail fuzz*
cąní *n*	*tobacco*
cąní sudá *cp*	*twisted tobacco*
cąníyatabi *n*	*chewing tobacco*
cą́šáša, cą́šášana *n-redup*	*red willow*
įyúhibi *n*	*tobacco mixed with red willow*
a'į́kpoǧa *vi3-refl, n*	*s/he blows smth* (medicine, perfume) *on him/herself; cedar; Indian perfume* (sweet pine, cedar)

Berries

waskúya, ~ wóskuya *n*	*berries, fruit; juice*
waskúyeja *n*	*berries*
wašáša *n*	*berry, berries* (generic)
wah'ą́kšija tawóde *cp*	*bearberry*
wįbazuką sába *cp*	*blackberry*
wįbazuką stéya, a'ų́yabi *ph, n*	*blueberry*
dágušašana *n-redup*	*buffalo berry*
wįyą́teja *n*	*cranberry*
wįcákneška *n*	*gooseberry*
taką́heja *n*	*raspberry*
wįbazoką *n*	*saskatoon berry*
Wįbazoką ugónes.	*Let us go search for saskatoon berries.*

wažúšteja *n*	*strawberry*
taspáspąna *n-redup*	*hawthorn berries; crabapple*
taspá *n*	*hawthorn fruit; apple; fruit* (in compounds)
Taspá nówa temyéwakiya.	*I made him eat all the apples.*
taspáhu *n*	*hawthorn bush*
taspácą *n*	*apple tree*

Crops and Other Edible Plants

pąǧí *n*	*potato*
Pąǧí šašá žená éyagu.	*Take those red potatoes.*
Pąǧí įbíhyabi.	*They boiled potatoes.*
pąǧí gakúkabi *cp*	*mashed potatoes*
pąǧí háska *n*	*parsnip*
pąǧíska *n*	*white Irish potato*
pąǧískuya *n*	*sweet potato*
wahpé įjáhibi *cp*	*salad*
wahpé tága *cp*	*cabbage*
wahpé ce'ága *cp*	*peppermint*
aǧúyabisu *n*	*wheat*
wįcánuhnuǧena *n*	*pumpkin*
hąwí wahcá *cp*	*sunflower*
típsinaǧi, píhpiǧana *n*	*carrot*
psį *n*	*rice, wild rice*
típšina, ~ típsina *n*	*turnip, wild turnip*
wakmúhazaskuya *n*	*sweetcorn*
wakmúhaza, ~ wakmúhąza *n*	*corn*
wakmúhazakneǧe *n*	*Indian corn*
nąpópomyabi *n-redup*	*popcorn*

wacóǧuǧu *n* Indian popcorn
wayáhoda *n* oats
ceyágadaga, ~ cayágadaga *n* wild mint, peppermint

27

Transporation and City Infrastructure

Means of Transportation

iyécįgayena, **iyécįgana**, **iyécįga**, **iyécįgena**, **iyécįgamani** *n*	*car, autmobile*
amógįyą, ~ **amúgiyą**, ~ **įmúgiya** *n*	*car, automobile*
Amógįyą žé wapíwacįšį.	*The car is not clean.*
Amúgiya né dágu yupíyašį.	*This car is worthless.*
amógįyą én yįgábi *ph*	*car seat*
amógįyą hú *cp*	*car tire, wheel*
hú mįmámina, **hú** *n*	*wheel*
įbákmįkma *n*	*wheel, tire; wheelbarrow*
yu'ówadA *vt2, n*	*s/he lights smth up; flashlight, car headlights*
įyúhomni *n*	*steering wheel*
įmóȟtage, ~ **įmóȟtaga** *n*	*bumper*
togáda įmóȟtage	*front bumper*
héktam įmóȟtage	*rear bumper*
iyécįgayena tí *cp*	*garage*

basí *vi1, vt1*	*s/he drives; s/he drives smth*
gíjibasi	*s/he drives for sb, drives sb around*
kpási	*s/he drives his/her own vehicle*
abási	*s/he drives sb, smth*
basíbi *n*	*driver*
įbási n	*driver's license*
wį́knisaba *n*	*motor oil, car oil*
wádagįyą *n*	*airplane, aircraft carrier*
mázagįyą *n*	*airplane*
įyécįga gįyéna *cp*	*airplane*
gįyáyąbi *n*	*airplane*
gįyékiyabi *n*	*airplane, car*
wádagįyą *cp*	*airport*
įwátokšu, otókšu, tokšú *n*	*truck, pickup truck, large vehicle*
Adé įwátokšu tága basíšį.	*Dad does not drive large trucks.*
įwátokšu tága *cp*	*large truck* (like a trailer van)
owáyawa otókšu *cp*	*school bus*
wáda įtókšu *cp*	*freight car*
wa'į́badįda *n*	*snowplow*
įwátokšu wa'į́badįda *cp*	*snowplow truck*
wáda *n*	*canoe, boat, ship; train, engine*
Wáda awáyaga.	*He is looking after the canoe.*
Wáda žé núzahą.	*The train is fast.*
mázawada	*train*
tąbáwada	*birchbark canoe*
mniwáda	*boat, ship*
wadó'įnažį *n*	*train station*
wadó, įwádopa *n*	*canoe*
wadópa *vi1*	*s/he paddles*
wan'į́dopa *n*	*paddle, oar*

214

wa'ániya hiyáya *cp*	*ski-doo*
wį́kni *n*	*fat, grease; oil, gasoline*
wį́kni įbápsų *cp*	*gas station*
ogícize maká agą́n wáda *ph*	*tank*
gaptáyA̧ *vt1, vi1*	*s/he/it knocks, hits smth down; the wind knocks, hits smth down; s/he has a car accident*

City Infrastructure

ocą́gu *n*	*road, street*
Ocą́gu gakná iyápebi.	*They are ambushed beside the road.*
Ocą́gu škaška omáwani.	*I travelled on a crooked road.*
ocą́guȟe *n*	*gravel road*
ocą́gusaba *n*	*paved road; drunkenness*
ocą́guna *n*	*path, trail*
cąwóhocągu *n*	*trail in the woods*
ocą́gu tága *cp*	*highway*
įbáweȟ ocą́gu *cp*	*crossroad*
amánibi *n*	*path*
makóškiška *n, vs*	*rough, bumpy road; it is a rough, bumpy road*
Ocą́gu okná yéšį, žé makóškiška.	*Do not go through that road, it is rough.*
owáyaco *n*	*court, courthouse*
Owáyaco ektá mnį́kta.	*I will be going to court.*
owáyacotąga *n*	*Supreme Court*
owácibi *n*	*dance hall, dance arbour*
wa'óyabi oyúȟpe *cp*	*post office*

omás'ape, ~ **omás'apa** n	*telegraph, telephone office*
oyáde omníciye, oyáde tí *cp*	*band office*
pežúda wašíjuti *cp*	*clinic, medical office*
owáyawa, wayáwa tíbi *cp, n*	*school, school house*
owáyawatąga *n*	*high school*
owácegiya *n*	*church* (building or institution
owácegiya tíbi *cp*	*church* (building)
caȟtí *n*	*house, building to store ice*
wópetų *vi₁-abs, n*	*s/he buys things; merchant*
owópetų tíbi, owópetų, ~	
owópetų *cp, n*	*store*
Owópetų tíbi imnámna.	*I am setting to go the store.*
Owópetų žedáhą ųkníbi.	*We came back home from the store.*
hayábi owópetų *cp*	*clothing store*
cąní owópetų *cp*	*tobacco, smoke shop*
máza owópetų *cp*	*hardware store*
omní owópetų *cp*	*liquor store, bar*
wóyude owópetų *cp*	*grocery store*
waȟpáya owópetų *cp*	*thrift store*
įnųba wiyópeyabi tíbi *np*	*thrift store, second-hand store*
hayábi owópetų tíbi *cp*	*clothing store*
tanó owópetų *cp*	*butcher shop*
owákpamni, ~ **owókpamni** *n*	*tribal agency, rations house*
tí *vi₁, n*	*s/he lives somewhere* (house, place, area); *house, place*
tín	*inside a house*
ti'ókšą, tiwókšą	*around the house, camp*
ti'íyaza	*from house to house; all throughout camp*

tíbi *n*	house, dwelling, any type of structure
wašíju tíbi, wašíjuti	house, framed house
tóhe, ~ **tíhe** *n*	his/her place, house, bed
cą'óti, ~ **cątíbi** *n*	log cabin, log house
į́yą wašíjuti *cp*	brick house
opšíje tíbi *cp*	mud house
tíbi tokšú *cp*	trailer house
o'écųna, o'écųna tíbi *n, cp*	gaming house, casino

Dóhąni o'écųna tíbi ektám né wa'íšį.   *I never went to the casino.*

Verbs of Departing, Coming, Arriving, and Travelling

Verbs for Departing

hiyú *vi1*	s/he departs, is setting to come here from there; it begins, appears, arises, turns into smth
Hiyú bo!	*Come here you all!*
Midáguyabi néci hiyú bo!	*My relatives come over here!*
iyáyA *vi2*	s/he sets to go from here, departs from here (before or shortly after departure)
Mitą́gena dóki inána he?	*My older sister, where are you setting to go?*
Ocą́gokna iyáya:ga.	*She was going along the road.*
knijú *vi1*	s/he departs, leaves to come back here
kiknÁ *vi1*	s/he leaves home
Kiknábi cén įmą́comni.	*They went back home so I am lonely.*
Kiknábi ųká nahą́h̃ bąyáhąbi stéya.	*They left home but still they can be heard yelling.*

Verbs for Coming and Arriving

ú *vi1*
Wa'úkta ųká mastústa.
Néci ú wo.

s/he goes, arrives here from there
I was to come but I am tired.
Come over here.

hí *vi1*
Nahánįštaš híbi.
Céǧa K'įna žedáhą yahí?

s/he arrives here from there
I wish they could of come.
Are you arriving from Carry The
Kettle?

yÁ *vi2*

Sám yá!
Įtó cąk'į mnį́kta.

s/he goes away from here, s/he
departed from here
Go away!
I think I will go get firewood.

í *vi1*
Duktéȟ í cá.
Ába waką žehą owácegiya žéci wa'í.

s/he arrives there from here
He went somewhere else I guess.
I went to church on Sunday.

Verbs for Returning

kú *vi1*
Wazíȟe ecíyadahą gúbi.

"Tída gú!" ecíjiya.

s/he comes back here
They left Cypress Hills to come
back here.
"Come back here!" I told you.

kní *vi1*

Tída kní.
Owópetų žedáhą ųkníbi.

s/he arrives back here; returns,
comes home
He comes home.
We came back home from the store.

kná *vi1*

Cída yakná he?

s/he goes, returns back to where s/he
is from
Are you going back home?

Yakná štén anų́k éduwą. | When you go back home look both ways.

kí *vi1* | s/he arrives back there (after leaving); returns back to where s/he is from

Aké tiyábi wakí cén. | Again I came back home.

Ecén wį́yą žé tída kí. | And so the woman returned back home.

maní, ~ máni *vi1* | s/he walks; s/he progresses, behaves as such in life; s/he accompanies, walks with sb

Inína mawánįkte no. | I will walk quietly.

Mį́togam mayáni oyágihi he? | Can you walk in front of me?

Ótąnaȟ máni wo. | Walk in a straight way.

ománi *vi1* | s/he goes for a walk, travels, wanders

Ocą́gu škašká omáwani. | I travelled on a crooked road.

ąm'ómani *vi1* | s/he/it walks around, travels during the day

ogáwįȟ ų́ *vi1* | s/he travels all over

28

Quantities

Cardinal and Ordinal Numbers

Lower Numbers (0-9)

dágunišį *num*	zero
wąží *num, dem*	one; *a*
Aké wąží émnagųkte no!	*I will give him one more!*
Cąsága wąží wabáksa.	*I broke a twig off.*
Wążína hugá cá.	*Only one was chief.*
nųba, nų́m *num, vs*	two; s/he/it is two; there are two
Dóba cogą́n nųba štén nųbáȟ.	*Four divided by two equals two.*
Nų́baȟ hokší gíji'įȟpaya.	*She had two miscarriages.*
Ą́ba nųba štén hį́kta.	*He will arrive in two days.*
nų́bacą *vimp*	it is a period of two days
Mikų́ ą́ba nų́bacą hí.	*My mother-in-law arrived two days ago.*
nų́bagiya *adv*	two by two, in two ways, in two different directions, locations
Nų́bagiya iyáyabi.	*They went on separate ways.*

númnanaȟ *adv*
   Númnanaȟ híbi.

nų́mnųbanaȟ *adv-redup*
newós *pro, dem*
   newós įwó'okma žéca
gawós *pro, dem*
   Gawós nų́ba a'ú.
yámni *num, vs*
   Cįjábi yámni mnuhá.
yámnina *num*
yámnigiya *adv*

   Yámnigiya éwaknągįkta.

yámniȟ *adv*
   Ptį́hą žéci wa'í yámniȟ.
dóba, dóm *num, vs*
   Į'íjuna dóba émnagu.
dóbana *num*
dóbagiya *adv*

   Dóbagiya né éknąga.
dóbaȟ *adv*
   Dóbaȟ yekíye no.
záptą *num, vs*
   Ecágen záptą apá hą́da hí.
zaptą́ȟ *adv*
záptąna *num*
šákpe *num, vs*
   Įyútabi šákpe nawážį.

only two
   Only two came.

only twice
these two
   these two pencils
those two yonder
   Bring these two yonder.
three; s/he/it is three; there are three
   I have three children.
only three
three by three, in three ways, in three
   different directions, locations
   I will put them in three different
   locations.
three times
   I went there three times last fall.
four; s/he/it is four; there are four
   I took four cups.
only four
four by four, in four ways, in four
   different directions, locations
   He put them in four different places.
four times
   He sent him out four times.
five; s/he/it is five; there are five
   He always arrives at five.
five times
only five
six; s/he/it is six; there are six
   I am six feet tall.

O'ápe šákpe ohą́.	*Boil for six hours.*
šakpéȟ *adv*	*six times*
šákpena *num*	*only six*
šagówį, iyúšna *num, vs*	*seven; s/he/it is seven; there are seven*
šaknóǧą *num, vs*	*eight; s/he/it is eight; there are eight*
šaknóǧąna *num*	*only eight*
napcúwąga *num, vs*	*nine; s/he/it is nine; there are nine*
napcúwągana *num*	*only nine*

Teens

wikcémna *num*	*ten*
agéwąži *num*	*eleven*
agénųba *num*	*twelve*
agéyamni *num*	*thirteen*
agédoba *num*	*fourteen*
agézaptą *num*	*fifteen*
agéšakpe *num*	*sixteen*
agéšagowį *num*	*seventeen*
agéšaknoǧą *num*	*eighteen*
agénapcuwąga *num*	*nineteen*

After 19 the cardinal numbers are formed by putting
the words in the following order:

wikcémna núm sám dóba	**wikcémna šákpe sám šákpe**
10 2 over 4	10 6 over 6
twenty-four	*sixty-six*

Twenties

wikcémna nų́m *num*	*twenty*
wikcémna nų́m sám wązí *num*	*twenty-one*
wikcémna nų́m sám nų́ba *num*	*twenty-two*
wikcémna nų́m sám yámni *num*	*twenty-three*
wikcémna nų́m sám dóba *num*	*twenty-four*
wikcémna nų́m sám záptą *num*	*twenty-five*
wikcémna nų́m sám šákpe *num*	*twenty-six*
wikcémna nų́m sám šagówį *num*	*twenty-seven*
wikcémna nų́m sám šaknóǧą *num*	*twenty-eight*
wikcémna nų́m sám napcúwąga *num*	*twenty-nine*

Decades

wikcémna yámni *num*	*thirty*
wikcémna dóba *num*	*forty*
wikcémna záptą *num*	*fifty*
wikcémna šákpe *num*	*sixty*
wikcémna šagówį *num*	*seventy*
wikcémna šaknóǧą *num*	*eighty*
wikcémna napcúwąga *num*	*ninety*
obáwįǧe *num*	*one hundred*

Ordinal Numbers

įjíwažį, įwą́žį *num*	*first*
įjínųba, įnų́ba *num*	*second*
įjíyamni, įyámni *num*	*third*

įjídoba *num*	*fourth*
įjízaptą *num*	*fifth*
įjíšakpe, įšákpe *num*	*sixth*
įjí'iyušna, įjíšagowį *num*	*seventh*
įjíšaknoğą *num*	*eighth*
įjínapcuwąga *num*	*ninth*
įjíwikcemna *num*	*tenth*
įjí'agezaptą *num*	*fifteenth*
įjíwikcemna šákpe *num*	*sixtieth*

Measuring and Weighing

įyútA vt2 — *s/he tests, tries, measures smth (food, drink, clothes, task)*

Húde žé įyútabi yámni. — *The base is three feet.*

Įyútabi yámni nážį. — *It stands three feet tall.*

Waníhą cą́'íyutabi yámni wagáksa. — *Last winter I chopped three cords of wood.*

įknúta *vti1-pos* — *s/he measures his/her own*

wíyuta *vi1-abs* — *s/he measures things*

mąkíyutabi *n* — *kilometre, land measurement, acre*

Agásąm ti'óda mąkíyutabi wikcémna šaknóğą. — *Harlem is 80 miles distant.*

Miníwaką mąkíyutabi wikcémna núm sám wąží. — *Manitou Beach is 21 miles distant.*

tacą́kiyutabi, si'íyutabi *n* — *foot measurement*

tkÁ *vs* — *s/he/it is heavy*

Dóna tké įníyuta he? — *How many times did he weigh you?*

Doháyą nitká he? — *How heavy are you?*

Tká įyútabi nidóna? — *How heavy are you?*

ehą́'i *vi1*

s/he reaches or arrives at a point
(place or time)

Dóna hą́ska ehą́ya'i?	*How tall are you?*
Tacą́kiyutabi šákpe ehąwá'i.	*I am 6 feet tall.*
Dóna ehą́'i he?	*What time is it?*
Dóna ehą́'i šten wówaši yecų́nikta?	*What time will you get off work?*
Wąží ehą́'i.	*It is one o'clock.*
Agéwąži sám hągé ehą́'i.	*It is eleven thirty.*
Waná ą́ba įdóba ehą́'i.	*It is now Thursday.*
Ą́bawaką ehą́'i.	*It is Sunday.*
Ą́ba įjíšakpe wįcógądu sųgágu hąwí.	*It is the sixth of November.*

ehą́ki *vt1-poss*

s/he reaches an age, is of a certain age

Waníyedu dóna ehą́yaki he?	*How old are you?*
Waníyedu dóna ehą́ki he?	*How old is s/he?*
Waníyedu wikcémna nų́ba sám	*S/he will be twenty-one years old.*
Waníyedu wikcémna dóba ehą́waki.	*I am forty years old.*

hą́skA *vs*

s/he is tall

Hokšína né tacą́kiyutabi záptą hą́ska.	*This boy is 5 feet tall.*
Tacą́kiyutabi šákpe mahą́ska.	*I am 6 feet tall.*
Tacą́kiyutabi šákpe nihą́ska.	*You are 6 feet tall.*

hągé *n*

half

Dóba sám hągé ehą́'i.	*It is four thirty.*
mázaska hągé	*fifty cents*

29

Space and Time

Spatial Relationships

nén *adv*
here (precise location near the speaker), *in a place*

Nén stustáyagen mągá.
I am sitting here bored.

Šųkcúk'ana nén ódabi.
There are many coyotes here.

néci *adv*
around here

Néci ú!
Come here!

Néci wa'ápe.
Wait over here.

nedápa *adv*
on this side

Nedápa yuptéjena.
Cut it shorter on this side.

nedápadahą *adv*
moving from here, behind, from this side; from the beginning, start

nédu *vimp*
it is here; this is the place

"Néduc," eyá.
"Here it is," he said.

néduȟ *vimp*
it is right here, this is exactly the place

néduna *adv*
near, close to here

nédunaȟ *adv*
very near, close to here

Nedám nédunaȟ wa'ų́.
I live close to here, over this way.

nehágeȟ *adv* — this long; this far off
    Nehágeȟ aktága. — He ran this far off.
nehágejA *vs* — s/he/it is about this high, tall, or far
žén *adv* — there
    Iyúha žén étibi. — People were camped there.
žéci *adv* — around there, over there, there
    Žéci wa'í žehą́. — I arrived over there.
    Mihų́ owáyawa žéci amá'įkta. — My mother will take me over there.
    žécipadahą — from over there
žéciya *adv* — over there, over that way
    žecíyadahą — from that direction, from over there
žecíyo *adv* — at the destination, at an end point
    Eháš žecíyo wa'í. — I arrived at the destination.
    žéciyota — that way
žedábaš *adv* — in that direction
žedáhą, ~ žedą́hą *adv, vs* — from there, from it; s/he/it is from there
    Céǧa K'ína žedáhą yahí? — Are you arriving from Carry The Kettle?

    Micį́kši ženídahąc. — My son, you are from there.
    žedáhąȟ — from that time
žedám *adv* — that way (away from speaker)
    Žedám édųwą! — Look that way!
žedápadahą *adv* — moving from there, that way
    Žedápadahą úbi. — They come from there.
žedápkiya *adv* — toward that direction
žédu *vimp* — it is there; that is the place
    žéduȟ — it is right there; that is exactly the place

    žédunaȟ — exactly there

žehágeȟ *adv*
only that far off, only that much
Obáwįǧe núba, žehágeȟ mak'ú.
$200, that is how much he gave me.

žehágeja *vs, adv, n*
it is that long, far, size; since then; distance, destination
Makóce makíyutabi dóba žehágeja.
The land is 10 kilometres long.
Gídąȟ žehágeja wa'í.
At last I reached the destination.

žektágiya *adv*
toward that direction (away from speaker)
Žektágiya iyáya.
He left in that direction.

gá *dem*
that over there
Šúga gá dágu dóku he?
What is that dog over there doing?

ganá *dem-pl*
those over there
Dágu ganá he?
What are those over there?

gán *adv*
over there
Įtó gán tiwįcoda tíbi.
Well, many families lived over there.

gakí *adv*
yonder, way over there
Gakí teháda owáne no.
I looked for it way over there.
Gakí wot'á.
He died over there.

duktén *adv*
where, at what place
Nikúši duktén tí?
Where does your grandmother live?
Duktén šúga žé wąnága he?
Where did you see that dog?
duktén túbi
place of birth

dukténi *adv*
nowhere
dukténiȟ
nowhere at all
dukténišį
it is nowhere

duktépadahą *adv*
from where

duktékten, duktékte *adv-redup*
here and there; occasionally
Duktékten cup'ó.
It is foggy here and there.

duktéȟ *adv*
somewhere
Duktéȟ wódįkte žéca oné!
Look for a place to eat!

duktédahą *adv*   *from where, where*

    Duktédahą yahí?   *From where did you arrive?*

duktédu *vimp*   *it happened somewhere as such*

    Duktéduȟtįyą?   *Where did it happened exactly?*

duktédugaš *adv*   *wherever, anywhere*

dóki *adv*   *where, where to; anywhere,*
          somewhere, to some place

    Nihį́kna dóki iyáya?   *Where did your husband go?*

    Dóki ya'íšį he?   *You did not go anywhere?*

dókiya *adv, vs*   *wherever; anywhere; where to*

    Wapáha žé dókiya?   *Where is the hat?*

    Cąšmúyabi dókiya?   *Where is the sugar?*

dókiyo *adv*   *in which direction, course*

    Dókiyo iyáya?   *In which direction did he go?*

    Wakpá žé dókiyo ȟaȟá.   *The river is flowing its course.*

kún *adv*   *down, downward, below*

    Kún ú.   *Come down.*

hokún *adv*   *down, below; downstairs*

    Hokún yubáǧe.   *He pulled it down.*

    Hokún yá!   *Go downstairs!*

į́hokun *adv*   *under, underneath smth*

    Į́hokun maníbi.   *They walked underneath it.*

kúdina, kúdiyena *adv*   *low, down, near the ground*

    Waná kúdiyena gaȟmóga.   *Now it is blowing close to the ground.*

gakún *adv*   *downward*

mahédu *vimp*   *it is deep inside*

    Mnikábi žé mahédu.   *The well is deep.*

mahéduȟ *adv*   *deeper, deep down inside*

    Dágu nówa mahéduȟ naȟmá.   *She hides everything way down.*

mahén *adv-cont, post*
  Nén mahén cąbúbų.
  Owį́ža mahén yįgá!
  mahén hayábi
  mahén hųská
  mahén ų́bi
  cahmáhen
  wamáhen
mahétkiya *adv*
  Mahétkiya badį́dašį.
mąkámahen *adv*

wągám, ~ **wągán** *adv*
  Wągám éknąga.
wągámkiya *adv*
  Wągámkiya yábi tehíga.
wągámneh *adv*
  Íyąhe wągámneh íbi.
  íwągam *adv, post*
  Taháge íwągam ta'óbi.
wągą́dahą *adv*
wągą́duwa *vs, adv*

  Wągą́duwa ecú.
wągą́duwa éknągA *vt1*
wągąduwah *adv*
  Wamní žé wągą́duwah gįyą́!

inside, in, within; under, underneath
  The wood is rotten here inside.
  Stay under the blanket!
  underwear
  long johns, thermal underwear
  underwear
  under ice
  under the snow
downward
  Do not push it too deep.
underground; under the ground;
  below the surface of the earth
up high, above, upright
  Put it upright.
uphill, upward
  It is hard to go uphill.
highest point, top, highest part of smth
  They went to the highest mountain.
  above smth
  He was wounded above the knee.[17]
from above
it is high, highly placed, of value;
  way above, way up there, high up
  He stacked it high up.
s/he promotes sb to a higher position
way up there, at the highest point
  The eagle flies the highest!

---

17   Drummond 1976.

wagáduwaȟtįyĄ *vs*
s/he/it is the highest, at the highest point

įjída *adv*
high above

  wįcá įjída hąska
  the tallest man

įjíma *adv*
next time, next

  Įjíma štén mnįkta.
  Next time I will go.

įjínažį *vii*
s/he/it stands above

gakná *adv*
beside, along sb, smth

  Gakná yįgá!
  Sit beside him!

  Nųpín gakná maníbi.
  They both are walking along.

įgákna *adv*
against, besides sb, smth

  Mígakna yįgá!
  Sit beside me!

mnigákna, ~ mnįjákna *adv*
beside the water, at the shore

tijákna *adv*
beside a dwelling, house

  Amúgįyą žé tijákna yįgá.
  The car is beside the house.

ki'úm *adv*
beside, alongside

  Šúga žé amúgiya ki'úm aktága.
  The dog ran alongside the car.

agą́n, ~ agám *post*
on top of smth, on it

  Agą́n bóǧa!
  Blow on it!

  Agám nážį.
  He stands on top.

timáhen *adv*
inside smth, in (building, car)

  Wí timáhen yigá.
  He is sitting in the tent.

  Šúga wąží iyécįgana timáhen ų́.
  There is a dog in the car.

timáhentahą *adv*
from indoors, from the inside

  Wíyą úkta timáhentahą.
  The woman will come from indoors.

tín *adv*
inside a house

  Tín úkta cįgá.
  She wants to come in.

tągán, tągáda *adv*
outside

  Tągán yá škáda wo.
  Go and play outside.

  Tągán a'óžąžą.
  It is sunny outside.

  Wanágaš tągán ecágen yągábi.
  Long ago they always stayed outside.

tágana *vs* — s/he/it is kind of big, grown up

tągápadahą, tągápada *adv* — from the outside

gaktá *adv* — near that yonder

kiyą́na *adv* — close, nearby

Kiyą́na ú. — He is coming close.

Kiyą́na híbi. — They are approaching.

togáda *adv* — ahead, in front, in the lead, in the first place; in the future, later

Togáda yá. — He is taking the lead.

Togáda žéci yá. — He will go over there late.

togám *adv* — ahead, in the lead

Togám ú. — He remains ahead.

Togám nážį. — He stood in front.

įtógam *adv* — in front of sb, smth; before time

Hųgá įtógam nawážį. — I stood in front of the chief.

kogám *adv* — in front, ahead, forward; across

Kogám aktága. — He ran ahead.

Wakpá kogám wanų́wą. — I swam across the river.

aháge *adv, vs* — last, last one; behind

Aháge mawáni. — I walk behind.

Todd ejé'enaȟ aháge. — Todd is the last one left.

hékta *adv* — back then, in the past

Hékta naháȟ pté óda žehą́. — There was still a lot of buffalo back then.

Né hékta nén aškán ḻhą́ktuwąbi nená ahí no. — Back in the recent past these Yankton Dakota came here.

héktam *adv* — behind, in the rear

Šúga héktam máni. — The dog is walking behind.

Héktam nážį nén. — He is standing here behind.

héktapadahą *adv*	*from behind*
ȟeyám *adv*	*in the back, behind*
Ȟeyám įnáwažįkte no.	*I will stand behind.*
nazám *adv*	*aside, at the back*
Nazám įnážį!	*Stand at the back!*
nazámpadahą	*from behind, from the back*
nazámpagena	*somewhere at the back; a little farther back*
nazámpagiya	*toward the back*
nazápa *post*	*in the back of smth, behind smth*
įnázam *adv*	*in the back of smth*
įnázapadahą *adv*	*from the back of smth, from behind smth*
ųzíhektam, ųzéktam *adv*	*backward*
ųzímani *viı*	*s/he walks backward*
ųzímaniya *adv*	*backward*
įdúgam *adv*	*backward, leaning back*
Įdúgam yįgá.	*He is sitting leaning back.*
ektám *post*	*there, in a place*
Dóhąni o'écųna tíbi ektám né wa'íšį.	*I never went to the casino.*

Conceptions of Time

ómaka, ~ omáka *n*	*year*
omáka'esą *adv*	*throughout the year, all year*
omákawąži *adv*	*annually*
Omákawąži amámneza.	*I have my annual check-up.*
omákawąži mas'ų́k'ubi	*annual treaty day*

wájaȟ *adv*
    Įtó wájaȟ iyópsija.

wájanaȟ *adv*
wihíyaye *n*
oką́ *vs, n*

    Oníką̇kta he? — Hą́, omáką̇kta.

néhą *adv*
    nehą́ktA
    nehą́n
nehą́du *vs*
    Nehą́du hą́da wóʼų̇dabi.
    nehą́duȟ
    nehą́duȟtįyĄ

nedápadahą *adv*

žéhą *adv*

    Komáškaškanahą žéhą wéksuya.

    Waníyedu yámni žéhą waníja.
žéhącʼehą *adv*
    Žéhącʼehą iyúha híbi.
žehą́dahą *adv*
    Žehą́dahą nén íšį.

one time, one time specifically; once
    For once, jump.[18]
only once; one more time
time
s/he has room, time; aisle, narrow
    path; vacant place
    Do you have time? —Yes, I have time.
at this time, now
    it is happening
    at this time; now, today
it is now; it took place at this time
    We ate at this time.
    now, about this time
    it is now specifically; it is at
        this time
moving from here, behind, from this
    side; from the beginning, start
then, at that time, at a certain point
    in time; last
    I remember when I was a
        teenage boy.
    He passed away three years ago.
at that time in the past
    They all arrived at that time.
from then on, and so now, since then
    He did not leave this place since
        then.

---

18   Fourstar 1978, 25.

žehą́du *vs*
    žehą́duga

    žehą́duȟ

žehą́ga *n*
    Dukác žehą́ga no.

žécan *adv*
    Žécan nén wa'ų́.
žehą́n *adv-cont*
    Žehą́n timáhen ú.
žehą́naga *conj*

    Žehą́naga agícida cuwíknąga
    šašábi žená awį́cahibi.
žehą́š *adv*
aškádu *vs*
téhą *adv*
    Téhą kníšį.
    Téhą mągá
    Téhą mįštíma.
ahágeȟ *adv*
    Ahágeȟ timáni wa'í.
    Ahágeȟ cén hí.
togáda *adv*

    Togáda yá.
    Togáda hí.

it was at that time, then
    it took/it will take place at about
    that time
    at that time specifically, right at
    that time
end of a story
    Supposedly this is the end of
    the story.
in the meantime, during that time, then
    In the meantime I stayed here.
at that time, just when
    At that time he came inside.
and so now, and after that, and at
    that time
    And after that, they brought in
    the RCMP.
but now
s/he/it is late
late; long time
    He got back late.
    I sat down for a long time.
    I have been asleep for a long time.
finally, at last
    I finally went for a visit.
    He arrived at last.
ahead, in front, in the lead, in the first
    place; in the future, later
    He is taking the lead.
    He came first.

Togáda žéci mná.

Togáda dágu ecánuȟtįyįkta?

I will go over there later.

*What will you do exactly in
the future?*

c'ehą, 'ehą *suff*

Hokšína žé hąhébic'ehą hí.

Tanó dóhąc'ehą núda?

back then, in the past, last

That boy arrived last night.

When did you eat meat?

hékta *adv*

Hékta naháȟ pté óda žehą.

back then, in the past

*There was still a lot of buffalo
back then.*

hékta odágugiciyabi

hékta odáguye

héktac'ehą

ancestors

ancestor

long time ago

wanágaš *adv*

Wanágaš waníja.

Wanágaš ecámų céyaga.

long ago

He passed away long ago.

I should have done that a long ago.

gicúni *vt1-irr*

Įbási žé gicúni.

Wací yécunįšį.

s/he quits an activity; it is finished

He quit driving.

You did not finish the dance.

ecágen *adv*

Ecágen pamáyazą.

Ecágen asásciya.

constantly, always, all the time

I have a constant headache.

I am always proud of you.

waná *adv*

Waná tída waknįkta.

Naháȟ waná he?

now, already

I am coming home now.

Are you ready yet?

jé, jé'e *part*

Híbi jé.

Įmáduka jé.

always, often

They come often.

I am always hungry.

éstena *adv*

Éstena gazógic'ų mnįkte no.

early, soon, right away

I will go play hockey soon.

tanį́n, tą́nį́na *adv*
Tanį́n togáda hí.
Tą́nį́na kpąyą́bi.

ahead of time, ahead of others; already
He arrived ahead of time.
They were already tanned.

Time of Day

Ȟtánihą *adv*
Ȟtánihą wį́yą nową́ žé snohwáya.

Ȟtánihą nína ganų́za hį́kna
mağážugeja.

hąhébic'ehą *adv*
Hokšína žé hąhébic'ehą hí.

hąyákeji *adv*
Hąyákeji nową́kta.
Hąyákeji dágu dókanų?
Hąyákeji mitúgaši įmų́ğakta.

hąyákena *adv*, *vimp*
Hąyákena úkta.
Hąyákena waštéc!
Waná hąyákena, gíkta!

hąyákena cogą́du *adv*
ą́ba nén, ą́ba né, ąbédu nén *adv*
Ą́ba né nína wašté cén hokúwa
ųyábi.

Ą́ba né wąží ehą́'i wahíkta.

Ą́ba nén maštáȟtįyąkta, gáyabi.

yesterday
I know the woman who sang yesterday.

Yesterday it was really windy and drizzling.

last night
That boy arrived last night.

tomorrow
He will sing tomorrow.
What are you doing tomorrow?
I will ask my grandfather tomorrow.

early morning; it is early morning
He will come this morning.
Good morning!
It is now early morning, get up!

midmorning
today
It is a nice day today thus we will go fishing.

I will arrive at one o'clock today.

Today will be the warmest day, it is said.

ąbédu *n* — *day*
  Ąbédu wóguga. — It is a beautiful day.
  Ąbédu nén osníšį he? — Is it not cold today?
  Ąbédu nén wówahtani cóna mawánįkta. — May I walk with no sins today.

wiyódahą *n* — *south*
  wiyódahą ektá — to the south; noon, midday
  wiyódahą wódabi — dinner

ȟtayédu *n, vimp* — *evening; it is evening*
  Ȟtayédu né amnágena. — The evening is still.
  Ȟtayédu cén tída waknįkta. — Because it is evening I will go home.

hąhébi *n, vimp* — *night; it is nighttime*
  Hąhébi dónacą žé nįštíma. — How many nights did you sleep there?
  Hąhébi háda cųwįktu tągán ománi. — Her daughter walks outside at nighttime.

hácogądu *adv* — *midnight, middle of the night*
  Hácogądu žehą wacíbi žedáhą wakní. — I came home from the dance at midnight.
  Įknúhahana hácogądu wékta. — Occasionally I wake up in the middle of the night.

sápa, sąm, ~ sám *adv* — *more, beyond, over*
  Ȟtánihą sápa wąmnágac. — I saw him the day before yesterday.

Days of the Week, Seasons, and Months

Days of the Week

ába įwąžį, ábawaką gicúni *cp* — Monday
ába įnúba *cp* — Tuesday

ą́ba įyámni *cp*	*Wednesday*
ą́ba įdóba *cp*	*Thursday*
ą́ba įzáptą, tacúba ą́ba,	
tanó yúdabišį *cp*	*Friday*
ą́ba yužáža, ą́ba tiyúžaža, otíyužaže,	
otíyužaža ą́ba, wowį́cak'u ą́ba *cp, n*	*Saturday*
ą́bawaką n	*Sunday*

Seasons

wédu *n, vimp*	*spring; it is spring*
Wédu cén dágu iyúhana gaspą́.	*In the spring everything is slushy.*
Wédu hą́da pağų́da žená nén iyáhąbi.	*In the spring those duck land here.*
wéhą *adv*	*last spring*
Wéhą timáni.	*She visited last spring*
Wéhą timáwįcagini.	*Last spring she visited her relatives.*
owédu *adv*	*in the spring time*
mnogédu *n, vimp*	*summer; it is summer*
Mnogédu hą́da wį́otibi.	*In the summer they live in a tent.*
mnogéhą *adv*	*last summer*
omnédu *adv*	*in the summer time*
ptąyédu *n*	*fall*
ptąyésą *adv*	*throughout the fall, all fall*
ptį́hą *adv*	*last fall*
Ptį́hą žéci wa'í.	*I went there last fall.*
wįcógądu *n*	*midwinter*
waníhą *adv*	*last winter*
Waníhą cą́'įyutabi yámni wagáksa.	*Last winter I chopped three cords of wood.*

waníyedu *n, vimp*   winter; year; it is winter

Waníyedu štén wó'ųknagabįkte no.   *Next winter we will tell stories.*

Waníyedu dóna eháki he?   *How old is he?*

Mató waníyedu ąbé'įštima.   *The bear sleeps during the*
winter days.

Waná waníyedu.   *Now it is winter.*

waníyedu cogą́na *adv*   *midwinter*

Months (hąwí)

	Pheasant Rump Nakoda	Fort Peck Nakoda[19]	Carry The Kettle[20]
January	witéȟi wí	wįcógądu	witéȟi wí
February	ąmhą́ska wí	ąmhą́ska	ąmhą́ska wí
March	wįcį́šta yazą́ wí	wįcį́šta yazą́ wí	wįcį́šta yazą́ wí
April	tabéȟ'a tawį́	tabéȟ'a tawį́	tabéȟ'a tawį́
May	įdú wiǧá hą́wi	įdú wiǧá	įdú wiǧá hą́wi
June	waȟpé wóšma wí	wahígušme wí	waȟpé wóšma wí
July	wašáša wí	wašáša	wašáša mnogén-cogą́du
August	cąpásaba wí	cąpásaba	cąpásaba hą́wi
September	waȟpé ǧí wí	waȟpé ǧiwí	waȟpé ǧí wí
October	tašnáheja hagíkta wí	tašnáheja hagíkta	tašnáheja hagíkta
November	wįcógądu sųgágu wí	cą'útka wí	cą'útka wí
December	wįcógądu wí	wįcógądu sųgágu	wįcógądu sųgágu

---

19   Ryan 1998, 40.
20   Haywahe 1992; Collette & Kennedy 2023.

30

Structural Words

Demonstratives and Pronouns

né *dem* — *this*

    Wa'óyabi né Nakón wįcášta ųgógijikmabi. — *We wrote this book for the Nakoda people.*

    Ohónageje! Né akída! — *Holy smokes! Check this out!*

nená *dem-pl* — *these*

    Wanágaš mitúgaši onówą nená ahíyayas'a. — *Long ago my grandfather used to sing these songs.*

    Wįkóške nená wayáwa tíbi aktágabi. — *These girls are running to school.*

nén *adv* — *here*

    Nén stustáyagen mągá. — *I am sitting here bored.*

    Šųkcúk'ana nén ódabi. — *There are many coyotes here.*

žé *dem* — *that, the*

    Wagágana žé tawácį síja. — *That old lady has a wicked mind.*

    Wáda žé yá. — *The train is going.*

žená *dem-pl* — *those*

    Wa'óyabi žená wabážužu. — *I erased it off the papers.*

    Wíyą žená ağúyábi gáğabi he? — *Are these women making bannock?*

žén *adv*   there

  Žén yįgá wómagiknąga.   *He sat there telling me his stories.*

  Ába aháge žén í.   *He went there on the last day.*

gá *dem*   that over there

  Šúga gá dágu dókų he?   What is that dog over there doing?

ganá *dem-pl*   those over there

  Dágu ganá he?   *What are those over there?*

gán *adv*   over there

  Įtó gán tiwįcoda tíbi.   *Well many families lived over there.*

wąží *num, art*   one; a, an

  Aké wąží émnagųkte no!   *I will give him one more!*

  Škoškóbena wąží núda he?   *Are you eating a banana?*

  Wa'ówabi wąžíȟ cíjahi.   *I brought you a book.*

cá *det*   such a person, such a kind, at such a
                                        time; a, an, the

  Wįcóyazą síja cá Įkcé wįcášta   *All of the Indigenous people*
    oyáde iyúha ecéyabi.   *suffered from a severe epidemic.*

  Šųkská cá awíwahamna.   *I dreamt about a specific white*
                                          horse.

miyé *pro*   I, myself

  Miyé žécen įmnúkcą duká ecúbįšį.   *According to me they did not do it.*

  Miyé wécįga.   *I want it for myself.*

niyé *pro*   you, yourself

  Niyé mayéksuya he?   *As for you, do you remember me?*

  Niyé omágipi.   *I am happy for you.*

iyé *pro*   he, himself, her, herself, themselves

  Iyé táwa žé ų́.   *He uses his own.*

  Iyé ejíyawakiya.   *I made him say something.*

ųgíye *pro.pl*   we, ourselves

  Ųgíye miní a'úbapsųbi.   *As for us, we were baptized.*

niyébi *pro.pl*   *you all, yourselves*

mį́š *pro*   *me too*

   Mį́š wówadįktehtįyą.   *I want to eat too.*

nį́š *pro*   *you too*

   Nį́š nąbénuzįkta.   *You too will shake his hand.*

į́š *pro*   *him, her, they, it too*

   Atkúgu, húgu į́š naháh̨ níbi.   *His father and mother too are still alive.*

   Pągí, tį́psina, wakmúhaza į́š špąyą́.   *She cooked potatoes, turnips, and corn too.*

ųgį́š *pro.pl*   *us too*

Indefinite Pronouns and Adverbs (D-words)

dágu *pro, quant, vs*   *thing, something; what; any, none; it is something*

   Gá dágu?   *What is that yonder?*

   Dágu ecácijimųkte no.   *I will do something for you.*

   Dágu dókanų? — Dágunišį!   *What are you doing? — Nothing at all!*

   Dágu yacíga he?   *What do you want?*

   Mitúgaši dágu nik'ú he?   *What did my grandfather give you?*

   Mázaska dágu ųk'úbišį.   *We did not receive any money.*

dóken *adv*   *how, what; in some way, whichever way or manner*

   Dóken ya'ų́? — Dąyą́ wa'ų́!   *How are you? — I am fine!*

   Dóken epį́kta he?   *How could I say this?*

   Dóken eníjiyabi?   *What is your name?*

   Dóken įnúkcą?   *What do you think about it?*

   Dóken ecúbi yacíga.   *Do it whichever way you want.*

dóki *adv* — where, where to; anywhere, somewhere, to some place

Nihį́kna dóki iyáya? — Where did your husband go?

Dóki ya'íšį he? — You did not go anywhere?

Dóki nį́kta hųštá žé nawáȟ'ų. — I heard you are leaving.

dókiya *adv, vs* — wherever; anywhere; where to

Honáǧina dókiya cén otápabi. — Flies follow him wherever he goes.[21]

Wapáha žé dókiya? — Where is the hat?

Cąšmúyabi dókiya? — Where is the sugar?

dókiyo *adv, n* — in which direction; direction, course

Dókiyo iyáya? — In which direction did he go?

Wakpá žé dókiyo ȟaȟá. — The river is flowing its course.

dóna *pro, quant, vs* — how many, what number; how much; several; s/he/it is so many

Dóna ehą́'i he? — What time is it?

Dóna hą́ska ehą́ya'i? — How tall are you?

Waníyedu dóna ehą́yaki he? — How old are you?

Mázaska dóna yacį́gabi he? — How much money will you want?

Nidónabi he? — How many are you?

duwé *pro, n, quant, vs* — who; person; nobody; s/he is sb

Duwé gicí yahí? — Who did you come with?

Duwé wąnága? — Who did you see?

Abáȟnan sąksája duwé nik'ú he? — Who gave you the silk dress?

Buscį́jabina nená duwé táwabi he? — Whose kittens are these?

Né duwé Mary. — This is Mary.

Duwé híšį. — Nobody came.

Madúwe he? — Who am I?

Žé duwé? — Who is that?

---

21   BigEagle 2019, 8.

dukté *pro*   *what, which one (of a set)*

    Dukté okmábi waštéyana?   *What colour do you like?*

    Dukté nitáwa?   *Which one is yours?*

    Dukté yaká kóšta.   *It does not matter which one*
                               you chose.

duktén *adv*   *where, at what place*

    Duktén yatí?   *Where do you live?*

    Hųská né duktén opéyatų he?   *Where did you buy these pants?*

    Duktén éwaknąga giksúyįkta šką. *Try to remember where I put them.*

Quantifiers

jónana *quant*   *few, little, small amount*

    Cąšmúyabi pšųkáką jónana mak'ú. *Give me a few candies.*

    Eyáš jónana mak'ú.   *Give me a small amount.*

iyúha *quant*   *all, every, one after the other; none*

    Amógįyą iyúha mnušnóga.   *I dismantled all the cars.*

    Ába nén iyúha ecámų.   *I do it every day.*

    Iyúha iyútąbišį.   *None of them tried to do it.*

iyúhana *quant*   *all, all of them, all of it*

    Iyúhana dąyą́ wódabi.   *They all ate well.*

    Šųktógeja iyúhana hįnápabi.   *All of the wolves appeared.*

    Iyúhana wacégiyabi.   *They pray in a mass.*

owá *quant*   *all (people, things); everybody*

    Owá ų́bi.   *They are all wearing it.*

    Owá mnagíciyąbi.   *People are grouped.*

    Owá dókaš dąyą́ ų́bįkta.   *Everybody will prosper.*

nówa *quant*   *all of these*

    Dáguškibina nówa nųwą́ iyáyabi. *All the children are going*
                                 swimming.

Įknúhana šúga nówa hįnápabi.

Suddenly all the dogs appeared.

Cá nówa škąšká.

All of the trees are shaking.

Mína nówa mnumá.

I sharpen all the knives.

kówa *quant*

all of those

ódA *quant, vs*

a lot, many, much; it is a lot,
there are many

Micíkši óda ųspékta.

My son will learn a lot.

Šųkcúk'ana nén ódabi.

There are many coyotes here.

Hékta naháň pté óda žehą.

There was still a lot of buffalo in
the past.

Partitives

abá *quant*

some, some of a group

Abá giksúyešį.

He does not remember some of it.

edáhą *quant*

some of that; some of a larger group

Waȟpé edáhą mak'ú!

Give me some tea!

Wicíjana né asábi edáhą cįgá.

This girl wants some milk.

Tanó edáhą manú.

He stole some pieces of meat.

dáguni *pro*

none, nothing

Dáguni yuhábišį.

Nothing belongs to them.

Hiyá, dáguni wacígešį.

No, I do not want anything.

duwéni, ~ **duwéna** *pro*

nobody, no one, none

Duwéni níšį.

No one survived.

Duwéni híšį.

Nobody came.

Conjunctions

híkna, hík *conj*

and, and then

Tín ú híkna wóda wo!

Come in and eat!

Amápa hį́kna mayúȟija. — *He hit me and he woke me up.*

Éyagu hį́kna žén éknąga. — *He took it and put it down there.*

Ų́šigiya nawáži̱ hį́kna wacéwagiya. — *I stand humbly and I pray.*

kó *conj* — *also, too, even*

   Nį́š kó! — *You too!*

   Mike kó hí. — *Mike also arrived.*

   Žécen kó eyá. — *She even said that.*

nągú̱, ~ nakú̱, ~ nągú *conj, adv* — *and, and also, in addition; more, anymore*

   Wahpé nągú̱ asą́bi mnuhá. — *I want tea and milk.*

   Wahpé, huȟnáȟyabi nągú̱ asą́bi mnuhá. — *I have tea, coffee, and also milk.*

   Nągú̱ wacíga. — *I want more.*

   Nągú̱ eyéši̱. — *Do not say it anymore.*

į́š *pro* — *s/he, it, they too, as well*

   Į́š ektá í. — *He went there too.*

   Nína į́š maǧážu. — *It rains a lot too.*

eštá *conj* — *or, either; whether it is the case or not*

   Tanó eštá wahą́bi yacíga he? — *Do you want meat or soup?*

   Į̱wį́camuǧa eštáš ecúbi he? — *I asked them whether they did it or not.*

ga'éca *conj* — *and then*

   Hí ga'éca awóknagabi. — *He arrived and then they talked about it.*

duká, oká, ų̱ká *conj* — *but, although, even though, despite*

   Haȟébi duká micį́kši nahą́ knį́ši̱. — *It is night time, but my son has not come home yet.*

   Iyé táwa oká éwejimnagu. — *It was hers but I took it from her.*

   Wahí duká wącímnage wahíši̱. — *I came but not to see you.*

štén *conj*

Įníduka štén, wóda wó.

Hąyákena štén aǧúyabisaga edáhą
  wacíga.

Hųgóȟa štén wíyų wo.

if...when, if...then; when, whenever
in, at, on, next

If you are hungry, then eat.

In the morning I want some toast.
Use it for a giveaway.

Adverbs

Time

aškán *adv*

Huhúžubina aškán nén wahí.

Aškán mitákọna šųkcíjana né k'ú.

recently, lately

I arrived here in Regina recently.

*My friend gave her this puppy
  recently.*

éstena *adv*

Éstena giktá.

Éstena amásni.

early, soon, right away

She wakes up early.

I recovered right away.

hąyákeji *adv*

Hąyákeji nowąkta.

Hąyákeji dágu dókanų?

Hąyákeji mitúgaši įmúǧakta.

tomorrow

He will sing tomorrow.

What are you doing tomorrow?

*I will ask my grandfather
  tomorrow.*

hąyákena *adv, vimp*

Hąyákena úkta.

Hąyákena waštéc!

Waná hąyákena, gíkta!

hąyákena cogądu

hąyákena wódabi

early morning; it is early morning

He will come this morning.

Good morning!

It is now early morning, get up!

midmorning

breakfast

hékta *adv*
back then, in the past

Hékta naháȟ pté óda žehą́.
There was still a lot of buffalo back then.

ȟtánihą *adv*
yesterday

Ȟtánihą t'į́kta.
She would have died yesterday.

Ȟtánihąc'ehą wakní.
I came back home yesterday.

Ȟtánihą šúga tągán gicízabi.
Yesterday the dogs were fighting outside.

įknúhana, įknúhąnaȟ *adv*
suddenly, instantly, all at once

Įknúhana šúga nówa hįnápabi.
Suddenly all the dogs appeared.

Įknúhanaȟ įdómamni!
Suddenly I felt dizzy!

naháȟ *adv*
still, yet

Naháȟ wagáǧįkte no!
I am still going to make it!

Naháȟ wówaši ecúbi.
They are still working.

Naháȟ waná he?
Are you ready yet?

nągáhą *adv*
now

Nągáhą wawápadįkta.
Now I will do some butchering.

Nągáhą nína wówaši ecú.
Now she is in labour.

téhą *adv*
late; long time

Téhą kníši.
He got back late.

Téhą mągá.
I sat down for a long time.

Téhą wącímnagešį.
I did not see you for a long time.

téhąc'ehą *adv*
long time ago

waná *adv*
now, already

Waná wóyadabįkte no.
You will eat now.

Waná tída waknį́kta.
I am coming home now.

Naháȟ waná he?
Are you ready yet?

wanágaš *adv*
long ago

Wanágaš wanį́ja.
He passed away long ago.

Wanágaš Šiyóša ektá wa'í.
I went to Red Pheasant long ago.

Place and Localization

agą́n, ~ **agám** *post* — on top of smth, on it
Agą́n bóǧa! — Blow on it!
Awódabi agą́n yúda! — Eat it at the table!
Agám nážį. — He stands on top.

ektá *post* — at, in, to a location, destination
Húgu Céǧa K'įna ektá tí. — Her mother lives at Carry The Kettle.

Wanągaš wazíhe ektá, étibi žén. — Long people were camped there in the Cypress Hills.

Iná tí ektá amáya'i. — Take me to mom's place.

én *post, adv* — in, into, on, onto, at, to; here, there
Įnį́bi én iyódąga. — They are sitting in the sweat lodge.

Céǧa K'įna én mątų́bi. — I was born in Carry The Kettle.
Mikúši owókšubi én ų́. — My grandmother is in the garden.

héktam *adv* — behind, in the rear
Šúǧa héktam máni. — The dog is walking behind.
Héktam nážį nén. — He is standing here behind.

hokún *adv* — down, below; downstairs
Hokún yubáǧe. — He pulled it down.
Hokún yá! — Go downstairs!

gakná *adv* — beside, along sb, smth
Gakná yįgá! — Sit beside him!
Nųpín gakná maníbi. — They both are walking along.

mahén *adv, post* — inside, in, within; under, underneath
Nén mahén cąbúbų. — The wood is rotten here inside.
Owį́ža mahén yįgá! — Stay under the blanket!

Structural Words

nén *adv*   here, in a place
  Nén úbįkta he?   *Will they be coming here?*
  Nén mayázą.   *I ache here.*
ókšą *adv*   around
  Ókšą úbi.   *They are all around.*
  Ókšą nén waką cá no!   *Everything around here is sacred!*
tągán, tągáda *adv*   outside
  Tągán osní he?   *Is it cold outside?*
  Tągán yá škáda wo.   *Go and play outside.*
  Tągán a'óžąžą.   *It is sunny outside.*
žén *adv*   there
  Iyúha žén étibi.   *People were camped there.*
  Ába aháge žén í.   *He went there on the last day.*

Manner

a'ínina, ~ ánina, ~ inína *adv*   *quietly, in silence*
  A'ínina yįgá!   *Sit quietly!*
  Ába né a'ínina yįgá.   *It's a quiet day today.*
awánųka *adv*   *accidentally*
  Tąȟca awánųka wakté.   *I accidentally killed a deer.*
cíga *adv*   *with energy, strenuously*
  Cíga wówada.   *I ate as fast as I could.*
  įyécįga *adv*   *by itself*
dąyą́, ~ dayą́ *vs, adv,*   *s/he/it is well, good, all right; well, properly*

  Eyáš dąyą́.   *I guess he is good.*
  Tawácį dąyą́šį.   *He is mentally disabled.*
  Dąyą́ wa'ų́.   *I am fine.*

dąyágen *adv*   carefully, fairly well, properly, with ease
  Wįcá žé dąyágen ókšą éduwą.   The man looked around carefully.
  Dąyágen ecų́.   He did it fairly well.
  Dąyágen įyútešį.   He did not measure it properly.
ektášį *adv*   wrongly
  Ektášį ecánų.   You did it wrongly.
  Ųmá né ektášį cažénada.   You said the wrong name.
įdú *adv*   just, simply, only
  Įdú ecámų.   I just did it.
  Įdú wacégiya wo!   Simply pray!
įnáȟniyena *adv*   hurriedly, in a hurry
  Įnáȟniyena wa'í.   I got there in a hurry.
  Įnáȟniyena tín hí.   He arrived in the house in a hurry.
įšnána *pro, adv, vs3*   by him/her/itself, alone; s/he is alone
  Įšnána o'énažį ektá í.   She went to town alone.
  Įšnána ecų́.   She did it on her own.
  Ȟó! Nįšnánašį.   Oh! You are not alone.
įwáštena, ~ owáštena *adv*   slowly, carefully, softly
  Įwáštena wagú.   I came back home slowly.
  Owáštena i'á.   Speak slowly.
waštéya *adv*   nicely, in a good manner, well
  Mitáwacį waštéya eháwa'i.   I reach my mindset, goal with a
                                   good heart.
kohána *adv*   quickly
  Kohána owá knuštą!   Finish them all quickly!
kokóna *adv*   quickly, fast
  Miyéš cądé kokóna iyámąpešį.   As for myself, my heart does not
                                   beat that fast.
naȟmáyena *adv*   secretly, furtively, quietly
  Naȟmáyena máni.   He walks furtively.

sakím *adv* — together, joined
    Sakím híbi. — They came here together.
    Hą́ba žé sakím éknąga. — Put the shoes together.

sijáya *adv* — badly, poorly
    Sijáya eyá. — He curses.
    Dágu sijáya ayákipakte no. — You will encounter something bad.

teȟíyą *adv* — with difficulty, poorly
    Teȟíyą yįgá. — He is in critical shape.

ų́šigiya *adv* — pitifully, humbly
    Midáguyabi nína ų́šigiya nážį bo! — My relatives stand very humbly!

wįjákeya *adv* — truthfully, honestly
    Nína wįjákeya i'á. — He spoke very truthfully.

yupíyagen *adv* — skillfully, handsomely
    Yupíyagen įknúza. — He dressed himself in fancy clothes.

Degree

eháš *adv* — too much, exceedingly; surely, quite
    Eháš nína skúya. — It is too sweet.
    Eháš štušténa óda ecų́. — She used too much salt.
    Eháš onį́kte wacį́. — He is quite a coward.

gahágeȟ *adv* — that far, not so far off

gídana, gídanaȟ *adv* — barely
    Gídana osní no. — It is barely cold.
    Ti'óba žé gídanaȟ yušpá yįgá. — The door is barely opened.

įyágasam *adv* — further, beyond

kapéyena *adv* — more
    Kapéyena wók'u wo. — Feed him more.

nína *adv*

very, really, a lot; intense, intensively; always

Nína cądéniwašte no.	You are very kind.
Nína wasnókye no.	She very clever.
Nína cóza.	It is very warm.
Nína cíga.	He wants it badly.

nísko *vs*

it is this size, much; it is as big as this

Miní niskó no.	It is this much water.
Eknága nísko kún!	Put this much down here!

sám, ~ sąm *post*

beyond, over, across; and, in addition to

Bahá sám žéci wa'í.	I went over the hill.
Sám yá!	Go away!
Dóba sám hągé ehą́'i.	It is four thirty.

sápana *adv*

farther on, over

Sápana yįgá!	Move over!

žecéš *adv*

only that (contrary to one's expectation)

Mázaska žecéš no!	That is all the money!
Žecéš wéksuya.	Only that I remember.

Interjections

Ahé! *interj*

expression of humility used at the beginning of prayers or songs

Dágeyešį! *interj* — Shh! Shut up! Don't talk!

Dágunišį! *interj* — Nothing!

Eyáš aké! *interj* — Not again!

hą *interj*

yes; hello! (female speaker)

Huȟnáȟyabi yacíga? — Há, edáhą wacíga.	Do you want coffee? — Yes, I want some.
Há, wanúȟ.	Yes, maybe.

Há jé! *interj*	*Yes, ok, mmh!*
Há jé žécen! *interj*	*Yes, ok, so!*
Hinága! *interj*	*Wait!*
Hiyá *interj*	*No!*
Hiyá cąníska įwékcukta.	*No, I will smoke my own cigarette.*
Híį́! *interj*	*Oh my!* (women's expression of surprise)
Hokwá! *interj*	*Not interested!*
Hokwá waná he?	*What's happening now?*
núške *interj*	*euh* (when a speaker is thinking about what to say)
Waná hinága!	*Wait now!*
Waktá! *interj*	*Beware!*

Verb Enclitics and Particles

Enclitics

-hą *encl*	continuative aspect
Mįšnąna mągáhą né tamúkašį.	*I dread being alone.*
Taníyešį įt'áhą.	*He is out of breath.*
-:ga *encl*	durative aspect
Dágu dókanų:ga?	*What have you been doing?*
Gą́na:ga hįníga.	*The older she got, the meaner she became.*
Įȟábi t'á:ga.	*They were laughing to death.*
-bi *encl*	3rd person plural animate
Wašínįc'inabi.	*They are acting like Whitemen.*
Duwé yúzabi he?	*Who did they arrest?*
Wayáwa gicúni híbi štén.	*They will come when school finishes.*

-na *encl*	diminutive (often used with actions done by babies)
Ų́kcana no!	*The baby farted!*
yuhána	*s/he (baby, small child) has sb, smth*
-s'a *encl*	habitual aspect
Buzáda škádabis'a.	*They always play on the shore.*
Mikúši dąyą́ gisų́s'a.	*My grandmother always braided her hair nicely.*
wódes'a	*eater; one who eats all the time*
-ktA *encl*	potential mood; future
Dóken ócijiyįkta?	*How can I help you?*
Dóhą štén įštímįkta?	*When will he sleep?*
Waná wó'ųdabįkte no!	*We are going to eat now!*
Gá yacíga štén cic'úkta.	*If you want that yonder I will give it to you.*
-šį *encl*	negation
Hiyá, mázaska mnuhéšį.	*No, I don't have money.*
Įštíma mnį́kktešį no!	*I don't want to sleep.*
Dáguni wąmnágešį no!	*I did not see any.*
-gen *encl*	negation
Snokwáyagen'.	*I do not care.*
Ecų́ktegen.	*He won't do it anyways.*
-s *encl*	let's
Ųškádadabinas.	*Let's all play.*
Omá'ųnis.	*Let's go for a walk.*

Particles

jé'e, jé *part*	*always, often*
Híbi jé.	*They come often.*

Įmáduka jé.

céyagA *part*

    Wa'úci céyaga.
    Micį́kši nihámna, nįknúžaža
    céyaga!

otį́'įgA, ~ **otį́gA**, ~ **otą́'įgA** *part*

    Ecúšį otį́'įga.
    Ų́šigabi otį́'įgešį.

ųkáš *part, conj*

    Mázaska mnuhá ųkáš no.
    Naȟ'ų́ ųkáš, aké epéšį ca.

hųštÁ *part*

    Kišnéyeciyabi hųštá.
    Cųwį́tku núm wįkóškebi hųštá.

he *part*

    Nidúwe he?
    Nągáhą tadé'ųye dágu he?
    Dágu nén okmábi he?

no *part*

    Wópina tága cic'ú no!
    Osą́kna'ųbi no!

c *part*

    Pežúdasije yuhác!
    Įštókmuz wayácibįktac!

I am always hungry.
*let's, should, must, ought to, might
as well*
    Let us dance.
    *My son you smell, you should wash
    yourself.*[22]
it seems, I think, apparently
    Apparently, he didn't do it.
    I do not think they are poor.
if, if only (marker of optative modality)
    If only I had money.
    *If he had been listening, I would
    not have to say it again.*
people say, they say, it is said
    You loved each other, it is said.
    *His two daughters were young girls,
    it is said.*
interrogative, question
    Who are you?
    What season are we in right now?
    What is drawn here?
declarative; statement (man speaking)
    I give you great thanks!
    We are lonesome!
declarative; statement
    He has bad medicine!
    You will dance with your eyes closed!

---

22   BigEagle 2019, 8.

' *part* — declarative (woman speaking)

Šųktógeja núba wąwícąmnaga'! — *I saw two wolves!*

Tątága'! — *They were big!*

ce *part* — declarative; statement (woman speaking)

Žéci mníkte ce. — *I'm going over there.*

wo *part* — imperative singular; order, command to one person (man speaking)

Dáguh nécen ecų́ wo! — *Why don't you do it this way!*

Wayáwa tíbi yá wo! — *Go to school!*

bo *part* — imperative plural; order commands to many people (man speaking)

Midáguyabi nážį bo! — *My relatives, stand up!*

Žéci yįgá bo! — *All of you, stand over there!*

Postpositions

ų́s, ų́ *post* — using it, with it, because of it

Sakyé ų́s mawáni. — *I walk with a cane.*

Wįhámne né ų́s tawáci dąyą́šį. — *He is moody because of this dream.*

Miyé ų́ hí. — *He came because of me.*

agą́n, ~ agám *post* — on top of smth, on it

Agą́n bóǧa! — *Blow on it!*

Awódabi agą́n yúda! — *Eat it at the table!*

įwągam *adv, post* — above smth

Įspáse įwągam ta'óbi. — *He was wounded above the point of the elbow.*

cóna *post, suff* — without, lacking, deprived of

Huȟnáȟyabi, asą́bi cóna waštéwana. — *I like coffee without milk.*

ektá *post*
Atkúgu Ktųsyą́ ektá tí.
Į́š ektá í.
Iná tí ektá amáya'i.
ektáktaš *post-redup*

ektám *post*
Dóhąni o'écųna tíbi ektám né wa'íšį.
én *post, adv*
Įnį́bi én iyódąga.
Mikúši owókšubi én ų́.
Én yįgá!
Gicí én wa'ų́šį.
iyákna *post*
Táno né iyákna wahą́bi gáǧabi.

mahén *adv-cont, post*
Nén mahén cąbúbų.
Owį́ža mahén yįgá!
nazápa *post*
okná *post*
Cą'į́tkų okná éknąga.
Oką́ okná žé mawáni.
Ti'óba žé okná tągán yá.
nókna
óhą *post*
Óhą hí.
Gábina óhą ecágen yįgá.
gicí *post*
Duwé gicí yahí?

at, in, to a location, destination
Her father lives in Wolseley.
He went there too.
Take me to mom's place.
at, in, to various locations or destinations; wherever
there, in a place
I never went to the casino.
in, into, on, onto, at, to; here, there
They are sitting in the sweat lodge.
My grandmother is in the garden.
Sit here!
I was not there with her.
together with smth, sb
They make a broth together with meat.
inside, in, within; under, underneath
The wood is rotten here inside.
Stay under the blanket!
in the back of smth, behind smth
in, through
He put it in the fire.
I walk through the aisle.
He goes out through the door.
through this
among, in the middle, in it
He arrives in the middle.
He always sits among the elders.
with sb, smth (single person or object)
Who did you come with?

Mitáwįju gicí wahį́kta.	*I will come with my wife.*
Mitášųga gicí iwá'a jé.	*I always talk to my horse.*
óm *post*	*with them*
Óm mawáni.	*I walk with them.*
Aké wíyąbi žé óm ų́.	*She hangs out with those women again.*
sám, ~ są́m *post*	*beyond, over, across; and, in addition to*
Bahá sám žéci wa'í.	*I went over the hill.*
Sám yá!	*Go away!*
Dóba sám hągé ehą́'i.	*It is four thirty.*
wikcémna nų́m sám dóba	*twenty-four*

Bibliography

BigEagle, Bronte. *The Legend of the T-Rex's Short Arms*. Saskatoon: Saskatchewan Indian Cultural Centre, 2017.

———. *The Legend of the Ankylosaurus*. Saskatoon: Saskatchewan Indian Cultural Centre, 2019.

Collette, Vincent, Armand McArthur, and Wilma Kennedy. *Nakón-iʾa wo! Beginning Nakoda*. Regina: University of Regina Press, 2019.

Collette, Vincent, and Wilma Kennedy. *A Concise Dictionary of Nakoda (Assiniboine)*. Lincoln: University of Nebraska Press, 2023.

Cumberland, Linda A. *A Grammar of Assiniboine: A Siouan Language of the Northern Plains*. PhD diss., Indiana University, 2005.

———. *Grammar of Assiniboine (Nakoda)*. Lincoln: University of Nebraska Press, 2024.

Drummond, Valerie E. *Carry-The-Kettle Assiniboine Texts*. Master's thesis, University of Toronto, 1976.

Fourstar, Jerome. *Assiniboine Dictionary*. Self-published, Wolf Point, MT, 1978.

Haywahe, John. *Four Seasons–Four Languages, Five Year Calendar* (Nakoda section). Edited by Jean Bellegarde and Marian Dinwoodie. Handbook. Fort Qu'Appelle: Touchwood File Hills' Qu'Appelle Tribal Council, 1992.

Parks, Douglas R., and Raymond J. DeMallie, eds. *Nakoda Stories from Fort Belknap Reservation, Montana*. Fort Belknap, MT: Hoteja Project and Indiana University American Indian Studies Research Institute, 2002.

———. *Assiniboine Narratives from Fort Belknap, Montana. Stories Told by George Shields Sr. Part 1. Interlinear Texts*. Bloomington: Indiana University American Indian Studies Research Institute, 2012a.

———. *Assiniboine Narratives from Fort Belknap, Montana. Stories Told by Rose Weasel. Part 1. Interlinear Texts*. Bloomington: Indiana University American Indian Studies Research Institute, 2012b.

Ryan, Kenny. *Nakona Language*. Fort Peck, MT: Fort Peck Community College, 1998.

About the Authors

Photo: M. Blackburn

Vincent Collette is a professor of linguistics at the Université du Québec à Chicoutimi, and the editor of *Nakón-i'a wo! Beginning Nakoda* and *A Concise Dictionary of Nakoda (Assiniboine)*. He is interested in Indigenous languages of North America, and specializes in historical linguistics, semantics, and morphology.

Photo: Neil Lahr

Tom Shawl was a Nakoda culture and language instructor at the Aannii Nakoda college in Fort Belknap and jr./sr. high in Harlem, Montana. He currently manages the Teeples IGA grocery store in Browning, Montana, and is an instructor for the YAM program based out of Montana State University.

Photo: Danyta Kennedy

Wilma Kennedy (1923–2020) Heȟága hóta'į wíyą (Echo of the elk woman) was an educator and activist from Carry The Kettle Nakoda First Nation. She was involved with the Nakoda community's culture and traditions, and co-authored *Nakón-i'a wo! Beginning Nakoda* and *A Concise Dictionary of Nakoda (Assiniboine)*.